Normalites

*The First Professionally Prepared Teachers
in the United States*

A volume in
Contemporary Research in Education
Terry A. Osborn, *Series Editor*

Normalites

*The First Professionally Prepared Teachers
in the United States*

Kelly Ann Kolodny

Framingham State University

INFORMATION AGE PUBLISHING, INC.
Charlotte, NC • www.infoagepub.com

Library of Congress Cataloging-in-Publication Data

A CIP record for this book is available from the Library of Congress
http://www.loc.gov

ISBN: 978-1-62396-688-1 (Paperback)
       978-1-62396-689-8 (Hardcover)
       978-1-62396-690-4 (ebook)

Cover image courtesy of Framingham State University, Archives and Special Collections, Framingham, MA.

Printed in the United States of America

Contents

Introduction

Establishment of the Normal School Movement and the First Students

In 1839, Lydia Stow, Mary Swift, and Louisa Harris, young women 15 to 17 years old, parted from their families to take part in a great new public initiative in teacher education as members of the first class of the first state normal school in the United States, established in Lexington, Massachusetts. Viewed by some to be a glorious educational revival, the first state normal school and those that followed were to successfully prepare individuals for teaching and successively strengthen the educational experiences of children. The normal school initiative offered both promise and possibilities for an evolving country, a union of 26 states in 1839, in terms of developing a learned and well informed citizenry. Indeed, some considered the institution of the normal school to be the "fountain of living waters, sending forth streams to refresh present and future ages" (Massachusetts Board of Education, 1840, p. 11).

The reality was, however, that the untraveled path in teacher education that Lydia Stow, Mary Swift and Louisa Harris embarked upon was anything but certain. Perceptions regarding the general sensibility of the initiative, levels of support for it, and future viability were unclear. Questions relating to who should control teacher preparation and who should be involved in the endeavor also added to the indeterminacy of the movement's future (Norton, 1926). Not only was the endeavor closely scrutinized, but a fierce

Normalites, pages vii–xviii

war was waged against it by opponents. Lydia Stow, Mary Swift, and Louisa Harris were in the limelight of this controversy. With some fundamental understanding of the criticism that surrounded their participation, these young women nonetheless helped pioneer the effort and engaged in formal content and pedagogical studies, as well as learning of a broader nature, in grounding of their teaching careers. They had hope, a mission, and a sense of duty, which shaped their life paths. It is these three noteworthy women who are the focus of this book. Though they were the forerunners in the teacher education movement, their stories are largely unknown. Understanding their accounts and experiences, however, provides a critical foreground to comprehending not only the complexity of the nineteenth century normal school movement but, more broadly, educational reform during this period.

Formation of State Sponsored Teacher Education

The path to standardized teacher preparation was the result of various robust forces that linked together in the nineteenth century. The idea of the Republican Motherhood, based on the premise that women could be educated to "raise good republican sons" for a developing country, emerged (Nash, 1997, p. 171). Founding father Benjamin Rush suggested that women should help instruct sons in the principles of government and liberty (Nash, 2005, p. 27). A virtuous citizenry also was considered necessary to protect a new nation against failure (Nash, 2005, p. 27). Beliefs and values such as virtue, propriety and dignity, were naturally thought to be delivered from women to children.

During this period a vision also grew that centered on the idea that women would work with the increasing number of children enrolled in the common schools, the precursor of the contemporary public school system. Based on the notion that all children, regardless of station or status, should receive a free, equal, and shared education, the common school model, first introduced in northeastern states, aimed to provide citizens with an opportunity to compete on equal terms in society (Spring, 2006, p. 35; Urban & Wagoner, 1996, pp. 96–117). The development of the common schools was deemed critical at a time when social cohesion appeared to be disappearing in an increasingly competitive social order (Wallace, 1996, p. 46). There was a heightened emphasis on preparing students for both personal and social duties. As the common schools took hold, some communities started to categorize ungraded district schools into primary, intermediate, grammar and high schools (Norton, 1926, p. xvii). It was an era marked by the formation of state school systems, during which schools increasingly moved towards centralization (Butts & Cremin, 1953, p. 241).

Teaching—historically a male dominated profession—was increasingly opened to women, a change strongly supported by notable reformers. Emma Willard, founder of the Troy Female Seminary in New York, in 1818, for example, argued that women were prone to patience and "the gentle arts of insinuation," and therefore were well suited to teach children (as cited in Ogren, 2005, p. 11). Horace Mann, who in 1838 became the first secretary of the Massachusetts Board of Education, believed that women had a "natural love of the society of children" and "superior gentleness," which enhanced their teaching abilities (as cited in Ogren, 2005, p. 12). Catherine Beecher, originator of the Hartford Female Seminary in Connecticut, viewed teaching to be the true and noble profession of a woman (Beecher, 1842). As nineteenth century urbanization and industrialization took hold, men became increasingly more connected to the public sphere of law, politics, manufacturing, and trade. Teaching, which was viewed by some as an extension of family and home, became to be seen as a role naturally connected to the private sphere of women. The ideological development of this two-sphere view of society is now recognized to not have accurately corresponded to historical or sociological realities, considering that men lived part of the day in the world of the private home. Likewise many women left the home to go out to work (Martin, 2011; Nash, 2005, pp. 9–12). Rather than viewing the two spheres as separate ones, an alternative is to see them as in flux, permeable, porous and negotiated (Sklar, 1995, p. xiii). Inhabiting the private sphere, for example, did not prevent women from voicing concerns about societal issues and/or writing essays for public journals and newspapers regarding pressing nineteenth century matters (Nash, 2005, p. 9). Though inquiry has brought forward questions related to the public and private sphere notion, the ideology attached to this belief system no doubt figured in the circumstances of nineteenth century women.

When women formally entered into common schools as teachers, their numbers grew quickly. By 1840 women held approximately 61% of the teaching positions in Massachusetts and between 30% and 50% in other New England states (Preston, 1993, p. 531). Between 1846 and 1856, the National Board of Popular Education sent nearly six hundred women to teach on the western frontier (Ogren, 2005, p. 12). By 1861, 80% of the teachers in Massachusetts were women (Preston, 1993, p. 531). Though women gained some entry into teaching in the 1600s and 1700s with dame schools and with some summer school work, the mid-1800s was viewed as the period of the feminization of teaching (Wallace, 1996, p. 46). Recognizing that there were differences in how the teaching practice unfolded across geographical areas of the country, women, aware of those distinctions, moved into this realm at unprecedented numbers (Ogren, 2005, p. 12). In a period when women had few career opportunities, women such as Lydia Stow, Mary Swift, and Louisa Harris were willing and eager to pursue the occupation of teacher.

Various factors, including class and race, shaped the experiences of nineteenth century women who entered into teaching. The majority of the women who joined the profession were White, of rural families, and of middling-classes (Biklen, 1990, p. 27; Conway, 2005, p. 135). Most entered teaching with little or no formal pedagogical preparation and a large number were only a few years older than some of their own students. Historian Jill Ker Conway (2005) has compellingly described them as remarkably youthful and not well educated in formal schooling (p. 135). Many had not even completed high school; they certainly had been denied access to most modes of higher education. Some private seminaries were the primary means of advanced education for women and usually only operated on a temporary basis for a few weeks to a couple of months (Nash, 2005, p. 5). In 1840 members of the Massachusetts Board of Education wrote in their annual report that "of those who offer themselves as teachers, a large number are destitute of an accurate and thorough acquaintance with the various branches of knowledge required by law to be taught in the schools. They neither read nor write, well; are deficient in the science of numbers; and have an imperfect knowledge of the grammar of our language" (Massachusetts Board of Education, 1840, pp. 8–9). In this context, Lydia Stow, Mary Swift, and Louis Harris—and others who became part of the small group of students who enrolled in the first normal schools—were indeed pioneers.

While instruction at a state normal school extended women's educational opportunities, it was promoted principally as the means to provide standardized and regulated teacher preparation in order to produce an assemblage of carefully trained educators to meet the needs of the growing number of common schools. Trusted to be an instrument of great good, state normal schools were designed to awaken the consciousness of aspiring educators (Ogren, 2005, pp. 4–5). Early educational reformers and advocates of these schools, such as James Carter, a Massachusetts legislator, believed that it would "do but little good to class the children" until there were instructors properly prepared to take charge of the classes (as cited in Norton, 1926, p. 227). Henry Barnard, first secretary of the Board of Education in Connecticut, believed that legislation was needed to make some provision for the better education and special training of teachers for their delicate and difficult labors (Barnard, 1851). The journey to the establishment of the first state normal school was one that took time and excited public interest. Social change can be difficult to achieve, particularly alterations that shaped an intensely public initiative such as the preparation of teachers.

Some of the first state normal schools established in the United States, such as the one that Lydia Stow, Mary Swift, and Louisa Harris attended, were for women only, whereas others that followed were coeducational. The normal school model drew from the Prussian state-supported system of teacher training which was established in 1819 and attracted worldwide attention (Ogren, 2005, p. 14). There the normal schools (called seminaries) grew at a steady rate, as well as attracted numerous students. Due to the reputation of these schools, commentary was published in the United States in the American Annals of Education and Instruction in 1831 by William Channing Woodbridge about the merits of this system (Ogren, 2005, p. 14). Woodbridge noted that, "School-keeping, in Germany, appears to be a very healthy employment," suggesting that the Prussian teacher training initiatives were yielding positive outcomes (Woodbridge, 1831, p. 257). The state normal school also was modeled after the French ecole normale, from which the name was derived (Fishburn, 1947, p. 3; Ogren, 2005). Though there were other institutions that provided teacher preparation in the nineteenth century, such as academies, private normal schools, and some departments of colleges, the state normal school model was unique in that it was devoted exclusively to teacher education. As the movement gained momentum, it eventually eclipsed other teacher training initiatives. The first state normal school established in Lexington, Massachusetts in 1839 by Horace Mann was quickly followed by ones in Barre and Bridgewater, Massachusetts during that same year. By 1870, eighteen states had at least one normal school. A total of thirty-nine state normal schools were located in New England, the mid-Atlantic states, the Midwest, and California. By the early twentieth century, there were 180 normal schools in states throughout the North, South, East, and West (Ogren, 2005, p.1). Not only did the state normal schools become a dominant force in teacher preparation, they were attended at unprecedented rates at the mid-point of the nineteenth century (Ogren, 2005, p. 57). They increasingly provided access to higher education for students, largely women, of different socio-economic backgrounds, races and ethnicities. Indeed, Lydia Stow, Mary Swift, and Louisa Harris lived to see normal schools established in almost every state in the Union, and an ever growing cadre of students who followed in their path in obtaining a state normal school education (Norton, 1926, p. xvi). Undoubtedly, this was an extraordinary development for them to witness.

Yet, despite the historical significance of the state normal school movement, both in terms of preparing "competent teachers" for the common schools as well as providing women with access to higher education and careers, it is unmistakable that gaps remain in our understanding of the experience. Exceptional research has examined the development of the movement as a whole; other studies have provided analysis of some of the leaders of the initiative, such as Horace Mann and Henry Barnard (MacMullen, 1991; Messerli, 1972; Ogren, 2005). There is a lack of rich, published information, however, about the first groups of students, women such as Lydia Stow, Mary Swift, and Louisa Harris, who took part in this initiative and drew from it throughout their lives. Indeed the general discussions about nineteenth century normal schools seem to ignore their experiences and lingering questions remain unanswered. Who were these women? What did they encounter during their normal school studies? How did these women perceive those occurrences? And how did they draw from their normal school preparation and experiences throughout their lives? It is curious that so little is known about these women with whom so much of the fate of the normal school movement rested. It is likewise problematic, as so much of what we understand about the normal school movement can only truly be understood in connection with the students who attended them, referred to by some as the minutemen of the new war on education (Norton, 1926, p. xvi). These women not only were pioneers in the movement, but through their involvement they were, in essence, part of the origin of it. In the early years of the twenty-first century, over 100,000 students are awarded baccalaureate degrees in education each year. Over 80,000 of these students are women (National Center for Educational Statistics, 2012). Their experiences have roots to the efforts of the first state normal schools, of which Lydia Stow, Mary Swift, and Louisa Harris were an integral and critical part. One of these three women would later refer to herself as a mere mortal of the immortal first class (L. Adams, personal communication, April 29, unknown year).

Approach and Theoretical Framework of Book

I utilized biographical methods as the approach for this writing. Megan Marshall, notable biographer of *The Peabody Sisters* and *Margaret Fuller,* wrote that a biography built on historical research "comes as close as any genre can to capturing the sense of what it felt like to be alive, in all the complexity that word suggests, at an earlier time" (Marshall, 2007). Biography provides an avenue in which one is allowed inside the life of another person who lived during a particular time, recording a special relationship to history of the time, while gaining insight into personal experiences

(Conway, 1996; Conway, 1998, p. 6). It is a well-defined tradition that allows one to see intersections between human agency and social structures (Kridel, 1998, p. 17). It can show how the part of "an individual action contributes to the whole experience" (Bullough, 1998, p. 25). As a tool, it has the power to touch hearts and minds; inevitably, biographies can be private and at times profound (Bullough, 1998, p. 22). They also can be deeply satisfying. Through bringing to light the stories of Lydia Stow, Mary Swift, and Louisa Harris in connection with the state normal school movement, I provide insights about the initiative through the experiences of three of the first students who were part of it and drew from it throughout their lives.

Themes of formal educational preparation and teaching are depicted in the life stories of these women. In this sense, I pull from traditional views about what educational pursuits entailed for them. I explore their formal curricular studies and pedagogical practices; however, I do not divorce other factors that also shaped their educational experiences and work. Educational philosopher Jane Roland Martin, who encourages a broad conception of education, writes that in instances of learning, wide-ranging encounters occur and capacities can become yoked together, and in other instances they become unyoked. In this process, individuals, institutions and cultures are changed (Martin, 2011, p. 23). Martin distinguishes between the deep structure of education and the broader interpretation. The deep structure often views and treats schools as the worthy educator of citizens; it is a truncated conception (Martin, 2011, p. 144). A broader interpretation considers cultural stock and how individuals, institutions, and occurrences also create educational and social change.

Drawing from Martin's work, I also depict themes of educational transformations, broadly conceived, in this book. The Second Great Awakening, the Civil War, the Women's Suffrage Movement and Industrialization, for example, occurred during this period, and naturally had an impact on the experiences of these women. Marital status, economic circumstances, work conditions, and political, social, and religious unrest also shaped their encounters. Social perceptions, understandably, bore weight on all three of these women during and after they completed their studies. A belief, for example, that "women's capacity for high intellectual attainment did not go hand in hand with a belief in full gender equality" persisted (Nash, 2005, p. 1). Though women, such as Lydia Stow, Mary Swift, and Louisa Harris, were seen as promising teachers, they also were viewed as cheap labor and received low wages. (Conway, 2005). Nineteenth century contexts yoked with the students' normal school experiences and shaped their life paths.

By taking a more open approach to understanding their educational encounters and transformations, I realized that it was a false dichotomy to separate the public lives of these women as teachers from their private and vice versa. Rather, I needed to examine their experiences holistically and in totality in order to understand the essence of their professional and personal lives. It is often when one experience unfolds in connection with another, that the intertwined nature of these occurrences builds the foundations of subsequent actions and events. Examining the lives of these three women in a holistic manner allowed me to obtain a clearer and more accurate picture regarding what it meant to be a "normalite," as these women called themselves. I better saw not only their context, but also their joys, inventiveness, creativity, activism, and moments of sadness. This approach allowed me to understand how tenets of care, concern and connection played prominently in their stories. It allowed me to see the unintended networks that formed as a result of their normal schools studies and how they drew from those networks throughout their lives while serving as teachers, professional leaders, and social activists. Nel Noddings (1995) has linked the tenets of care, concern and connection to the full range of human talents, competence, and to the contribution of positive influences to society. Though these ideas often are left out of the normal school narrative, they are critical to comprehend. These experiences were what enabled the normalites to endure and move forward at different times during their schooling and thereafter.

Lydia Stow, Mary Swift, and Louisa Harris became teachers upon completing their studies. Their work unfolded in common schools, private seminaries and at the Perkins Institution for the Blind in Massachusetts. Two of these women, Lydia Stow and Mary Swift, left the profession after a short time, married and started families, which too is typical of the historical work patterns of women and teaching. Most nineteenth century women teachers, particularly those who taught younger children, only stayed employed for three to four years (Conway, 2005, p. 136). The stories of Lydia Stow and Mary Swift are much more complicated, however, than a cursory look at such data would suggest. It was through understanding their lives in context that their roles in the field of education become vivid, as well as how they drew from their normal school studies. Lydia Stow and Mary Swift left teaching in terms of paid employment, yet they stayed connected to the field and shaped it in profound ways. Lydia Stow, for example, became an abolitionist associated with Frederick Douglass and Sojourner Truth; became the first woman school board member in Fall River, Massachusetts at a time when women were just crossing the threshold into these roles; and founder of a women's union that provided social and educational services for working women and girls in the mills of that city. Mary Swift became involved in the field of blind and deaf education and though she was not formally employed as a teacher once she married, she continually touched the lives of many blind and deaf students, including the well-known Laura Dewey Bridgman and Helen Keller. She also was a school board member, appointed to serve on a special advisory committee for the Industrial School for Girls in Lancaster, Massachusetts and a founder and tireless advocate of the Boston Young Women's Christian Association (YWCA), subsequently assuming a national advocacy role with this organization, which too provided social and educational services for working women. Their experiences suggest that although women of the nineteenth century were expected to leave teaching once they married, they were able to stay connected to the field, broadly conceived, through participation in women's organizations and alternative avenues. Louisa Harris, in contrast, did not marry nor leave the teaching profession. Her story provides another important lens to view the experiences of the early teachers educated at state normal schools. It reveals how life unfolded for one woman who remained single, boarded around, and at times interfaced with the stereotypes that surrounded the term "spinster."

Research Process

Researching and writing about the lives of these three women extended over ten years. I initially became interested in their stories when I joined the Education Department at Framingham State University, which evolved from the first U.S. state normal school in Lexington, Massachusetts and held an interesting history in teacher education. I taught foundations of education and in that course explored topics such as the normal school movement. With my interest piqued, I set about learning and writing about the women of the first class, including Lydia Stow, Mary Swift, and Louisa Harris.

To piece together and recover the stories of these three women, I examined journals, letters, poetry, school board reports, meeting records, deeds, and newspaper accounts. I naturally began my research at Framingham State University where the Archives and Special Collections contains a copy of Mary Swift's bound journals depicting her normal school studies, as well as the hand written journals of Louisa Harris and Lydia Stow. These journals, which differ in the time during which they were kept, record daily events, interpretations, and personal reflections, while also disclosing the consciousness of these women (Biklen, 1990). The Archives and Special Collections also holds records from the first graduating class, containing the accounts of their reunions, marriages, birth of children, and life work.

I also conducted on-site research at the American Antiquarian Society, the Henry W. and Albert A. Berg Collection of the New York Public Library,

Boston Public Library rare books room, Concord Public Library, Dedham Historical Society, Fall River Historical Society, Fall River Public Library, Haverford College, Independent Association of Framingham State Alumni, Lexington Historical Society, Massachusetts Historical Society, Nantucket Historical Association, National Archives and Records Administration in Washington, DC, the Perkins School for the Blind, Rhode Island Historical Society, the Schlesinger Library at Harvard University, and Washington University in St. Louis. Archivists at the Gilder Lehrman Institute of American History, Houghton Library at Harvard University, Oberlin College, and the University of Rochester also sent me materials. Each of these institutions yielded materials which helped me to recover the stories of Lydia Stow, Mary Swift, and Louisa Harris.

At times, my access to information came about in unexpected ways as I met individuals at historical societies or other institutions who put me in touch with others who helped me with this research. Through these introductions, for example, I became connected with the Fall River Women's Union, which one of the women I researched helped to found, and was allowed to see their historical records. Through another incidental connection, I visited a woman who held in her home the records of a women's club dating back to the 1890s, which proved to be a fruitful source of information. Another time I found myself sifting through records in an attic in a home for senior citizens, the land for which was donated by one of the women I researched. Alone in that attic, I found the original land deed that she and her husband signed. There were times when these personal contacts, strangers to me at the beginning of the research process, encouraged me to move forward with a helpful email or a kind greeting card for which I am very grateful.

A rare find was made when I visited a used bookstore through the Internet. I purchased Records of the First Class of the First State Normal School in America: Established at Lexington, Massachusetts 1839 compiled by Mary Swift, which proved to be the original copy that belonged to her (Lamson, 1903). My excitement was overwhelming when I realized that, in addition to class records, it contained some hand-written poems from her normal school peers as well as Swift's notes of classmates' obituaries. These obituaries and poems suggested close lifelong connections with normal school peers; a theme I realized permeated their lives. The New England Genealogical Society also was an excellent source of information regarding the vital records of these women and their families. Visits to neighborhoods in which these women lived, the normal school where they studied, places they taught at and traveled to, and their gravesites rounded out the research.

After these materials were collected and reviewed I began the task of piecing together their lives. Their stories are informative, involved, and layered. They merit critical examination and reexamination, and provide invaluable insight into the normal school movement through the experiences of three of the first students. Though it would have been appealing to carefully research and write about all of the women who were in the first class of Lexington students, I felt constrained to limit my research to three. Though in understanding these women's experiences I also learned about the others and was able to bring in pieces of their stories in this writing.

Arranged chronologically and in four parts, this book explores the experiences of Lydia Stow, Mary Swift, and Louisa Harris during their normal school studies, their entrance into the world and commencement of their careers, the transitions in their personal and professional lives, and the building of their life work. Throughout these periods, their formal educational experiences, as well as broader moments of transformation, are considered and how life paths were shaped. Writing their narratives was not an exercise in glorifying lives, but rather one in which details and complexities were examined. Phenomena were pulled together that often are considered unrelated. Their stories help deepen our understanding of the nineteenth century state normal school movement, and more broadly educational reform during this period, and what participation entailed and how life unfolded for three of these women who were true originators in this venture.

Acknowledgments

This book would not have been possible without the encouragement and support of many individuals. I would like to thank my editor, Dr. Terry Osborn, Dean of Education, University of South Florida at Sarasota Manatee, who accepted this work as part of his book series with Information Age Publishing and graciously answered my questions about the publishing process. A number of individuals read different versions of this book. I am particularly grateful to Dr. Robert Grant, Professor Emeritus of Framingham State University, who provided meticulous comments. Dr. Helen Heineman, President Emerita of Framingham State University, Dr. Peter Dittami, Framingham State University, Ms. Louise Dittami, Dr. Daniel Mulcahy, Central Connecticut State University and Dr. Mary Lee Morrison, President Emerita of PaxEducare also read versions and provided important suggestions. Dr. Gerald Gutek, Professor Emeritus of Loyola University, offered advice regarding the process of developing a book prospectus. I also am appreciative of the superb support that Lauren Conley provided with the endnotes and reference sections of this book. Ms. Wendy Wiggins provided tremendous assistance with copyediting.

A number of archivists, curators and supervisors of historical collections helped with various aspects of this project. In particular, I would like to thank Ms. Colleen Previte, Framingham State University, Ms. Jan Seymour Ford, Perkins School for the Blind, Mr. Michael Martins and Mr. Dennis Binette, Fall River Historical Society, Ms. Marilyn Manzella, Independent Association of Framingham State Alumni, Ms. Anna Cook, Massachusetts Historical Society and Ms. Linda Schofield, Fall River Women's Union. I would like to thank the administration at Framingham State, as well as my colleagues in the Education Department and wider university community who listened to ideas about this book. Colleagues often shape our lives in deep and meaningful ways. Though words at times go unspoken about how much colleagues come to mean to us, their care and kindness can be transformative. I am grateful to have met individuals who have touched my life in this regard. I am especially appreciative of the women who work in the Education Department Office: Ms. Carol Nichols, Ms. Sandy Shaw, and Ms. Cindy Flores. My university students also have inspired me to move forward with this book. We often learn as much from our students, as they do from us. Faculty and friends I met while I was a student at Clark University, Rhode Island College and the University of Connecticut have provided various sources of inspiration for this project, as well as the acquaintances I have come to know at the New England Philosophy of Education Society (NEPES), the Society for Educating Women (SEW) and the Massachusetts State University Council of Presidents' Standing Committee on Professional Education (SCOPE).

Most importantly, I would like to thank my family. My parents, Frank and Kerry, and my in-laws, Janet and Ed, have shared their convictions and encouragement. I am fortunate to be connected to caring siblings, sister and brother-in-laws and nieces and nephews. To my children, Joshua, Anna Grace and Jonathan, I am deeply appreciative of your energy, wisdom, kindness, compassion and love of laughter. To my husband Doug, I am thankful for your love and for the life we have built together. This book is for Doug, Joshua, Anna Grace, and Jonathan.

PART **I**

Normal School Studies

1

Becoming Normalites

In July of 1839, the first state normal school opened in Lexington, Massachusetts. Its establishment was led by Horace Mann, the Secretary of the Massachusetts Board of Education, and funded by Edmund Dwight, viewed by some to be a "merchant prince" due to his financial generosity of $10,000 (Framingham State Alumnae Association, 1914, p. 10). Dwight's gift, conditioned on a like amount of funding to be put forward by the General Court, was passed on April 19, 1838, and signed by Governor Edward Everett of Massachusetts (Framingham State Alumnae Association, 1959, p. 2). Cyrus Peirce was recruited to serve as principal of Lexington Normal School. Peirce had gained a promising reputation based on his uncommon success with both teaching in the common schools on the island of Nantucket and promoting their goals (Massachusetts Board of Education, 1840, p. 5). Though Peirce was a minister, he felt called to teach rather than preach. Accompanying Cyrus Peirce to his new position in Lexington was his wife, Harriet Coffin Peirce, an intelligent woman who had been one of his former students.

Normalites, pages 3–18
Copyright © 2014 by Information Age Publishing

Lexington, the site for the school, was designated as such as a result of a thorough appraisal of towns and connected resources in order to determine the best location for the first normal school (Norton, 1926, p. 259). Lexington citizens secured a suitable building (the site of the former Lexington Academy) on a three-year lease. They also agreed to provide one thousand dollars for books and other materials, and subsequently were given the honor of serving as the site of the founding of this great new movement (Framingham State Alumnae Association, 1959, p. 2). Situated in a white, two-story facility on a corner of the Lexington Common, this notable institution was a simple shelter with modest furnishings, though its surroundings were rich in historical context. The town of Lexington was the renowned location of the first battle which started the American Revolution. On April 19, 1775, British Redcoats, on a mission to capture military stores in nearby Concord, came into conflict with Captain John Parker and a group of militiamen as they marched through the Lexington Common. It was there that a first shot was fired and the American Revolution began (Beyer, 2011, pp. 9–10).

Like two-thirds of the nineteenth century Massachusetts population, Lexington residents were primarily farmers or artisans (Kollen, 2004, p. 37). Due to its location as a waypoint between northern New England and nearby Boston, the town was centered in a busy crossroad of commercial activity where wagons full of cheese, butter and produce passed through en route to Boston from New Hampshire and Vermont. The local Buckman and Munroe taverns and town center stores were bustling with activity (Kollen, 2004, p. 37). Located a few hundred yards from the normal school building, situated on the green grass in the center of Lexington, was the oft visited column of grey granite, a monument erected in recognition of the Battle of 1775. Inscribed with a brief account of this battle, it linked the confrontation in Lexington to ideas of freedom and sovereignty sought by the United States from England (Beyer, 2011, pp. 42–43).

It rained on July 8, 1839, the school's opening day. Rain would later come to signify good luck in New England, but in the nineteenth century precipitation lent itself to difficult travel conditions. The normal school opened during the summer season, at a time when it was more probable for women to obtain teaching positions as men worked in farming. (Massachusetts Board of Education, 1840, pp. 5–6). The combination of these factors contributed to low turn-out. The first students who arrived at the normal school, three in total on the opening day, offered diminutive hope to the possibilities that the movement offered in teacher education. It was in these events that "the origin, the source, the punctum saliens of the Normal Schools of Massachusetts," and throughout the United States arose (Framingham State Alumnae Association, 1914, p. 10).

Figure 1.1   Normal School Building in Lexington, Massachusetts. Drawn by Electa Lincoln, Member of the Class of 1843. Courtesy of Framingham State University, Archives and Special Collections, Framingham, MA.

Lydia Stow

Lydia Stow, one of the first three students who enrolled at the normal school, hailed from Dedham, Massachusetts, a town located about 20 miles south of Lexington (State Normal School Framingham, 1900, p. 11). At the young age of 17 and weighing approximately 130 pounds with curly hair, Lydia knew that she would become a teacher and contribute to the Union through her work (L. Stow, personal communication, journal entry, April 16, 1842). Many members of her family and friends believed that teaching was an opportunity to meld young minds and contribute to the future of the nation. It was a role for which some felt that young women were particularly suited, since women, so it was believed at the time, possessed high levels of patience and perseverance. It was a path to progress on which Lydia would travel toward the day when she would assume a school of her own and teach her own students. However, she likely did not wish away her situation at the normal school, as she valued her studies and took pleasure in meeting and learning with the other scholars.

Though not from a wealthy family, Lydia was afforded the opportunity to enter the normal school because tuition was free as long as one agreed to teach in the common schools in Massachusetts upon completing the program. Lydia also received emotional support from her extended family of grandmothers, aunts, uncles, and cousins to move forward with her plans (L. Stow, personal communication, journal entries, 1840–1842). Her official recommendation for entrance into the school came from M. T. Garner, who was the teacher of a private school in Dedham, Massachusetts. Stated simply, he wrote:

> This certifies that Miss Lydia Ann Stowe [*sic*] has been under my instruction several months and is a young lady possessing good intellectual capacity, correct moral principles, and an unblemished character. M. T. Gardner. Dedham Private School, July 18th, 1839.

Though it was her official recommendation, it was drafted after Lydia commenced studies. The recommendation clearly depicted ideals of Republican Motherhood in that it focused on Lydia's virtues and character.

Confident participation in her studies did not come easily to Lydia (Fox, 2000, p. 67). She questioned her abilities, although her grandmothers and aunts likely suggested to her that she was quick with learning and would excel at school, both which proved to be the case. Though bright, Lydia's life had been shaped by tragedy, which may have contributed to her feelings of intellectual uncertainty. Her father, Timothy Stow Jr., died when she was one year old and she had no memory of him (Hanson, 1997a, p. 465). Lydia's mother, Lydia Foord Stow, was his third wife; his first two wives had passed at young ages due to illness (Hanson, 1997a, p. 465). Timothy married Lydia Foord in 1818, and together they had at least three children, one of whom died at only two days old (Hanson, 1997a, p. 466). Though death of children due to illness was not uncommon, Lydia felt that her early years were marked by pronounced uncertainty due to the death of her father. When he died at age 45, her mother was forced to advertise the rental of their house and husband's shop in the Village Register in Dedham.

TO BE LET

And possession given immediately, a convenient tenement for a small family. Also, the shop lately occupied by Timothy Stow, Jun. deceased, as a Carpenter's Shop, on the old Providence road, and within half a mile of the Court House—rent low. For further particulars inquire of the subscriber on the premises, or of Mr. Enos Foord, at his office in the Court House.

LYDIA STOW

Dedham, Sept. 30, 1824 (Village Register, September 30, 1824).

Note: Enos Foord, referenced in this advertisement, was Lydia's maternal uncle.

As Lydia grew up, she watched her mother struggle with the challenges connected to being a widow and single parent. The death of her father, however, was not the end of Lydia's encounters with loss and sorrow. When she was 11, Lydia lost her mother, who died at the age of 36 (Hanson, 1997a). The epitaph recorded for Lydia's mother, which came from Job 19:25, read, "I know that my redeemer liveth" (Hill, 1896, p. 288). Lydia became an orphan at that point along with her older sister Mary Stow, her only sibling still alive and with whom Lydia was very close. The earliest of Lydia's years, cruel years, seemed staged to prepare her for a life of either sorrow or a life of overcoming pain. Lydia hoped it would be the latter. She knew that it was through trials that one would draw on one's strength.

After her mother died, Lydia lived in Dedham, Massachusetts with her maternal grandmother Hannah, her aunts Sophia and Esther who had not married, and sister Mary (L. Stow, personal communication, journal entries, 1840–1842). Her Uncle Enos, his wife Elizabeth Davenport Foord, and their family also may have resided with them at times. Her mother's family was large, since a sizeable number of her siblings had lived past childhood (Hanson, 1997a). The extended Stow family, who also lived in town, continued to visit with Lydia and took an interest in her life. Enveloped in the arms of her large, extended family, she experienced some respite from the losses that had consumed her earlier childhood.

Dedham, Lydia's home, was a growing town with a large acreage. In the early 1800s a stage turnpike had been built that connected Boston and Providence and crossed Dedham. The construction of that roadway was followed by one that connected Dedham to Hartford, Connecticut. Stagecoaches, drawn by four horses, could cover a 42 mile route in three hours and 27 minutes (Austin, 1912). Their degree of efficiency was eclipsed when the railroad later came. With depots in Dedham, the town boomed as a transportation center (Austin, 1912, p. 89). Yet, it still sustained elements of natural beauty that Lydia appreciated. Inspiration Rock, possibly also called Powder House Rock due to the erection of a building that was used to store gunpowder, was situated above the town on a hill and provided not only a view of the village, but of the Blue Hills in the distance. The state name of Massachusetts came from Massachuseuks, which translated meant the place of the great hills (the Blue Hills range). The area had been inhabited for over ten thousand years by Native Americans, prior to the arrival of the European settlers (Wilson, 2003, p. 324). Upon looking at the hills, Lydia would notice and appreciate the bluish hue that she saw. At times, she found a sunny side of a mossy boulder at Inspiration Rock, and while listening to the whispering of the pines, took in the scenery surrounding her (L. Stow, personal communication, journal entry, February 12, 1842). She cherished those views.

Figure 1.2   Powder House Rock, Dedham, Massachusetts. Courtesy of the Dedham Historical Society, Dedham, MA.

Lydia's family was well established in Dedham. Her maternal grandfather, James Foord, had served as a private in the American Revolution (Hilldred, 1876, p. 130; Tuttle, 1897, pp. 42–43). Originally from Milton, Massachusetts, he settled in Dedham and made a living as a farmer, school teacher and then as registrar of deeds. Her Uncle Enos Foord was elected registrar when her grandfather no longer wished to continue in this role. Enos Foord was also the treasurer for the local bank (Tuttle, 1897, pp. 42–43). It is likely that Lydia's family learned about the normal school movement through her Uncle Enos' connections with Horace Mann. Prior to his appointment to Secretary of the Board of Education, Mann had worked as a lawyer in Dedham. Horace Mann and Enos Foord both worked as justices of the peace in Dedham in 1829 (Massachusetts General Government, 1829, p. 78). Enos Foord was said to be a man of decided opinions. "All real improvements found in him an active supporter, mere novelties received from him little favor" (Tuttle, 1897, p. 43). If these sentiments are accurate, it is likely that Enos Foord would have supported the normal school movement, as it was conceived to prepare qualified teachers, subsequently providing a better education for children.

Both of Lydia's aunts with whom she resided, Esther and Sophia, her late mother's sisters, were teachers. Esther was a reader of the very best books (Slafter, 1905, p. 127). Her Aunt Sophia Foord served as a teacher at the first intermediate school in Dedham. Intermediate schools were for older children who completed their primary studies, but had not transitioned into a high school. Aunt Sophia was considered an extremely learned, though somewhat eccentric woman (Slafter, 1905, p. 133). She showed an interest in the teachings of Ralph Waldo Emerson and obtained a copy of an oration he delivered for the Phi Beta Kappa Society at a Harvard commencement exercise in Cambridge in 1837 that focused on the American scholar (Foord, 1837). Specifically, the address considered a scholar's relationship with nature, a perspective that drew from Transcendentalism. Aunt Sophia Foord also was acquainted with the notable Transcendentalist Bronson Alcott and showed an interest in his work. Alcott was a teacher and educational philosopher who followed the teachings of Swiss pedagogue Johann Pestalozzi. Alcott started the Temple School in Boston in the 1830s, through which he became well known for his original teaching methods. One of his school assistants, Elizabeth Palmer Peabody, published *A Record of Mr. Alcott's School* in 1835 (Peabody, 1835). In the years that followed in the 1840s, Lydia's Aunt Sophia would become increasingly connected to Alcott and become the governess of his children, including Louisa May Alcott (Saxton, 1977, p. 159). Lydia was pleased that she had the support of her Aunt Sophia, who encouraged her to continue with her studies and inspired her to pursue a normal school education. Her Aunt Sophia had a particularly strong influence over her.

Though she did not live with her father's side of the family, the Stow family, her interactions with them were warm as well (L. Stow, personal communication, journal entries, 1840–1842). Her grandmother Prudence was a resilient woman who had been married to Timothy Stow Sr., a lieutenant and captain in the militia. They were founders and active members of the Orthodox Church in Dedham which was established in the early part of the nineteenth century (Hanson, 1990). This was a split from the First Parish Church to which Lydia's parents belonged and remained members. Dedham had received some fame as a result of the Dedham Decision, decided by the Massachusetts Supreme Judicial Court in 1820. This decision focused on the church's division over the calling of a controversial new minister to the First Parish Church, a liberal Unitarian named Alvan Lamson who had been educated at Philips Academy and Harvard University. His appointment resulted in a large portion of the church members withdrawing their membership (Tuttle, 1901, p. 35–38). The ruling decided which group was entitled to the church property, for which the Supreme Judicial Court ruled that it is the group that remains, even if it is a minority that constitutes the rights to the property (Harris, 2003, pp. 149–151). Reverend Lamson once said, likely out of frustration, that Dedham has the quiet of a graveyard, but without its peace. He still preached in Dedham in 1839;

Lydia regularly attended his services, though there were times when she saw that he preached largely to empty seats (L. Stow, personal communication, journal entry, March 27, 1842). In total, Reverend Lamson preached in Dedham for 42 years (Tuttle, 1901, p. 35).

Lydia was loyal to the character and principles of her family and participated in their understanding of how the world should be. She was particularly aware of the lessons learned from her grandmother and aunts from the Foord side of the family. In general, they believed that equality, kindness, compassion and like action were necessary for progress to occur in society. They were involved in reform-minded activities, such as temperance and abolitionism. They participated in anti-slavery gatherings and were thought of highly by some for their work in this area. Lydia's Aunt Sophia was the subject of praise in a letter from an acquaintance, L. M. Robbins, for her work in abolitionism at the time that Lydia commenced her normal school studies. The letter addressed to Maria Weston Chapman of Boston read:

August 7th 1839

Dear Maria

I hope you are now able to yield your poor arm without pain. I am very anxious to hear how you do. This note will be handed you by Sophia Ford [sic], a relative of the Davenports that Caroline loved so well. She is from Dedham an abolitionist of the *right sort*. She is working diligently for the fair in October, has great ingenuity & perseverance.... She sees very clearly the ground of the new organization ...

I met her by accident at her sick aunts & asked what she was working.... I was really delighted to meet a sister in the *faith* & asked her to go home with me. She did & stayed for an hour or two. She wants to see you & I want to have her.

Yours most affectionately,

L. M. Robbins

(L. M. Robbins, personal communication, August 7, 1839)

Maria Weston Chapman, at that time, had been elected to the executive committee of the American Anti-Slavery Society which was founded by William Lloyd Garrison and Arthur Tappan in 1833. By 1838, there were over 1,000 chapters of the society and 250,000 members. Chapman, who was the editor of the anti-slavery journal titled *Non-Resistant*, also authored *Write and Wrong in Massachusetts*, a book that explored the disagreements within the Massachusetts anti-slavery society. These dissensions involved a split within church clergy. Members such as William Lloyd Garrison believed that any church member who supported slavery should be excommunicated from the church. Others believed that this was not the right path to follow (Chapman, 1839). The introduction of Lydia's Aunt Sophia to Maria Weston Chapman suggests that the family was connected to those considered by some to be radical abolitionists.

On an earlier occasion, Lydia's Aunt Esther Foord, in a letter received in 1812 from a relative, also was encouraged to "make very good improvement in everything that may be usefull [sic] for you, time passes swift away and we must endeavor to do all we can for the good of ourselves and our fellow creatures" (L. Blake, personal communication, January 26, 1812). There was a strong moral impulse in the family. Lydia grew up hearing about reform and abolitionist meetings and then, when she reached the appropriate age, participated in them as well.

The historic monument in Lexington was one of Lydia's first areas of exploration when she arrived at the normal school in July 1839. She remembered her curiosity and excitement when she read the carefully set inscription, which she copied diligently into her journal. Though the quest for freedom of the country was an event that many felt had been accomplished through the success of the American Revolution, Lydia questioned this idea. She knew that freedom for *all* in the country had not been achieved and that this liberty was something that still was being fought for. As a young woman, Lydia had a grasp of these ideas, but she could not know how they would shape events in the coming years as unrest spread between the slave and nonslave states.

Mary Swift

Mary Swift arrived at the normal school on July 10, 1839; two days after Lydia commenced her studies. Confident, sensitive, a bit anxious, as well as forthright about her thoughts, she wore her plain dark brown hair parted in the middle and pulled back in a bun. Her long, thin face was full of expression. It appeared that her dark blue eyes, bursting with discernment, led one into the depth of her being.

Mary was the daughter of Dr. Paul Swift and Dorcas Gardner Swift, Quakers from Nantucket. Her mother's family was one of the largest on the island. It dated back to 1624 when Thomas Gardner left England and immigrated to Gloucester, Massachusetts. Within a few years of his arrival in Gloucester, Gardner relatives were living on Nantucket. Her father, who practiced medicine on the island, was a doctor of solid reputation. His words of praise for an "eye-water" solution used to treat sore and inflamed eyes had been used in an advertisement in 1831 and 1832 in the Hopkinsian Magazine (Thompson, 1832, p. 448). Not a native Nantucket islander, Paul Swift initially was from Sandwich, Massachusetts. His ancestors had immigrated to New England from England in the seventeenth century. He may have been referred to as a "coof" by Nantucketers, meaning he was a Cape Codder (Philbrick, 2001, p. 10). However, when he and Mary's mother married on September 5, 1821, at the monthly meeting of the Quakers in Nantucket surrounded by 58 family members and friends, Nantucket became the home of the newly joined couple. Children quickly followed. Mary was the oldest of their four daughters, born a year after their marriage in 1822. Her sister, Catherine, was born in 1824. Susan was born in 1827 and Elisabeth, nicknamed Lizzie, in 1831 (Nantucket Historical Association, 2013).

The Quaker community, or the Society of Friends as they called themselves, was a flourishing group on the island. At times, they outnumbered other religious denominations there such as the Congregationalists. By the mid-eighteenth century, a Quaker meeting house was constructed on Nantucket to house two thousand people, a large portion of the island's population. To meeting, Quaker men wore long dark coats and wide brimmed hats. Women, in comparison, wore long, plain dresses and bonnets. There were many components of Quakerism to which Mary felt connected. They were pacifists. The Quakers denied the authority not only of a clergy but also the primacy of scripture as the sole expression of God's will. They believed that an individual could access the spirit without access to ceremony and liturgy. The spirit was understood to be truth. The Quakers depended on their "own experience of God's presence" (Philbrick, 2001, p. 8). They practiced a direct and pragmatic approach to one's relationship with God, which was familiar to Mary. Since Quaker women were not excluded from debates about public issues, but rather encouraged to play an active role in the community, Mary's mother assumed a leadership role in the Society of Friends. Although there were many aspects of her religion to which Mary felt drawn, she recognized that the Quaker community on Nantucket had started to experience disjuncture and factions developed (Leach & Gow, 1997). This likely concerned her.

In the nineteenth century, Nantucket was informally designated the whaling capital of the world. More than 150 ships came and went from the island in search of whales, hunted primarily for their blubber, from which oil for lamps, soaps and candles were produced. With the price of whale oil rising steadily in the early nineteenth century, the business was lucrative and numerous boat building shops were built on the island that supported the industry, as well as boarding houses for the seamen (Philbrick, 2001, p. 1). Mary's great grandfather owned a ship, named Johanna, which was seized by the French prior to 1800. Her family had sought restitution but it was never received and resulted in unrest (D. G. Swift, personal communication, unknown date). As a result of the thriving whaling industry, seventeen oil and nineteen candle factories also were established on the island. Nantucket whale oil was said to light the streets of London and Paris. Though Nantucket Quakers practiced pacifism, many also hunted whales. This may seem like a contradiction; however, their religious beliefs suggested that man had dominion over the seas (Philbrick, 2001, p. 9). In addition to the whaling industry, Mary's childhood was formed by other aspects of island life. The carefully set cobblestone streets of beautifully rounded grey-toned stones had been set to ease travel conditions. The red painted or grey weathered, shingled homes were topped with roof platforms that allowed families, with the use of spyglasses, to spot incoming ships (Philbrick, 2001, p. 3). These spyglasses also were used at night to look at stars. When a comet was seen, it often was interpreted as a sign that something unusual was about to happen (Philbrick, 2001, p. 4). The pristine Nantucket beaches were striking, showcasing different types of sand shaped by the ocean's waves and currents. The local stores provided opportunity for community members to meet and talk and the athenaeum offered an array of books which were available for study, as well as providing a space for public lectures (Philbrick, 1994, pp. 9–11). To Mary, Nantucket—a thriving community of 10,000 residents— was home, a place of connection, friends and family.

Mary first met Cyrus Peirce, principal of the normal school, when she was a student at his private school in Nantucket. It was a successful and lucrative school, with a steady number of scholars, where she studied a basic English curriculum, as well as classics such as Greek and Latin (May,

Figure 1.3   Waterfront View of Nantucket in the Early to Mid 1800s. Courtesy of Nantucket Historical Association, GPN2734, Nantucket, MA.

1857, p. 8). While Mary studied with Peirce at his private school, she likely met and knew Maria Mitchell who prepared there at about this same time (Gormley, 1995). Maria Mitchell would later become the first woman astronomer in the United States. Though Peirce was not originally from Nantucket, he settled on the island when he married Harriet Coffin. The Coffin family was one of the few families on the island who were larger than the Gardner family. It also was one of the most prominent. Harriet's distant ancestor, Tristam Coffin, was part of the group of original purchasers of the island from a Mr. Thomas Mayhew in 1659, who had been deeded the island in 1642 by the English authorities who were in control of the land from the coast of Maine to New York (Philbrick, 1994, p. 35).

Seventeen years old when she started her studies in Lexington, Mary knew that she was part of a great experiment in formal teacher education. Educational experiments were not new to Mary, however; she had encountered them prior to her start at the normal school. Before 1818, Nantucket did not have common schools. Children attended private schools or Cent Schools which were open to the younger children who paid one cent for each session (Nantucket Historical Association, 1905, p. 42). Not all families could afford to pay for the education of their children, however, so in 1818 a small number of common schools were opened and were free of charge. Cyrus Peirce, along with his brother-in-law Samuel Jenks, had been instrumental in starting these schools on the island. Common schools were segregated while Mary was growing up. Black children attended the African Church, also referred to as the African School, located at an area of the island called New Guinea. Attempts to integrate the Black children from the African School into the island's common schools were voted down (Linebaugh, 1978). The vote went against appeals made by Peirce for integrated schools (May, 1857, p. 17). While many of the Nantucket Quakers opposed slavery, there was less of a commitment to social equality and to having children of different races attend school together. One of Mary's relatives from her mother's side of the family, Anna Gardner, taught at the African School (Karttunen, 2005, p. 82). When Anna had been a child, her parents Oliver and Hannah Gardner had concealed fugitive slave Arthur Cooper and his family in their house when a slave catcher was on the island looking for them (Karttunen, 2005, p. 76). Anna Gardner subsequently became active in the island's anti-slavery meetings. As Anna Gardner fought for school integration and for the rights of slaves, she stopped attending the Quaker meetings and thereafter was formally "disowned" (Karttunen, 2005, p 144).

In Lexington, Mary realized that once again she was in the midst of an unsettled and controversial educational experience. The future of the normal school was uncertain. Would it succeed? In July of 1839 only one other normal school was scheduled to open, in Barre, Massachusetts. Mary's mother, Dorcas Swift, had a background in teaching, having served in 1819 as an assistant teacher, without pay, at the Moses Brown School, a Friends Boarding School, in Providence, Rhode Island (Kelsey, 1919, pp. 51–52). Unlike her mother's preparation for teaching, however, Mary's was to be more formal, monitored and closely connected to the work of the common schools, and she would be paid for her efforts. There were many facets to Mary; undoubtedly she was a complex person. One could imagine her future as a successful teacher, the deliverer of a refined speech in front of a crowd of people, as well as one who could sit in blissful quietness with a young baby on her lap, all activities she would later undertake.

Louisa Harris

Louisa Harris, a third normal school student, arrived at the start of the second term in October 1839. When she entered the school, the sun-drenched summer days had turned to crisp autumn ones. Trees that overflowed with leaves of bright reds, oranges and yellows surrounded the general vicinity, creating the quintessential picture of a New England autumn. Tall and reserved in appearance, Louisa was nevertheless social in nature. Her first days at the normal school were lonely, however. The normal school scholars engaged in conversation with her, yet she was at first excluded from the easy camaraderie of young people who have spent time with each other. Louisa would later write in her journal that, "A school girl's first evening among strangers is not a pleasant one" (L. Harris, personal communication, journal entry, October 16, 1850). Though Louisa was studying to be a teacher, she still viewed herself as a school girl when she commenced her studies at age 15. She was one of the youngest of the normal school students.

Louisa was the daughter of Captain Michael and Susanna Stevens Harris, originally from Needham, Massachusetts, who married on November 25th in 1802 (Harris, 1861, p. 32). In his twenties, Louisa's father, a prominent citizen, had been described as a precocious office holder who filled positions of importance in the town and parish, in addition to being a militia captain (Clarke, 1912, p. 688). Her mother had been active in church in Needham (Clarke, 1912, p. 284). After Louisa's parents married, they relocated to Roxbury, Massachusetts, at that time an independent township that bordered on Boston. Elbridge, born in 1805, was Louisa's oldest brother and a person she admired greatly. Her brothers Warren, Granville, and Michael and sisters Lucy, Jane and Laura were born between 1807 and 1818. In 1824, the year Louisa was born, another one of her brothers, Hiram Walker Harris, died at the age of four (Harris, 1861, p. 33).

Louisa had not known her mother's parents, her maternal grandparents Ephraim and Sybil Stevens of Needham, as they died before she was born (Hanson, 1997b, pp. 200–201). Though not known to her in person, some of their history was part of family lore, such as her grandfather's position as a sergeant in the Lexington Alarm (Clarke, 1912, p. 454). Broadly spoken about, the Lexington Alarm was the set of events of April 19, 1775 which contributed to the Battle of Lexington. Militia companies from other towns which responded upon hearing news of the Battle in Lexington never fought in the famous morning Battle. They either fought at Concord, or along Battle Road, the route from Boston on which the British had marched. Some townsmen never participated in any fighting. Nonetheless, these patriots were often recorded as responding to the "Lexington Alarm" (Phillips, 1997). The status of Louisa's grandfather with regard to where and how he fought in the Lexington Alarm is unknown, but he participated. Her grandfather also had worked as a surveyor of highways and superintendent of streets (Clarke, 1912).

Louisa's paternal grandparents, Michael Sr. and Mary Harris, were married in 1775, a year before the Declaration of Independence was signed. They produced a large family of nine to ten children, providing Louisa with a sizeable number of aunts, uncles and cousins (Hanson, 1997b, p. 45). These grandparents, too, did not live to the time of Louisa's birth.

Roxbury, Louisa's home community, had grown from a small town dotted with farms, tanneries and mills, into a more populated urban neighborhood. A period of noticeable transition took place between 1820 and 1839. Alterations were made in the boundaries of Boston and Roxbury through legislative acts. Construction took place on some of the roads and stone was laid to ease travel conditions. All of the roads in Roxbury received names at this time and some of the streets also were lighted. Tremont Street, a large throughway to Boston, opened into the community. A local newspaper was started and a board of health was established (Winsor, 1881, pp. 571-588).

During this time, Roxbury also was the location of notable visitors. When the Marquis de Lafayette, a French aristocrat who served as a general in the American Revolution under George Washington, visited the United States in 1824, he was entertained by Governor Bustis at his residence in Roxbury at the Governor Shirley Mansion. On Lafayette's arrival in Roxbury, bells were rung and artillery discharged. His visit took place during the same year that Louisa was born. The two-hundredth anniversary of Roxbury was celebrated in 1830, when Louisa was six years old, with parades and processions and an address delivered by the General H. A.S. Dearborn, a former member of the Massachusetts state house of representatives and Massachusetts senate (Winsor, 1881, pp. 571–580). Roxbury was a commu-

Figure 1.4   Roxbury, Massachusetts in the Late 1800s. Courtesy of the Trustees of the Boston Public Library Print Department, Boston, MA.

nity Louisa would feel closely connected to for most of her adult years. It would be a place where she would live, teach, and become part of a close-knit social network.

Three other new scholars also arrived at the normal school in Lexington on the day that Louisa commenced her studies (State Normal School Framingham, 1900, pp. 11–12). Sara Wyman was from Roxbury, Louisa's home town and someone with whom she was acquainted. Eliza and Rebecca Pennell, sisters, came from Wrentham and were the nieces of Horace Mann. They resided with their mother, also named Rebecca Pennell, who was very close to Mann, whom she addressed in her letters as her dear, dear brother (R. Pennell, personal communication, April 3, 1833). Since the Pennell sisters' father was deceased, Mann assumed an attentive role with his nieces. In a letter to Mann in April of 1833, the elder Rebecca, wrote her brother that she did not wish anyone "to love you more than my children do" (R. Pennell, personal communication, April 3, 1833). Mann was a person of great respect and prestige. It was an honor to have Mann's nieces take part in the school. Mary Davis from Lexington, Sarah Sparrell from Medford, and Adeline Ireson from Cambridge, also enrolled, followed by six other young women (State Normal School Framingham, 1900, pp. 11–12). Two of these women were sisters, Eliza and Hannah

Rogers, from Billerica. Another student, Susan Burdick, was from Nantucket and likely acquainted with Mary Swift's islander family. Susanna Woodman came from Boston and Abby Kimball from Dracut (State Normal School Framingham, 1900, pp. 11–12).

The first class of normal school students steadily grew to 25 in the first year. Almost all of these students came from Massachusetts towns and cities, though one traveled from New Hampshire. The formal learning experiences of the normal school students were set to unfold, as well as a more profound experience based on shared values, goals, and the excitement of being part of a transformative movement. This would result in deep, life-long friendships, networks and connections among the first class of "normalites." Lydia Stow in January of 1840 recorded in her journal that "the word normal implies that we should have order and system." To be a normalite was to be someone who was a guide and custodian for such order and system. The sense of connection among the normalites was different from a familial nature, but it was strong and would grow over time. As this sense of connection grew, the life work that the normalites would engage in also would evolve.

2

Formal and Informal Learning Experiences

The days that unfolded in 1839 inevitably were a time of change and adjustment for the normal school students. They were away from family and friends and that which was familiar to them. In turn, they became acquainted with new contexts. They studied academic content and pedagogy, as well as met peers and new mentors. These students were not empty vessels waiting to be filled with material. Their agencies, rather, loomed large. They made choices, intervened in various situations, and demonstrated resilience. An examination of their experiences helps one move beyond a one dimensional view of the nineteenth century normal school movement, to more of a holistic one. A review of the learning which unfolded for these women also helps to reveal the transformations which took place for them, as well as for those whom they encountered.

As the semester began in the summer of 1839, the students learned the school rules and customs. School was in session from Monday through Saturday. Each day commenced at 8 a.m. and continued to noon. This was

Normalites, pages 19–34
Copyright © 2014 by Information Age Publishing

followed by a two-hour break, after which class resumed at 2 p.m. and continued to 5 p.m. The students adhered to these hours, with some marginal divergences, as well as made the necessary adjustments when the set schedules changed (Norton, 1926).

During the school day, the students followed a formal subject matter curriculum focused on composition, enunciation, bookkeeping, arithmetic, grammar, geography, and moral and natural philosophy. The academic content at the normal school was a mix of disciplines, but often of a rudimentary level. Cyrus Peirce, who was both the principal and sole instructor, felt that many of the students were deeply deficient in areas of basic academic knowledge, though early on he reflected that Lydia Stow and Mary Swift were promising students (as cited in Norton, 1926, p. 6). When Louisa Harris joined the school at the start of the second term, no immediate assessment of her potential was offered, although Peirce believed that when Louisa and other students entered his class, "the prospects of the school seem to brighten a little" (as cited in Norton, 1926, p. 10).

Classes primarily were held in the chamber of the building known as the "school room," an area that was lacking in ventilation and had no stove, a challenge that Peirce sought to correct (Norton, 1926, p. 6). Furnishings likewise were scarce. Some chairs, a table, blackboard and a prized globe—with an off-white background on which continents and countries were depicted—were the primary equipment. Though basic comforts were lacking in the classroom, Mary Swift would later write that "its emptiness was yet to be filled with a power that should reach throughout our country" (Lamson, 1903, p. 188).

Peirce presented the subject matter carefully to the students; as he was responsible for all content areas this was a demanding task. On Friday, August 9, 1839, he conducted a lesson about light refraction and reflection and discussed the reason for appearances of rainbows. Following that lesson, students took part in a natural history lesson and learned about classification of animals according to genera, orders, and species (Norton, 1926, p. 85). On Monday, August 12, 1839, lessons about light reflection continued. On that day, Peirce told a story about his friend who passed a house late during the evening. He thought the house was unoccupied but saw a bright light burning within. When he approached the house, however, the light disappeared. The light that he thought he saw in the house was actually a reflection from another house in the neighborhood (Norton, 1926, p. 8).

The academic content that the students pursued was necessary, but at times they perceived it to be taxing. In January 1840, for example, they completed a review in algebra. One of her most trying subjects, Lydia Stow recorded in her journal that, "I almost despair over ever mastering you!" (L. Stow, personal communication, journal entry, January 7, 1840). A month later on February 12, 1840, again reflecting on her Algebra abilities, Lydia penned in her journal, "Oh, how I wish my organ of calculation was large" (L. Stow, personal communication, journal entry, February 12, 1840). It was disheartening to make so many failures in one subject area. Yet, Lydia felt she would persevere. She believed that mastery of knowledge should not be the same for normal school scholars as it is for little children. Little children believe that their duties have ended when they have learned their lessons, but to teach requires much more. Lydia also knew that many doubted whether girls should be taught mathematics, as some of the nineteenth century masses doubted the propriety of educating a woman for full participation in society. However, Lydia Stow knew that there could never be a high state of civilized society where women were not educated (L. Stow, personal communication, journal entry, February 29, 1840). Lydia also was likely aware that "support for the growth of educational opportunities for women did not imply a concomitant belief in legal, political or economic equality" (Nash, 2005, p. 1). Lydia had not yet learned her algebra lessons. She would persist. In addition to experiencing difficulties with algebra, Lydia questioned other areas of her academic abilities, though her overall quality of work was strong. It was a lack of confidence, rather than a lack of proficiency.

Unlike many of the other students, Mary Swift found the curriculum manageable and aspired to learn more. In evenings in a corner of the normal school building, Mary quietly studied Greek with Peirce. She had studied both Latin and Greek with Peirce when she was a student at his private school on Nantucket. While at the normal school, Peirce did not want her to forget her previous work in Greek so he asked her if she would like to prepare three lessons a week that she could recite to him during the evening hours. With a candle on a desk, Mary continued to study what she referred to as the Greek Testament with Peirce (Lamson, 1903, pp. 193–194). The Greek Testament was the Christian New Testament, which primarily had been written in Greek and produced by Erasmus, a Catholic priest and humanist, in the sixteenth century. At times, Mary recorded in her journal that she felt refreshed with her continued study of Greek (Norton, 1926, p. 175).

Louisa Harris, as did others, appeared to enjoy specific components of the normal school studies, such as the reading and writing exercises. Louisa also appreciated the more social aspects of the curriculum. In her journal, she reflected on which students were present and absent in the schoolroom, and occasionally on the temperament of her peers. At times, in her journal, she admitted that she was more focused on the "frivolity" of the day (L. Harris, personal communication, journal entry, September 14, 1840). When Louisa reflected on the "frivolity of the day" she demonstrated an understanding that there was an artificially constructed, dualistic sense of their undertakings at the normal school. Through their studies they were preparing to teach in the common schools, yet the students also were experiencing new contexts and growing in a broad social sense. Louisa, at one point, recorded in her journal that she had spent some time practicing politeness, perhaps to balance her blunt nature (L. Harris, personal communication, journal entry, September 14, 1840). She found that she sympathized too easily with her peers. At another time, she wrote in her journal, "What will become of me if I do if I do not learn to restrain my feelings? Never in my life did I find it so difficult as late" (L. Harris, personal communication, journal entry, December 9, 1840).

During afternoon classes, students were provided with lectures about pedagogy. It appears that Peirce had a keen belief in the critical roles of both subject matter and pedagogical practice in the preparation of teachers. He did not appear to promote one over the other but understood that preparation in both areas were required of effective teachers (Norton, 1926).

While Peirce was preparing his students for future teaching careers, he also was preparing to open a model school for the neighborhood children at which the normalites would assume some teaching responsibility. In Prussia, from which some of the features of the state normal school evolved, model schools were utilized. William Woodbridge Channing, in the *American Annals of Education and Instruction*, described these schools as places where teachers learned to coordinate all aspects of teaching, to teach using a variety of disciplinary methods, govern the class and learn about the "peculiarities" of children and work with them accordingly. When the model school was opened in Lexington in October 1839, it was attended by children of both sexes. Between the ages six and ten, these children were drawn from the different districts of Lexington (Norton, 1926, p. 9). Normal school students were assigned the role of superintendent of the model school for short periods. Mary Swift was selected as the first superintendent. Peirce may have first selected Mary because he knew her well from when she was a student at his school on Nantucket and held her in high regard. Assistant teachers, fellow normalites, also worked with her. On December 30, 1839, when the role of superintendent was transferred to another normalite, Peirce wrote in his journal, "Under Miss Swift it has done well." He also wrote that "care is necessary lest in the change of teachers from time to time it sink, and decline and fail" (as cited in Norton, 1926, p. 22). Peirce visited the model school regularly, which was located on the first floor of the normal school building, and offered guidance on instruction and administration (Massachusetts Board of Education, 1840, p. 6).

In his instruction of pedagogical practices on August 21, 1839, Peirce asked the question, "Can the proper object of schools be secured without appeal to corporal punishments and rewards or premiums?" The normalites each provided an opinion on the use of corporal punishment; some agreed with the employment of it while others did not. Peirce adamantly did not support corporal punishment (as cited in Norton, 1926, p. 94). But although Peirce did not agree with it, corporal punishment was widely practiced in the nineteenth century. This was an outcome of earlier Puritan belief systems, including Calvinist ideologies of the innate depravity of children that led to the inevitable use of the "rod" (Glen, 1984, pp. 107–108). Calvinists believed that the sovereign grace of God was necessary for salvation and that physical punishment was used in leading children to this path. Fear, discipline, and obedience were viewed by some as the guiding standards of this conception of child nature (Butts & Cremin, 1953, p. 66). Peirce, in contrast, held a more benevolent view of human nature. Horace Mann, likewise, considered corporal punishment an evil which should be avoided (Mann, 1840, pp. 45–48).

On the afternoon of Saturday, August 31, 1839, there was a discussion that focused on teaching methods, particularly the practice of allowing scholars to exchange or switch seats as they liked. Peirce expressed his opposition to this practice. He believed that allowing students to exchange seats should be avoided. It turned the attention of the students toward the arrangement of seats, rather than toward the learning at hand. It laid a foundation that lent itself to competition and strife. He believed that there was harm done in holding up anything as better than knowledge.

Peirce also thought that a good school must be orderly; whatever its object or title, or whoever its teacher may be. He felt that a school may be pleasant, and even inviting, but order was necessary to make it a good one. He told the normal school students that "the work of Education is a work of order. Order was Heaven's first law" (as cited in Norton, 1926, p. 100). Peirce believed that children, much as they like freedom, are fond of order and system. He believed that this was the cause of their admiration of regular geometric figures, such as the circle. He felt that children were better served by an orderly school, and "if you wish to please them, confine them to rules. This will also be more satisfactory to yourselves as you will be more successful and will know that nothing is neglected" (as cited in Norton, 1926, pp. 100–101). Teaching methods were reviewed regularly throughout the normalites' studies, at times in connection with a text they referred to as "Abbott's Teacher." The full title of this book was *Moral Influences Employed in the Instruction and Government of the Young,* written by Jacob Abbott. The book was intended to provide an overview of the organization and arrangement of a school (Abbott, 1875). It was particularly useful in helping young teachers in conducting their classes.

The normalites learned about the societal expectations connected with teaching. Peirce stressed the need for punctuality when teaching school. He conveyed to the students that they should "not be satisfied with being pretty punctual. Perfection is everything" (as cited in Norton, 1926, p.102). The students knew that he was concerned that a few of them had arrived late to lessons on occasion. Perhaps this particular lesson was an opportunity to reestablish Peirce's expectations regarding starting school promptly. Peirce also explained his views about the dress of teachers. He felt that teachers should not be negligent in their dress. He asked, what right do teachers have to appear in society in an unkempt manner and offend the eyes of others? He told the students that teachers should walk lightly, move gently, and speak softly. One touch of the bell is better than many (Norton, 1926, pp. 99–102). Peirce's sentiments were similar to the perspectives of many in society, filled with clear assumptions about the expectations of women. Some of the normal school students, however, were not sure if Peirce was aware of current fashion styles. A few months after starting her normal school studies, Mary Swift, for example, reflected on Peirce's remarks about the tightness of dresses worn by some of the students, thinking it was the fashion at that time. She recorded in her journal that "He probably has not heard that the wisdom or some other good quality of the age has substituted the reverse fashion for the present time" (as cited in Norton, 1926, p. 84). When she recorded this in her journal, she knew that Peirce would read the sentiment as he regularly reviewed and responded to their writing. It would be read as a cordial challenge. In the years to come, Mary would continue to exhibit her willingness to challenge circumstances which she found inaccurate or unfair. At times, Mary included questions in her journal, asking Peirce, for example, how the new normal school, established in Barre, Massachusetts in 1839, was progressing (Norton, 1926, p. 105).

In Massachusetts, normal schools were intentionally established in different geographical areas so they would best serve the many school districts and towns in the state (Herbst, 1989, p. 60). Peirce reported to the students that the new normal school in Barre, a co-educational school under the direction of Reverend Samuel Newman, had 45 students. Twenty-three were males and 22 were females. Another normal school later opened in Bridgewater, where 30 pupils attended under the supervision of Colonel Nicholas Tillinghast (L. Stow, personal communication, journal entry, November 24, 1840; Massachusetts Board of Education, 1840, pp. 6–7). The start to the normal school movement was experimental, commenced for a three year trial and carefully monitored (Norton, 1926, p. xiv). Horace Mann had stated publicly that "ignorance, bigotry and economy were arrayed against them" (as cited in Norton, 1926, p. xiv). The normal school students were well aware of their role in this great experiment.

As their studies proceeded, the students contributed to the formal curriculum by sharing sentiments. Peirce had encouraged them to share sentiments as it allowed them to practice their reading and gain skills in enunciation and oration (Norton, 1926, p. 165). Expression of these sentiments was important to the students as they also allowed them to share a wide range of ideas and shape the focus of the curriculum. Once a sentiment was put forward, it would create reflection and dialogue. The sentiments also were recorded in the students' journals. On November 4, 1840 Eliza Pennell, niece of Horace Mann and sister of Rebecca Pennell, said, "By indulging certain thoughts we unconsciously weave the web of our existence" (L. Harris, personal communication, journal entry, November 4, 1840). Another student, a month earlier, had suggested that "where the rose grows, the thorn flourishes" (L. Harris, personal communication, journal entry, October 5, 1840). Lydia Stow, on November 30, 1840, provided the sentiment that "It is the world within, the world that you can modify and regulate, that makes your character and destiny, and we the impassive world without" (L. Stow, personal communication, journal entry, November 30, 1840). Lydia's reflections on the importance of character would grow over time. Although more quiet in nature than some of the other normalites, Lydia was speculative. She would later be described by Mary Swift as having faith in liberty of speech for all (Lamson, 1903, p. 37). Mary Stodder, another normal school student and friend of Lydia, Mary, and Louisa, in contrast, read a cure for love one day. "Take a year of sense, half a grain of prudence, a dram of understanding, one ounce of patience, a pound of resolution and a handful of dislike, intermix them and fold them in the slumber of your brain for 24 hours. Then set them on the slow fire of hatred and strain them clear from the drug of melancholy. Sweeten them with forgetfulness, then put them in the bottle of your heart, stopping them down with the cork of sound judgment, then let them stand 14 days in the water of cold affection. This rightly made and properly applied is the most effective remedy in the universe and was never known to fail" (L. Harris, personal communication, journal entry, November 4, 1840). Louisa Harris' reaction to this sentiment was curious. She thought that this remedy had been offered just in time. Though they were public exemplars of the normal school movement, they also were young women for whom matters of romance, courtship, and matrimony were much on their minds. On November 12, 1840, when it was learned that a normalite was to be married, Louisa wrote in her journal, "Miss Amanda Parks is to be married this evening, the first normalite to whom such a catastrophe has occurred" (L. Harris, personal communication, journal entry, November 12, 1840). Marriage was not an undertaking Louisa would have considered at that time; she was preparing to teach, an important social role for which she had equipped herself. The profession would provide her with some income, as well as independence.

The normalites began the practice of writing questions for Mr. Peirce which they placed on the center table. He often answered them at the start of the day. In his instruction Peirce hoped to awaken freedom of inquiry and discussion (Norton, 1926, p. 8). On February 21, 1840, one scholar wrote what Lydia Stow thought was a particularly interesting question. "Is there any difference between reverence and respect?" (L. Stow, personal communication, journal entry, February 21, 1840). Peirce remarked that they both applied to the same class but that reverence was of a higher order. Another scholar asked a question on January 11, 1840, which, in contrast, did not appear to be too pleasing to their principal. The question was if there was any advantage that resulted from studying the globe. Lydia Stow recorded in her journal that "Mr. P. said he thought there were advantages, he had never heard nor seen anything written to convince him of the contrary. It gives a knowledge of the situation of countries, their continent and also some knowledge of astronomy, latitude and longitude" (L. Stow, personal communication, journal entry, January 11, 1840). One can imagine how Peirce reacted to this question, with a measured response, probably as he looked on at the prized globe in the classroom.

At other times informal conversation flowed from topics that they were studying. After a reading lesson in February 1840, in which the term "forlorn hope" was discussed, the topic of whaling came up. Peirce recalled a boat that left Nantucket on a whaling voyage and the unfortunate circumstances connected with that trip. Lydia Stow felt so shocked that she recorded in her journal that the events were "truly appalling to the stoutest heart" (L. Stow, personal communication, journal entry, February 21, 1840). Though the exact whaling voyage that Peirce discussed is unknown, it was perhaps connected to the famed whaleship Essex, a story widely familiar to Nantucketers. In 1819, the Essex left Nantucket to hunt for sperm whale. In the South Pacific, however, the ship was rammed by a sperm whale and subsequently sunk. In three small surviving boats, the 20 member crew tried to reach South America, afraid of cannibalism they thought was practiced on the islands they passed. Only eight of this crew survived, and they were forced to eat the bodies of their dead shipmates in order to stay alive during the ordeal (Philbrick, 2001).

The journals the normalites kept were written with care. The skills of Lydia Stow, Mary Swift and Louisa Harris in journal writing demonstrated a strong command of prose and composition, with the ability to clearly encapsulate the ideas of lessons, experiences and events. Mary Swift's journal would later be described by researchers who read her writing in the centuries to come as copious and systematic (Norton, 1926, p. xx). Her entries were long, causing her at one point to conscientiously shorten her entries as she was running out of journal paper. Peirce read these journals with diligence. On January 7, 1840, he returned their journals and commented that he thought they were in fine shape, but also felt that the scholars spent too much time on their writing to the neglect of their other duties (L. Stow, personal communication, journal entry, January 7, 1840). Periodically, he would insert a comment in a journal. On one occasion, in the journal of Lydia Stow, he asked her if she could use darker ink and if she could reduce the amount of blank space she left on the pages (L. Stow, personal communication, journal entry, January 25, 1840). On another occasion, when Lydia failed to record a summary of a lecture, he wrote with sarcasm that "these remarks are interesting" (L. Stow, personal communication, journal entry, December 17, 1840). As Peirce read the journals carefully, going through each page by page, he did not respond in great detail to their writing, but his brief comments suggested that he was attentive. Though dutiful, Peirce at times was discouraged when he read them and learned that the students did not fully understand the essence of the lessons that he delivered.

Scriptures were read each day at the normal school. In the nineteenth century, religion was still closely connected to public curriculum. As a former Unitarian minister, Peirce was comfortable leading the scholars in religious study. Periodically Peirce reflected on a parable, such as the story of the five loaves and two fishes (Norton, 1926, p. 83). There also were occasions when Peirce would preach in a nearby church. Christianity shaped his views and at times, biased his instruction. On one occasion the students read a short biography of Socrates. He was a philosopher whom Peirce appeared to appreciate, telling the students that he was "one of the most worthy heathen characters that ever lived" (L. Stow, personal communication, journal entry, February 27, 1840). Though appreciative of Socrates, Peirce, in his comments, drew attention to Christian religious beliefs and the fact that Socrates did not share them. Socrates, therefore, was a "heathen." During that same lesson Peirce also disclosed to the students that Socrates had been unhappy in his matrimonial connection and described Socrates' wife as a scold. He portrayed an incident when Socrates was one day sitting under the window of his apartment, taking his ease. His wife, perceiving this, took a vessel of water and poured it over his head. Peirce told the students that Socrates replied that, "one would not expect a shower after so much thunder" (L. Stow, personal communication, journal entry, February 27, 1840). Gender roles also were considered, often stereotypically, in the teachings of the classroom.

In addition to taking part in the designated academic classes during the day hours, students adhered to the required evening study periods, though they bent the rules on occasion. On Thursday, January 8, 1840, Lydia Stow wrote, "Our evening hours were carefully observed by most. I made communication during the evening not through the mechanism of my lips. However, a smile or even a look will often convey much meaning" (L. Stow, personal communication, journal entry, January 8, 1840). Peirce believed that if the students observed the required study hours, they would accomplish small miracles (L. Stow, personal communication, journal entry, January 10, 1840). The students, in turn, at times felt that the study hours were an imposition. They often preferred social pursuits.

As students assembled in the classroom each morning, they naturally assessed the scene around them. Peirce's unruly brown hair rested above his ears and neck line. His thick eyebrows and firmly set nose drew attention to the seriousness of his expression. His walk was distinct. The sound of his footsteps announced his presence. He lacked a clear, sonorous voice, but when he spoke it was said that one could hear the inspiration of his soul (May, 1857, p. 25). He commanded respect, but was kind. Due to his paternal nature, the scholars called him Father Peirce (May, 1857, p. 25). He was pleased to be in his position as principal of the normal school, a school of special recognition. However, the scholars knew that Peirce was equally proud of his work in the field of education. He had spent over thirty years as a teacher, and also served as a Unitarian minister for a time after he graduated from Harvard College and Harvard Divinity School. Though he was a minister, his passion was education. In addition to his work as principal and primary teacher, he maintained all of the correspondence for the normal school and oversaw and physically helped with the janitorial responsibilities of the building. Early on in 1839, he wrote in his journal that a wood shed was being constructed for the normal school building, presumably which he supervised. His dedication to the school was unmistakable (Norton, 1926, p. 6).

At times the students marveled at Peirce's indefatigable energy. They feared, and later knew that they tried his patience with what they would later say was young and saucy conduct (L. Stow, personal communication, journal entries, 1840–1842). As they were young in age, they also were youthful at heart. There were one or two scholars who Mr. Peirce did not believe were suited for teaching at all. They lacked the academic foundation, as well as the temperament and drive for teaching. When Peirce asked questions related to his teachings, these particular students often could not provide a response (Norton, 1926, p. 14). The normalites were thankful that Peirce had the support of his wife, Harriet. She was affectionate toward the students, who were like daughters to her. They, in turn, called her Mother Peirce. The Peirces had no children of their own (May, 1857).

When school was not in session, the normalites were expected to take part in physical exercise or a suitable recreational activity, as an extension of their curricular experiences. Physical exercise, it was thought, helped one relieve nervous energies. It also was believed that it prevented conditions such as dropsy, which was a swelling of tissues, such as those found in the feet, due to excess water retention. On January 8, 1840, Lydia Stow recorded in her journal that "Mr. P spoke of the importance of attending to physical exercise. If we attempt to study at the long recess, we but partially abstract our minds and lose much good, where as if we exercise our bodily powers and then our mental, we should accomplish much more" (L. Stow, personal communication, journal entry, January 8, 1840). Mary Swift's father, Dr. Paul Swift, also talked about the importance of exercise with the normalites when he visited the normal school (Norton, 1926, p. 28). The normalites found exercising together to be pleasant, particularly at the end of a hot summer day when the heat abated (Norton, 1926, p. 96). On occasion, excursions would take the students on long walks, such as an outing to a church in West Cambridge, a saunter of eleven miles. This particular excursion had received reluctant approval from Peirce, as it was a lengthy journey. When the normalites returned, Peirce felt that they were too tired from the trek (as cited in Norton, 1926, p. 5). The students even tried to find time to exercise together in cold temperatures. They named one of the hills that they visited "Normal Hill." Sometimes their attention was attracted to streams of water that etched their way down the slopes, perhaps from melting snow. When a small waterfall was seen, it sparked dialogue about the wonders of Niagara Falls. They wondered if they would have the opportunity to see this wondrous site with its pulsating water and strong force (L. Stow, personal communication, journal entry, February 22, 1840).

On Sundays the students took part in public worship. They attended services at the nearby Unitarian Meeting House, a large, plain rectangular building with three stories of windows, box pews, and a pulpit that rose eight feet above the floor (Norton, 1926, p. xx). The normalites reflected on the sermons, often in their journals. On August 25, 1839, for example, Reverend Buckingham preached from Genesis about the Garden of Eden in the morning and from Job during the afternoon. Mary Swift put off recording notes about the sermon on that occasion, causing her to reflect on the bad habits of procrastination (as cited in Norton, 1926, p. 96). Mary was perhaps her own greatest critic, often seeming to push herself to do more. On occasion, a guest minister preached. Reverend Damon from West Cambridge, presumably father of normal school student Hannah Damon, preached on September 13, 1840 (L. Harris, personal communication, journal entry, September 13, 1840). On the day of Sabbath, the students were mindful not to engage in any type of academic study, as this had been discouraged by Peirce (L. Stow, personal communication, journal entry, July 21, 1840).

Though there was excitement surrounding the normal school movement, the day to day experiences were not always stimulating. On August 31, 1839, Mary Swift penned in her journal "that time waits for no man and it appears that he has left us far behind." She felt some initial qualms about her decision to enroll in the normal school although she suspected that those feelings would pass (as cited in Norton, 1926, p. 99). On another occasion, Louisa Harris wrote in her journal, "The school room seems not so pleasant as formerly to me at best, and from appearances I should judge it was the same with others" (L. Harris, personal communication, journal entry, September 17, 1840). The lessons the normal school scholars undertook differed in content, but the routine often was the same. Louisa Harris at times felt that it would be more pleasant to be with her family (L. Harris, personal communication, journal entry, September 17, 1840). She reflected on the platonic year, the longest cycle known to astronomers, and wrote that she believed in it due to her normal school studies. In that same journal entry she wrote that "things are beginning to be acted over again. For I don't perceive any difference between today and yesterday" (L. Harris, personal communication, journal entry, September 24, 1840). On September 22, 1840, Louisa's spirits changed briefly, however, because the previous evening the normal school students had spent the time singing, dancing, talking and laughing. They had such a wonderful relaxed evening and were so enamored of these activities that they awoke the next morning and danced again (L. Harris, personal communication, journal entry, September 22, 1840). The stress of their studies was relieved by playful interactions among young friends. Sometimes, however, their dancing brought forth complaints. A building steward complained on more than one occasion about this type of activity. In December of 1840, the students also had begun to play cards. When Peirce learned of the activity, he told them that he hoped it would not continue in their "consecrated" walls (L. Harris, personal communication, journal entry, December 8, 1840).

At Peirce's request, the scholars started to assemble in the sitting room each morning following their breakfast where they would read scriptures and sing a hymn (L. Harris, personal communication, journal entry, September 12, 1840). This room was small, however, creating a sense of discomfort (L. Harris, personal communication, journal entry, September 12, 1840). Due to shortcomings in some of the students' efforts with their studies, Peirce also felt he needed to strengthen the regulations surrounding their schoolwork. As a result, a bell was rung each morning to announce the start of sessions (L. Harris, personal communication, journal entry, September 14, 1840). It became known as the sacred bell, an object that Louisa Harris would grasp on one occasion and ring in defiance. On September 26, 1840, she recorded in her journal that, "In the afternoon accomplished that which my hands and propensities have long desired to do, and which required nothing but a mischievous aid to enable me to make the attempt, ventured to pull the bell nape" (L. Harris, personal communication, journal entry, September 26, 1840). Peirce, due to the perceived defects of the students, regulated evening study hours more carefully, and stretched them from 7 p.m. to 9 p.m. In addition, he requested a half an hour in the morning during which students would review the lessons from the previous evening. Louisa Harris recorded in her journal that, "think's... that's rather more time than the studious king devoted to such business" (L. Harris, personal communication, journal entry, September 12, 1840). At times, Louisa Harris ceased participation in the required study hours and instead took time to write letters to family (L. Harris, personal communication, journal entry. September 18, 1840). Peirce told the students that he felt it would be a departure from duty if they wrote letters during school hours. He also asked that if a letter arrived during the school day that it should not be read until after school hours. It was a great temptation for the students when a letter was placed before them and they had to wait to open it (L. Stow, personal communication, journal entry, February 29, 1840). The students placed a good deal of importance on their correspondence with and from friends and family. Louisa Harris recorded her feelings about letter writing during study hours in her journal, knowing Peirce would read them.

In the same, small sitting room in which the students started their day, they often would reconvene in the evenings and sit by a fire, at times commiserating with each other (L. Harris, personal communication, journal entry, September 14, 1840). During evening hours, students also talked, shared news and plans. One topic of discussion was Squire Phinney, a neighbor, who was keenly interested in the American Revolution (Norton, 1926, p. 104). In Lexington, there were still a few residents left who had been there when William Dawes' and Paul Revere's famous rides took place. Revere, who became the more famous of the two men, had alerted the colonial militia of the advance of the British troops from Boston in 1775.

After crossing the Charles River, he landed in Charlestown and rode to Lexington by horse, alerting almost every house en route of the approach of the British Regulars (Beyer, 2011). Some residents also remembered the Minutemen who were among the first to fight in the American Revolution (Norton, 1926, p. xxii). The history of Lexington was of compelling interest. In a letter in August of 1839 to his former students on Nantucket, Peirce penned, "I can almost jump from my window upon the soil which was first moistened by blood spilled in the opening of the Great Drama which led to our glorious independence, as it is called and I am within a stone's cast of the monument erected to the memory of the first martyrs to American Liberty" (C. Peirce, personal communication, August 5, 1839).

The students established a society, with elected officers, the object of which was mental improvement (L. Stow, personal communication, journal entry, January 18, 1840). In the evening, they would convene and discuss a chapter from a book, such as one by Silvio Pellico (L. Stow, personal communication, journal entry, November 28, 1840). Pellico was an Italian author who wrote tragedies. Considered a revolutionary, Pellico also was imprisoned for a time and wrote about his experiences (Pellico, 1931). At other times, the normalites would sew together. The establishment of the society suggests that they were willing to invest in their studies and shape them.

In all endeavors, Cyrus Peirce encouraged his students to live to the truth (Lamson, 1903, p. 25). This was a directive Peirce had used with his former students on Nantucket and used it almost daily at the Lexington Normal School (May, 1857, p. 21). It had defined his own studies when Peirce was a student. Whiling studying, Peirce would read academic material until he had learned the truth of it (May, 1857, p. 6). It was an idea that the normal school students embraced and one that they would carry forward. It was part of the normal school impulse, yet not one that was recorded in official curricular materials. Since their enrollment was small, Mr. Peirce also told them that "strength does not come in numbers" (Lamson, 1903, p. 5). This suggested to them that by succeeding in their undertaking they would have the ability to spearhead formal teacher preparation throughout the United States. In all undertakings, Peirce urged the students to do their best, or to "do it with all their might" (L. Stow, personal communication, journal entry, June 11, 1840).

As formal educational experiences proceeded at the normal school, so did informal learning opportunities. Students soon formed close bonds with each other. As many of the students including Lydia, Mary, and Louisa boarded together at the normal school, they saw each other regularly outside of their classes. Two dollars a week, plus washing duties, was the boarding fee for students (Norton, 1926, p. xiix). Those who did not secure boarding at the normal school secured lodging in homes in the surrounding community. Though these students who lived in the neighborhood area were relatively close to the normal school, weather, such as a violent snow storm which occurred on December 6, 1840 and resulted in high snow banks, made their attendance difficult at times (L. Harris, personal communication, journal, December 6, 1840).

Because the normalites lived as well as attended school with each other, their academic and personal lives were bound together. It was in this informal context that other moments unfolded which also shaped the normalites' interactions. At the start of January in 1840, for example, Lydia Stow recalled that she woke up and wished her fellow scholars a happy new year. The students were often together on special days, including Christmas and New Year's Day. The year of 1840 Lydia felt would be a memorable time, as she was with her friends. New Year's Day of that year brought the coldest weather that they had encountered since they started their studies, with the temperature standing at one degree below zero (L. Stow, personal communication, journal entry, January 1, 1840). Two weeks before, on December 15, 1839, Mary Swift had awakened Lydia to see the first snow of the season (Norton, 1926, p. 166). When it was particularly cold, the normalites tried to remain in bed as long as possible to keep warm. The variable and rapid changeability of New England weather played a role in their lives; it not only signified changes of the seasons, but also the possibilities within and constraints brought by them. Early morning moonlight walks became a time of quiet connection for the students. On October 13, 1840, Lydia Stow wrote in her journal that she rose before five and enjoyed a walk in the moonlight with a normal school peer. She felt that "it was beautiful" and they extended their walk until 6 a.m. (L. Stow, personal communication, journal entry, October 13, 1840). The beauty of nature brought joy to the normalites. Nature also helped the normalites learn about each other. When Lydia Stow tended a turtle that she found with care, Louisa Harris reflected on Lydia's conscientious nature (L. Harris, personal communication, journal entry, September 8, 1840).

There were times when scholars became ill. Mary Swift, for example, was not well in late January 1840 and left for a few weeks to stay with the Reverend O. A. Dodge, a Baptist minister, and his family (L. Stow, personal communication, journal entry, February 2, 1840). While Mary was away due to sickness, Cyrus Peirce felt a loss. Mary's father, Dr. Swift, traveled from Nantucket to check on her progress. He attributed Mary's illness to over-exertion. In his middle years, Dr. Swift had turned reflective. On his forty-fifth birthday the previous year, he pondered on that event and wrote, "I looked forward to this period as the summit of human perfection, as a period when the mental powers have not failed in energy yet having had the benefits of experience" (P. Swift, personal communication, March 2, 1839). In his reflections, however, Dr. Swift acknowledged that death had taken from him some of his best friends (P. Swift, personal communication, March 2, 1839). Dr. Swift was concerned about Mary's health which, coupled with his strong willed nature, compelled him to personally assess the situation regarding his daughter. As Mary grew better, Lydia felt particularly pleased that she would have the benefit of Mary's company for a few months longer. Following Mary's illness, Peirce told the students that he did not want them to neglect their health while they attended to their studies. He further said, "Above all things, I wish you peace among yourselves. Whatever else you may do, do not lose your harmony and peace of mind" (L. Stow, personal communication, journal entry, March 18, 1840). In sharing these words, Peirce likely reflected on his own sacrifices which he had made to oversee the first state normal school.

There inevitably were times when students became frustrated with each other. On one occasion, an unnamed student grabbed another student named Mary Haskell and used her long hair to tie her to a particular, though presently unknown, area in the normal school. It was only with a pair of scissors that the student was set free. Since the student who was tied to a particular area had beautiful red hair, her perpetrator kept a lock of hair which she wrote in a note that she would cherish (Lamson, 1903, p. 7). It was an event that the students would remember for years to come. In 1839 and 1840, however, the students still were young. They had future opportunities to grow in learning and in wisdom.

The students became sisters in learning, normalites (L. Stow, personal communication, journal entries, 1840–1842). The sense of connection between the normalites was different from one of a familial nature, but it was strong and would continue to grow over time, as their experiences as normalites metamorphosed into deep friendships and networks. Lydia Stow, Mary Swift, and Louisa Harris would remain connected and close throughout the remainder of their lives.

3

Excursions and Visitors

The normalites became familiar with their neighbors and surrounding community during their time at the normal school. In the company of Mr. Peirce and other normalites, they traveled to special events and attended public lectures and conventions during which they experienced new contexts and situations. Visitors also frequented the school to give talks and lectures. The normalites viewed these occasions as ones during which the students mingled and acquired information from "dignified and learned men." They held "animated discussions" marked by "free interchange of thought" (L. Harris, personal communication, journal entry, February 26, 1842). The normalites subsequently acquired new insights from the outside world, introductions to influential people, and abilities to conduct intellectual discourse. These excursions and meetings with visitors shaped the normalites' experiences and future life work. These interactions, in various ways, also shaped those who the normalites met.

One of the first trips took place on August 28, 1839, when Lydia Stow and Mary Swift traveled to the Harvard College commencement exercises with Peirce, his sister and niece. There they met crowds of attendees

Normalites, pages 35–44
Copyright © 2014 by Information Age Publishing

35

dressed in finery; some women wore bonnets while others wore veils. Music played and processions were led. Spectators laughed at the recitation of humorous poems. There was a banquet dinner and a visit to the 50,000 volume college library. It was at the commencement exercises that they heard Samuel Eliot, a Harvard graduate who went on to become a president of Trinity College in Connecticut, deliver a fine oration entitled, "The Old Age of the Scholar." Mary Swift's recorded notes about this oration are likely the most descriptive that remain in existence (Norton, 1926, p. xxi). Mary, however, preferred the reading of a poem by Thomas Dawes of Cambridge to Eliot's speech. Mary, Lydia, and Cyrus Peirce returned again to Harvard College the next day to attend the meeting of the B. K. Society, the first name of the Phi Beta Kappa Society, at which they witnessed a procession headed by the Governor (Norton, 1926, p. 97). During this particular outing they also visited the Mount Auburn Cemetery, where as Mary recorded in her journal, they saw the tomb of Johann Spurhzeim, a German physician who traveled extensively in Europe and the United States promoting phrenology, a philosophical movement that gained prominence in New England in the nineteenth century (Norton, 1926, p. 99). Phrenology was based on the concept that the brain was the organ of the mind, and that certain brain areas have localized functions (Spurzheim, 1846). The distinguishing feature of phrenology was the belief that the sizes of brain areas were meaningful and could be inferred by examining the skull of an individual. Spurhzeim died in Boston in 1832 of typhoid fever. His brain was removed and preserved in alcohol and his tomb established in Mount Auburn.

On January 15, 1840, the normal school students attended the dedication of a new church in East Lexington. Lydia Stow described the building as small, but a picture of neatness and simplicity. Ralph Waldo Emerson from Concord delivered the keynote address, which lasted almost three hours (L. Stow, personal communication, journal entry, January 15, 1840). By 1840, Emerson had become one of the nineteenth century's most notable speakers and writers as a proponent of Transcendentalism, an intellectual movement with roots in the philosophical teachings of Immanuel Kant. Emerson's focus was on the inner spiritual essence of humans. He had gained fame after he delivered a speech regarding *The American Scholar* in 1837. Emerson also had anonymously published an essay titled *Nature* in 1836, which was based on the idea that divinity diffuses all nature. By 1841, he published another essay titled the *Over-Soul* which, written with grace and sophistication, focused on the immortal nature of the human soul, and the relationship of the soul to others, the world and universe (Richardson, 1995). The message of the *Over-Soul* was one that touched not only nineteenth century New Englanders, but one that would be considered in the centuries to follow.

The normalites continued to become immersed in the surrounding community. On January 19, 1840 they heard a sermon delivered by the Reverend Caleb Stetson. In his sermon, Stetson brought news of the death of Dr. Charles Follen, an abolitionist and strong supporter of the state normal school movement from the East Village in Lexington, who had died, along with his only son, in a steamship accident (L. Stow, personal communication, journal entry, January 19, 1840). Follen's son had been a student in the model school connected to the Lexington normal school.

The normalites had heard Dr. Follen lead a prayer when Governor Edward Everett of Massachusetts visited the school in October of 1839 (Norton, 1926, p. 127). On that day, the first day that Louisa Harris started her studies, Governor Everett appeared at the school to commence the start of the second term and addressed the students and surrounding community of Lexington at the Unitarian Church, nearly filled to capacity (Norton, 1926, p. 124). The program included a hymn read by Reverend Dodge, viewed by Cyrus Peirce to be a best friend of the normal school, and a prayer by Dr. Follen (Norton, 1926, p. 42). Then came Everett's address (Norton, 1926, p. 124). His emphasis was to celebrate the start of the second term of the normal school, still in its infancy. Everett told the audience that the term "normal" came from the word *norma*, a Latin word for rule or direction. He suggested that the principles taught in the normal school, and the manner by which students were taught to use those principles in their own teaching, are models for others. He summarized the history of the normal school movement throughout the world, taking particular note of the system that was in practice in Prussia (Norton, 1926, p. 124). He reflected on the goal of normal schools, which was to provide children with teachers who are educated in substance and in practice. He said it was critical for teachers to be educated in common branches of knowledge and to be able to impart instruction capably. They had to understand the role of government, and they had to gain some practice experience in model schools (Norton, 1926, pp. 124–127). That very day Louisa Harris sensed that life had changed for her in a matter of hours. As she saw it, she was on an ocean voyage, on a great journey. She wondered where it would bring her. At the conclusion of Everett's address, he toured the normal school building before leaving (Norton, 1926, pp. 124–127). A few months later, at Dr. Follen's funeral, Reverend Stetson observed that "our joys, our hopes, our sorrows and crosses are closely bound together" (L. Stow, personal communication, journal entry, January 19, 1840). It was a sentiment Louisa could easily relate to, as life has a way of encapsulating different events, episodes, and emotions in tandem.

There were other notable individuals who visited the normal school. Since the normal school movement was experimental, there was wide interest from both within and outside the state. On March 19, 1840, Henry Barnard, Secretary of the Board of Education in Connecticut, and six other "gentlemen" visited to observe the practices utilized with the students (L. Stow, personal communication, journal entry, March 19, 1840). The students were apprehensive in the presence of this formidable group of visitors. It appeared as if they were being called before a daunting array, meaning that they felt apprehension about meeting such a powerful assembly. After observation of some of their lessons, Henry Barnard remarked on recent steps being taken to discontinue the normal schools in Lexington and Barre, Massachusetts. He shared with the students that the Lexington school, being the first state normal school, was hailed by Massachusetts and other states as a "morning star of a brighter and more glorious day" (L. Stow, personal communication, journal entry, March 19, 1840). He told them that great responsibility rested upon those who were the first to go out from the school. He beseeched them to understand that the public would expect much of them and that they needed to appeal to higher and holier motives than many teachers do. They were figures of notice in the public eye.

Horace Mann also visited frequently. At times he would join in the lessons that were presented to the students. In addition to his involvement in the normal school movement, he liked to keep up with his two nieces, Rebecca and Eliza Pennell, who were students at the institution. They were close to their uncle. They also had become close to the other normalites, including Mary Swift, Lydia Stow, and Louisa Harris.

Dr. Samuel Gridley Howe from the Perkins Institution for the Blind likewise was a frequent guest. The Perkins Institution was the first school for the blind in the United States, established in 1829 and initially named the New England Asylum for the Blind. Howe's interest in the normal school was no doubt related to his close connections with his friend Horace Mann with whom he had been classmates at Brown University. In 1840, as members of the Massachusetts legislature moved to abolish the normal schools and refund the money that Edmund Dwight had put forward for the endeavor, Dr. Howe wrote a letter in support of the schools, lending assistance to Mann. This letter, which he wrote on March 9, 1840, was sent to Thomas A. Greene who was a member of the minority committee along with a John Shaw, who provided support for the movement (Combe, 1841, p. 282).

Mr. Greene,

Sir, I have received your note, in which you ask my opinion of the Normal School at Lexington, and I cheerfully comply with your request.

I can express my opinion more confidently, because I have more than once visited the School; because I have examined the pupils, in their various branches of study; and because I have had other opportunities of knowing the principles of the system of instruction. . . .

I have said, sir, that the pupils were thoroughly acquainted with the various branches of an English education, as far as they advance in them, and they bore well a very severe examination . . . At the Lexington School, the moral nature is as much cultivated as the intellectual, and the training of each goes on at the same time.

There is one point of view, however, in which this School particularly interested me, and in which it presented a beautiful moral spectable, the memory of which will dwell long in my mind; it was the fact, that every pupil seemed impressed with a deep sense of the importance of the calling which she was to follow; they seemed to feel that at least the temporal weal or wo of hundreds of human beings might be dependent upon the fidelity with which they should perform their duty as teachers. . . .

With much respect, truly yours,

Samuel G. Howe

(as cited in Norton, 1926, p. 274).

It is interesting that in Howe's letter he describes teaching as "a calling." Intrinsic to teaching, suggested Howe, was a higher purpose, a commitment to a grander mission.

Samuel May, an educational reformer, abolitionist, and advocate of women's rights who also was the brother-in-law of Bronson Alcott, often visited the normal school. May would later become the normal school principal in 1842 for a period of two years, when Peirce temporarily stepped down from that role. May, along with other notable individuals such as Horace Mann, also served as a board member of the Perkins Institution which was directed by Dr. Howe. These educational reformers were closely connected by work and friendship. They provided each other with nourishment and sustenance in their independent yet mutual endeavors. These were relationships the normal school students noticed.

Close connections between the normal school at Lexington and the Perkins Institution brought about other changes. In November 1839, one of the teachers from the Perkins Institution, Lydia Drew, decided to enroll at the Lexington school. She likely had been encouraged by Dr. Howe to pursue a normal school education. When Mary Swift first met Lydia, she was surprised to learn that she already was a teacher. On October 1, 1839, Mary wrote in her journal,

> A gentleman and lady called, she looks like a "to be" scholar.—P.M. What a poor guesser for a Yankee! The gentleman was Dr. Howe the superintendent of the blind institution in South Boston and the lady one of his teachers. (as cited in Norton, 1926, p. 123)

In her twenties, Lydia Drew was the oldest student at the normal school (State Normal School Framingham, 1900, pp. 11–12). When she arrived at Thanksgiving she wrote to her mother to describe her experiences in Lexington.

> Lexington Nov. 28th, 39
>
> My Dear Mother,
>
> It is Thanksgiving Day. I supposed—however, if I had not been told of it by the ringing of the church-gong bell, I should not have known it. I came out to Lexington on Tuesday and found the young ladies preparing to leave school to go home to spend the Thanksgiving. There will be a vacation for the remainder of the week, a few of the young ladies remain so I am not entirely alone. But what do you think I had for Thanksgiving dinner? Now don't envy me the luxury—fried pork and potatoes with brown head, and a bread plum pudding. How I thought of the nice time you were having at home....
>
> I like Lexington very much. This school is delightful so far as much I can judge for so short a time. The young ladies who compose the school are very pleasant and happy. I think I shall be very well contented....
>
> I remain your affectionate daughter,
>
> Lydia
>
> (L. Drew, personal communication, November 28, 1839).

Though Ms. Drew liked her fellow students, normalites, over time she grew to see that they could test limits. In 1840, Drew wrote to Dr. Howe, "I do not think it is possible to have no trouble. The young ladies of the school are not all considerate, and are apt to take more liberties in a boarding house than they would at home" (L. Drew, personal communication, March 6, 1840). As Drew became acquainted with the normalites, she shared stories with them about Dr. Howe and the Perkins Institution, which proved to be interesting and informative.

The visits of Howe, his student Lydia Drew, and others connected to the Perkins Institution exposed the normal school students to educational ideas that they had not yet considered. On March 7, 1840, for example, a Miss Howe, likely the sister of Samuel Gridley Howe as she lived with him, visited the normal school with Laura Dewey Bridgman, a student from Perkins (Norton, 1926, p. 208). Laura had arrived at the Perkins Institution on October 12, 1837, at the age of seven years, two months prior to her eighth birthday. Although she had been born with the ability to see and hear, she contracted scarlet fever when she was two and became blind and deaf. She also was left with a severely limited sense of smell and could barely distinguish between different foods by aroma. Laura's two sisters had also caught the horrible fever, but had not survived. Laura's parents, Daniel and Harmony Bridgman, nursed their remaining daughter back to health over the course of the next few years, during which she was confined to her bed (Gitter, 2001, pp. 3–4). She was described by some who met her as child with a "scrofulous" temperament, meaning that she was run-down and considered morally deficient. Yet Laura also had a strong will to please her parents. In efforts to communicate with Laura, her parents used some rudimentary gestures, such as patting her on the head, to portray their wishes to her (Gitter, 2001, pp. 47–52). Prior to enrolling at the Perkins Institution, however, Laura had largely been unable to communicate with the outside world. Her mind was said to dwell in darkness and stillness. She largely stayed by her mother's side, only to leave her for short periods to spend time with her father (Freeberg, 2001, p. 18).

Dr. Howe had learned of Laura's circumstances, and visited her parents in Hanover, New Hampshire in order to persuade them that Laura would be well served at the Perkins Institution. Howe was familiar with another child, Julia Brace, who also had lost her sense of sight and hearing, and resided at the Asylum for Deaf-Mutes in Hartford, Connecticut (Freeberg, 2001, p. 26). Julia had made some progress with learning to communicate with the outside world and Dr. Howe was eager to have Laura achieve this same success. Laura's parents agreed, though likely with trepidation and mixed emotions, that she could attend the Perkins Institution. Howe and others subsequently were successful in helping Laura learn to communicate. Howe's achievements with Laura Bridgman gained him a measure of fame. She was written about in newspaper and magazine articles, and his work with Laura was widely discussed in the United States, as well as across the Atlantic in Europe (Freeberg, 2001; Gitter, 2001; Lamson, 1881). When Laura visited the normal school in 1840, Lydia Stow recorded in her journal that it was "mysterious how a being destitute of three of the five senses can thus evince such knowledge. Oh, how much happiness is this child by having been instructed in common things. Her powers of memory are very strong" (L. Stow, personal communication, journal entry, March 7, 1840). Mary Swift, likewise, thought it was remarkable that this communication with this child had opened up the world to her. Mary did not yet know how her own life would become deeply shaped by Laura.

Under the direction of Peirce, the normal school students periodically took a break from their studies and visited nearby schools or attended education related meetings. One such occasion occurred on September 22, 1840, when they had the opportunity to take part in the County Educational Convention. Conventions were directed by law and attended by the Secretary of the Board of Education from each county of the Commonwealth. These assemblies were considered to be in accordance with the character of the political institutions in the United States with the "aim to effect the great objects of human society, as far as possible, by the voluntary action of the people . . . which look to government only, for such measure of aid and organization, as is needed to call into the highest action the enlightened sense of the community" (Massachusetts Board of Education, 1840, pp. 4–5). Attendance varied at the meetings at which diverse subjects connected to education were discussed (Massachusetts Board of Education, 1840, p. 3).

On September 22, 1840, Reverend Caleb Stetson from Medford opened the convention with prayer. Broad questions thereafter were considered by the attendees. Dialogue often turned to the role of parents in their children's education. Should parents be more interested in procuring a fine horse or cow than in the morals of their children? One participant believed that the current state of social affairs should fill parents and society with confusion and shame. Other topics of discussion frequently included the proper qualifications of teachers. One question that was considered was whether a child should be compelled to study against his or her will. Reverend Stetson reflected on schooling in England, where he said lessons were literally flogged into children. He said that if these measures were adopted in New England there would likely be a rebellion. An alternative, he suggested, was to walk into a school room and to tell the children that you bring them the noblest gift, that of learning. Stetson suggested that with learning, you bring one power. He said, "I cannot bring in my left hand the rod and in my right I bring thee the gift" (L. Harris, personal communication, journal entry, September 22, 1840).

It was clear to Louisa Harris that Peirce did not agree with some of the tenets of the discussion that took place during the September 22 meeting, and he was not shy about proposing alternative thoughts. Peirce said he was surprised that the question regarding whether a child should be compelled to study was brought forward and that he thought it was absurd. He said this is like preparing a banquet and compelling the guests to eat, when they did not desire the food. Mr. Frost, a participant at the convention who became upset with Peirce said that he did not see the analogy between the two ideas. Though the disagreement was dropped, Peirce would address the idea of compelling students to study when the normalites were back at school (L. Harris, personal communication, journal entry, October 3, 1840). Committee appointments were made during the convention and men (only men) from various towns and cities in the surrounding area were elected to posts. After the convention, Louisa Harris wrote in her journal she could not take in-depth notes as she did not enjoy the discussion, nor could she understand the beautiful language that was used (L. Harris, personal communication, journal entry, September 22, 1840).

Other events for the normal school scholars included visits and lectures from phrenologists. In Edinburgh, Scotland, a phrenological society had been established with George Combe, a student of Spurhzeim, serving as a leading defender of its views. The developments of this group crossed the Atlantic to New England in the nineteenth century. Walton Felch, a phrenologist, visited the normal school on one occasion and lectured about it from 6:30 p.m. until 10 p.m. After the lecture concluded, he examined the heads of many students. In some cases, Felch's descriptions of the scholars, based on his examinations, appeared to be quite accurate. Peirce said that Felch had "hit the nail on the head" when he described the character of Mary Swift, saying that her organs of self-esteem, love of approbation and mirthfulness were not number one in size (as cited in Norton, 1926, p. 151).

At times, notable transcendentalists were invited to visit the students. In July of 1840, some of the students had put forward questions to Peirce about the subject of transcendentalism. Since Peirce felt that he was little acquainted with the topic, he invited Bronson Alcott and his brother-in-law Samuel May to deliver a lecture to the students (L. Stow, personal communication, journal entry, July 25, 1840). When Bronson Alcott visited the normal school later that month, he gently rebuked Peirce for what he perceived as being impatient with his students—an interesting exchange for the students to witness. Later reflecting on this incident, Peirce thought that Bronson Alcott was "just" in doing this (as cited in Norton, 1926, p. 50). On August 7, 1840, the students also conversed on the topic of transcendentalism with Reverend Caleb Stetson. Lydia Stow, reflecting on transcendentalism, recorded in her journal that Mr. Stetson "speaks to something in me that did not come through the senses. Why do I receive it? Because I have something of the divine within me which makes me feel that he is a spiritual teacher. If I had not this I could understand no more than the horse does through his senses. We must be possessed of something that transcends the senses. I have some of the divine nature. God has made man in his own image. It is truly by allowing this, that we can hear God's voice in the whirlwind, in the storm, in the unsprung trees, and in the still small voice of conscience, or see him in the shining sun and stars" (L. Stow, personal communication, journal entry, August 7, 1840).

Visits from family were also a common occurrence. Early on during her normal school studies in August of 1839, Lydia Stow's sister, Mary Stow, visited her. Her Aunt Sophia Foord likewise called at the normal school on November 22, 1839 (Norton, 1926, p. 17). When the students began to leave the normal school and to teach at schools of their own, the remaining normalites visited them, often with Peirce. On July 23, 1840, Lydia Stow recorded in her journal that she had visited the schools of Mary Stodder and Hannah Damon, two Lexington normal school graduates, and was not enthusiastic about what she observed.

> Went to visit Misses Stodder's & Damon's schools. Did not have much opportunity to see Miss D's school, as she had dismissed most of her scholars. Miss S School was quite small, but if this is a specimen of her school as it usually is, I should despair if I was in her place. If I am to have such a school, may my first day of teaching be my last. (L. Stow, personal communication, journal entry, July 23, 1840)

These excursions and on-going visitors were of interest to the normalites. The normalites likewise were of profound interest to visitors and to others they met during excursions. The normalites were considered the inventions of the normal school experience, an undertaking which, if successful, was to shape the preparation of teachers throughout Massachusetts and the country. Indeed, in the years that followed their participation in the normal school, leading educational reformers would begin to advocate for national normal schools and a federal department of public instruction. There were increased calls for centrally collected school data which would be disseminated nationally. This information was considered vital to the country and to those laboring to improve educational systems (Warren, 1974, pp. 47–48).

4

Partings

As the months passed in 1839 and 1840, the normalites recognized that their time at the school would come to a conclusion and that they would leave their school and assume teaching positions. In their teaching, and in their broader life work, they would "Live to the Truth," as Cyrus Peirce, Father Peirce, had so often guided them to do. Their partings, however, were bittersweet. It was a juncture in their lives that would be met with both excitement and sorrow.

In February 1840, Lydia Stow expressed these feelings in her journal. "I could not [but] be reminded of the period which is not very far distant, when many of thee whom we dearly love will separate from this place never more to attend to those instructions which we are now listening to day by day" (L. Stow, personal communication, journal entry, February 1840) Later in the month, she reflected in her journal, "Never have I passed, it seems to me such a happy one. And now, take all and all shall I again see such an one" (L. Stow, personal communication, journal entry, February 29, 1840). A month later, on March 26th, Lydia looked around the classroom, discerning that all were present on that day. However, as she assessed the scene,

Normalites, pages 45–49
Copyright © 2014 by Information Age Publishing
45

she reflected that she would "have to think that ere long, this seat and this, that one and that will be deprived of its occupants. This is saddening" (L. Stow, personal communication, journal entry, March 26, 1840). Peirce often spoke to the students about the importance of their normal school work and about being well acquainted with the common branches of study. He stressed the importance of "feeling an interest and love in the occupation." Lydia reflected that she felt a great responsibility toward the work she was called forth to do in the capacity of teacher. "How important it is then that you be qualified for the station" (L. Stow, personal communication, journal entry, March 28, 1840). Yet, she was not ready to depart. On February 26, 1840, as the scholars took part in an evening reading group, Peirce called Lydia aside. He read her a letter he had received from a gentleman in Ashburnham, a rural town in northern central Massachusetts. The writer of the letter was seeking a teacher for a school of 60 students beginning the following summer, and sought Peirce's recommendation for someone to fill the position. Peirce carefully summarized the preferences and requirements to Lydia and asked her if she would like to accept the offer. Almost immediately, she declined. She felt that her present time was better spent as a pupil than as a teacher (L. Stow, personal communication, journal entry, February 26, 1840). The thought of teaching 60 students was daunting, especially since she did not have any substantial teaching experience. Perhaps she also felt she was not yet ready to transition to the role of authority figure. Teaching in a rural setting also presented difficulties with regard to boarding options—and to top it off—the pay was low. Peirce quietly accepted Lydia's response and moved on to see if another scholar, Hannah Damon, would be interested in the position (L. Stow, personal communication, journal entry, February 26, 1840). It is unknown if Hannah accepted the arrangement.

Mary Swift was the first student to conclude her normal school studies on April 4, 1840 (State Normal School Framingham, 1900, pp. 11–12). Peirce would later hand-write her a formal certificate of completion. Since Mary's father, Dr. Paul Swift, believed her previous illness had resulted from ardent study and preparation, he wanted her to rest; to regain her strength before obtaining a teaching position. Mary's preparations for departure occurred during the same time that the future of the normal school was decided. In the preceding months, ongoing visits from Horace Mann, Samuel Gridley Howe, Samuel May, and Henry Barnard had caused unease among the scholars. Peirce's explanations for these visitations were not altogether convincing, and students felt that he was not direct with them about their purpose. Mary Swift wondered, "Do the gentlemen think that we are going to believe every story, they tell us?" (as cited in Norton, 1926, p. 212).

Then on Friday, March 20, 1840—which Mary recorded in her journal as a stormy day on which she felt destitute of "foreign company"—the uncertainty that had weighed them down since the start of their studies was brought suddenly to an end. As if preparing for the proverbial parting of the clouds, Peirce announced that the state legislature had decided, by a majority of 63 votes that the normal schools would continue to be funded and recognized. Though there were three primary reasons of opposition to the normal school movement including sectarianism or religious affiliations, expense and political parties, those in favor of the normal schools had prevailed. Peirce told the students that if they "begin to teach and fail, that it would be remembered more than three instances of success" (as cited in Norton, 1926, p. 214).

The night before Mary Swift left, Peirce and the students gathered around her and sang Auld Lang Syne (L. Stow, personal communication, journal entry, April 5, 1840). It likely was a moment of beauty, as well as one of deep emotion. Mary had formed close friendships and connections among the normal school group, and her peers and teacher conveyed to her that they would not forget her in her absence.

Louisa Harris departed next on December 22, 1840. The last entries of her journal included pages in which notes of "good bye" were recorded. In one place, she wrote, "the music was like the memory of past joys; sweet, but mournful to the soul" (L. Harris, personal communication, journal entry, December 1840). Lydia Stow had previously recorded in her journal that when Louisa was away, "she makes a vacancy both in our circle in the schoolroom and out of it, which will not soon be filled" (L. Stow, personal communication, journal entry, October 15, 1840). After Louisa's departure from the school, her absence was noticed.

Lydia Stow was the last of the three women to complete her normal school studies on March 24, 1841 (State Normal School Framingham, 1900, pp. 11–12). Of these three women, she had spent the most time at the normal school, taking pleasure in the studies and in her interactions with her peers.

During their studies, the normal school students had been exposed to both academic and pedagogical content. They were examined, guided carefully while they prepared for the work of teacher, employment they often referred to as a duty. They were keenly aware of the importance of their studies and of their future work. Though they were young and impressionable when they started their studies, between the ages of 15 and 17, they developed maturity and self-confidence. As students, they questioned practices that they thought were unreasonable and recorded their reflections about those circumstances. They were influenced by their studies, yet they also created many effects in this process. As they learned from their school principal and took note from leading educational reformers, they also contributed to the learning process. Examples are found in the questions they asked and in the sentiments they shared.

In some regards, the public spotlight that surrounded these young women and their future work overshadowed the more personal aspects of their experiences. They had come together from different towns and backgrounds, yet they had become sisters in learning. They grew to care about each other and formed lifelong friendships as well as what would now be considered professional networks that would influence their future endeavors. As Louisa Harris would later write in her journal, no longer were their glances at each other those that strangers would share, but rather ones of loved normal sisters (L. Harris, personal communication, journal entry, October 16, 1842). Societal structures and norms, self-imposed boundaries, as well as differences in backgrounds often create parameters and constraints in how human beings interact and relate to each other. At times, a human yearns to know another, but is stopped because it would be stepping out of the standard expectations. Boundaries, at times, are put in place. However, the sharing of a common purpose and goal can strengthen human ties of care and connection. The normalites recognized that public men, including political and religious leaders and educational reformers, had steered their path. However, in the process of obtaining a normal school education, they created a female communal network. These bonds developed during a time when changes were rapidly unfolding in the prospects available to young women, which further added to elements that cemented their cohesion. This was an experience for them, an education, which was free of bureaucratic constraints.

The first group of normal school students grew to 25 over the course of the first year (State Normal School Framingham, 1900, pp. 11–12). In comparison, at that time, there were 3,000 public or common schools, most one-room structures, in Massachusetts. Nonetheless, upon completion of their studies at Lexington, the normalites were carefully tracked in Annual Reports of the Massachusetts Board of Education. In 1841, the seven Board of Education members for the Commonwealth of Massachusetts issued a report that included high praise for the teachers produced by the Lexington Normal School.

> This school has been in operation about eighteen months. The interest and devotion to the purpose for which the institution was established, have been very gratifying during the whole period, and at no time more so than at present. The progress of the pupils generally in those branches of knowledge

required to be taught in our schools, has been in the highest degree flatter-
ing, and the clearness and exactness of their information will be of great advantage to them in their professional duties hereafter. In the principles and
practice of the art of teaching also, they have made quite as rapid proficiency, as any judicious friend of the system could have anticipated.... Several
pupils of this institution have been employed as teachers, since completing
their studies there. Their success has been for the most part remarkable,
and acknowledged to be such by all who have had opportunities of observing their schools. (Massachusetts Board of Education, 1841, p. 4)

In 1843 and 1844, the state board of education again gathered information about the normal school graduates, as some continued to doubt the
utility of the normal schools, a presumption that reformers wanted to se-
curely put to rest (Massachusetts Board of Education, 1845, pp. 27–44). Educational reformer Samuel May wished to emphasize the practicality of the
normal schools with regard to teacher preparation for common schools. In
the 1844 Board of Education report, he wrote that it was from the success
or failures of those who went on to teach in the common schools that the
effectiveness of the normal schools could be inferred. In this and other
reports, there were individual testimonials included, many from notable
reformers and school committee members, about specific graduates (Massachusetts Board of Education, 1844, pp. 22–34).

In addition to being highlighted in the early reports of the Massachusetts Board of Education Lydia Stow, Mary Swift, Louisa Harris, and other normal school graduates were discussed in later reports of the United
States Department of Education, which was established briefly in 1867 for
a period of about one year through the efforts of Charles Brooks, a strong
advocate of the normal schools, and other educational reformers (Warren, 1974, pp. 77–86). The United States Department of Education would
not permanently become a Cabinet level department until 1979. The normalites also were written about in *The American Journal of Education*, a publication overseen by Henry Barnard (Warren, 1974, p. 94). Eyes were upon
them, as they were members of the first class of the first state normal school.
The normal school movement, particularly the first school, would later be
referred to as the mustard seed which would give growth to a mighty tree,
the leaves of which "were for the healing of nations" (Framingham State
Alumnae Association, 1914, p. 21). Just as the eyes of the public were upon
them, the eyes of the normalites were upon one another as they entered
into the world of teaching.

PART II

Entrance Into the World and Commencement of Teaching

5

First Teaching Positions

An understanding of the post schooling experiences of the first normalites is critical to obtaining a full and holistic view of the start of formal state sponsored teacher preparation in the United States. Rather than viewing the normalites in a narrow sense as women who taught for a few years after their studies, married and then left the profession, a more complex picture emerges when the timeline is extended and analyzed. Questions relating to how the normalites drew from their normal school experience and how they utilize those experiences in their work with others are answered.

When the normalites commenced their first teaching positions, they faced changes. No longer school girls, they moved into roles in which they drew from their academic and pedagogical preparation. As professionally prepared educators, they experienced new responsibilities. They developed connections with their own students, questioned teaching practices, and developed a sense of autonomy and authenticity. They also encountered constraints as they worked with new mentors and, often, strict school boards. Massachusetts law required supervision of schools, usually by a com-

Normalites, pages 53–74
Copyright © 2014 by Information Age Publishing

mittee that included the minister and others who served as town officials. Visits from and to these school boards were official affairs (Johnson, 1904, p. 101). In this context, the formal experiences that Lydia Stow, Mary Swift, and Louisa Harris were introduced to in Lexington provided good preparation for their professional lives. They also remained attached and visited with their sister normalites, at their schools and homes, drawing strength, advice, and ideas from their shared experiences.

Lydia Stow

Upon completing her studies, Lydia Stow returned to Dedham to live with her grandmother Foord and her Aunt Esther. Her Aunt Sophia had since left the Dedham household to live and teach in Fall River. Lydia's return to Dedham followed an unexpected attack of scarlet fever during the Christmas season in 1840 from which Lydia needed to recuperate (L. Stow, personal communication, journal entry, December 25, 1840). The affections and tender natures of her grandmother and aunt were pleasing to Lydia, though she missed the scholars from the normal school. After her recovery, Lydia took a teaching position in Dedham and taught in a one room school house. It is likely that her school was small and constructed on land that was not considered valuable, which was typical of nineteenth century public school facilities. The summer sun and winter winds often had free play of these structures (Johnson, 1904, pp. 102–103). Lydia had actually been offered positions in two schools, the other in Fall River. She chose the one in Dedham while her sister Mary accepted the Fall River assignment (L. Stow, personal communication, journal entry, October 11, 1841).

Lydia recorded in her journal that she felt trepidation the first time she came before her class. Her school numbered only 20 pupils, a number she believed she could serve well. As time passed, Lydia's commitment to her teaching grew, and she hoped her dedication to teaching would be matched by a similar desire to learn by her pupils. Although there certainly were trials to her patience, exacerbated by her lack of experience in managing student behavior, she had internalized Cyrus Peirce's disapproval of corporal punishment, and succeeded without resorting to that as a disciplinary measure. Truthfully, however, she had been tempted a time or two. She, however, had seen the good effect of mild measures and refrained. Her first assignment was a summer school that commenced in April of 1841. In rural areas, summer schools were more likely to be attended by younger children as older youth were often engaged in work on farms. During winter sessions, the older children attended school, as they were not needed as much for farm chores (Bernard & Vinovskis, 1977, p. 337). Summer schools, attended by younger students, also were more likely to be taught by women, though teaching was becoming more feminized in general in the 1800s. This was the context in which Lydia began her teaching career. It also was with some reluctance that she left her students when her school session closed in October of 1841 (L. Stow, personal communication, journal entry, October 11, 1841).

On the last day of her summer school session, Lydia received an unexpected visit from Harriet Peirce who was visiting a cousin in the area (L. Stow, personal communication, journal entry, October 12, 1841). Lydia enjoyed reconnecting with Mrs. Peirce, a woman who had assumed a maternal influence in her life, and who brought an update on the news of the normal school. She related to Lydia that their number had grown to 35 scholars. There was some sad news as well. She told Lydia that one of the new scholars and a relative of Mrs. Peirce, Amelia Coffin, had died suddenly of typhus fever (L. Stow, personal communication, journal entry, October 12, 1841). When Amelia died, another normal school student, Susan Johnson, recorded in her journal her dismay over what had occurred. "Can it be she is no longer to be one of our number? It is seemingly impossible. Never the less it is so, and we must be resigned to it, and comfort ourselves in the promise that Earth has no sorrow that Heaven cannot cure" (S. Johnson, personal communication, journal entry, October 10, 1841). Though Amelia was not from the first class of students at the normal school, the news of her death had reached the ears of normal school sisters, including Lydia.

During the evening hours of Mrs. Peirce's visit, they attended a local temperance meeting (L. Stow, personal communication, journal entry, October 12, 1841). Temperance meetings were common occurrences in Dedham, often held in the two local churches and also in the town hall. The gatherings focused on keeping families away from the vice of drink. Sometimes men spoke about their own unfortunate pasts with drinking. Other times a child might speak about not deserting a father even if he had fallen to a state of drunkenness, but rather using that situation to administer to him. Peirce, when he had lectured the scholars at the normal school about temperance, had advised them that, "Pupils, I hope you will never give your hand or heart to one whoever puts to his lips the intoxicating cup" (L. Stow, personal communication, journal entry, October 10, 1840). He was considered by his students to be an earnest, perhaps fanatical, advocate of temperance and believed in complete abstinence. Even fishermen who engaged in long whaling voyages, Peirce felt should avoid alcohol (May, 1857, p. 14). Lydia found attendance in temperance gatherings to be thought-provoking. As she recorded in her journal about the meeting she and Mrs. Peirce attended, "The lecture was very excellent. I hope that every rum seller in town was present for they thought the speaker had great ins [influence] upon them" (L. Stow, personal communication, journal entry, October 12, 1841). Lydia, like Cyrus Peirce, believed in complete abstinence. Not prone to drinking coffee or tea, Lydia's drink of choice was field water. However, she at one point wrote in her journal that she would "not scandalize those who use cider & wine if they get caught," suggesting a more tolerant attitude toward this behavior (L. Stow, personal communication, journal entry, March 19, 1842).

In October 1841, at the time her summer school position ended, Lydia's paternal Uncle Nathan brought to her attention a new school position. She declined to accept it, however, deciding that this would probably be her last free winter when she could enjoy time to read books (L. Stow, personal communication, journal entry, October 13, 1841). Her decision was accepted by her uncle. It was during this time that Lydia's grandmother Stow died. Lydia recorded in journal that she sat in the dark stillness of the night on November 24, 1841 with her grandmother, knowing that she did not have much longer to live. As she sat there, Lydia listened to her grandmother's labored breathing, which lasted several hours until 2 a.m. when she eased into a quiet sleep. It was the second time in Lydia's life that she had kept watch over a sick bed at night (L. Stow, personal communication, journal entry, November 24, 1841). The first time was that which preceded her mother's death. Lydia did not want her grandmother to suffer any longer. She was 86 years old. Her husband, Lydia's grandfather, had died at similar age. Lydia felt that her grandmother would be happy when her soul could meet the good and just individuals who had died before her. Lydia believed that her grandmother's soul would enter into communion with those of the family who had preceded her in death. She questioned if it would be right to lament her grandmother's withdrawal from life, even though she knew that she would miss her (L. Stow, personal communication, journal entry, November 23, 1841).

There were few times when Lydia had time alone during the winter that followed. On those rare occasions when she did have time by herself, she welcomed it but only for brief interludes. She preferred to be surrounded by family and friends, and recorded in her journal that "solitude has charms for me for awhile but be it uninterrupted I fear I might become melancholy" (L. Stow, personal communication, journal entry, October 27, 1841). During those free months she attended a singing school, though she felt that she did not have a singing voice. She took French lessons and enjoyed the state of "blessed singleness" (L. Stow, personal communication, journal entry, November 20, 1841). The term "blessed singleness" drew attention to the idea that there could be uncertainty of happiness in marriage. Although unspoken, Lydia's preparation and credentials for a career in teaching must have influenced her attitude toward matrimony. Financially independent women were not as reliant on marriage for support or self-respect (Freeman & Klaus, 1984, pp. 394–414).

In early November 1841, members of Lydia's family traveled to Fall River to visit relatives. Lydia declined to go with them and instead traveled cheerfully to Roxbury to see Louisa Harris at the primary school where she was teaching. Lydia had missed Louisa and was anxious to reconnect. In her journal she recorded, "I found some children around the door who ran in to inform their teacher of the arrival of a woman. Spent the remainder of the afternoon with her and saw the antinormalism in using the stick on the hands of one of the pupils. Too bad" (L. Stow, personal communication, journal entry, November 3, 1841). Lydia was surprised that Louisa had resorted to such tactics. What would Mr. Peirce think? During their schooling, they had been advised to avoid corporal punishment. Since corporal punishment was not in keeping with a normal school education, Lydia connected the practice with "antinormalism." Internally, Lydia and other normal school students sought the approval of their mentor and teacher, Mr. Peirce. Yet, the movement away from corporal punishment was a slow undertaking. Nineteenth century women teachers were less docile than they were reported to be (Preston, 1993, p. 549). Louisa Harris' own journals, however, seem to support that her primary methods of discipline were to keep students after school, or to keep them quiet in their seats for a period of time (L. Harris, personal communication, journal entry, March 1, 1842). Thus, what Lydia witnessed may have been out of character from Louisa's avowed disciplinary practices.

In the afternoon of her visit, Lydia and Louisa traveled to see Sarah Wyman, another of their peers from Lexington who was especially close to Louisa. While visiting Sarah's school in Roxbury, Lydia observed that the students were quite clean and neat, more so than the students at Louisa's school. She recorded in her journal, however, that they were "left more still than I should judge necessary. It must be hard for such little children to be always sitting square in their seats. The school was not as orderly as usual and no wonder as there could be no fire built. Poor little creatures could not keep still" (L. Stow, personal communication, journal entry, November 3, 1841). During her visit to Wyman's school, Lydia worked with the children and helped them with printing letters on their slates. She reflected that she "had not had the trials in my summer's experience that these girls have" (L. Stow, personal communication, journal entry, November 3, 1841). Lydia spent additional time at Louisa's school. In contrast to the school in which Sarah Wyman taught, the children in Louisa's school were poor and the conditions difficult. She had to remind herself not to engage in too much mirthfulness with Louisa, though it was difficult at times, since Louisa was lively and good spirited by nature. However, her personality did not necessarily reflect what Louisa felt inside (L. Stow, personal communication, journal entry, November 3, 1841). Louisa experienced both high and low points in her emotions. Louisa's friendships were deeply important to her and helped her battle feelings of depression.

Following her visit with Louisa, Lydia continued her travels to the Perkins Institution in South Boston. The primary purpose for her visit was to see Mary Swift, who had assumed a position there. On her arrival, however, she was surprised and pleased to see Lydia Drew, her former classmate who had left the Perkins Institution to study at the Lexington Normal School. Lydia Drew had resumed her work at Perkins after finishing her normal school studies. Eliza Rogers, another scholar from the normal school, also had become a Perkins teacher and Lydia was happy to see her as well. Upon her arrival, however, Lydia was given the news that Mary was sick and confined to her room. Mary and Lydia did have a chance to visit, however. Upon hearing of Lydia's arrival, Mary indicated that she was feeling better and that it was only the long work days at Perkins that had worn her out (L. Stow, personal communication, journal entry, November 4, 1841).

The day of Lydia's visit was an Exhibition Day, so her friends could not spend too much time with her. Each week on Saturdays, hundreds of individuals traveled to the Perkins Institution for Exhibition Day, at which they observed Laura Dewey Bridgman read, write and talk with a manual alphabet (L. Stow, personal communication, journal entry, November 4, 1841). The public was fascinated with the idea that the isolation "experienced by the deaf and blind, could, in large measure, be overcome" (Freeberg, 2001, p. 2). There was also, in that time period, an increased public demand for novelty for which Laura's predicament and overcoming of that predicament held some lure. Lydia's former classmates were thus engaged in preparing for the many individuals who would visit Laura Bridgman's "exhibit." Many who traveled to the exhibit hoped for a souvenir, "an autograph or a piece of knitting—made by Laura's own hand," and the fulfillment of those requests fell to the Perkins staff (Freeberg, 2001, p. 2). During Exhibition Days, Perkins' founder, Samuel Gridley Howe, also lectured on the sacred obligation that society had to the blind, by which he solicited additional funds for the institution (Freeberg, 2001, p. 15).

Figure 5.1 Bust of Laura Dewey Bridgman created by Sophia Peabody. Courtesy of Perkins School for the Blind, MA.

While Lydia was at the exhibition she observed a bust made of white marble that an artist named Sophia Peabody, who would later marry Nathaniel Hawthorne, had created of Laura Dewey Bridgman. Lydia was introduced to Sophia Peabody's sister, Elizabeth Peabody, a writer, who attended the exhibit on that day (L.Stow, personal communication, journal entry, November 5, 1841). Elizabeth Peabody hoped to enter into an arrangement with Dr. Howe to produce and sell the bust her sister created of Bridgman.

In 1841 Peabody wrote to Howe with such a proposal.

My dear sir,

My sister Sophia asked me several days since to write you a note & tell you what we thought about selling the busts of Laura.

In the first place it is obvious that it would be well to have the busts sold at the Institution at whatever price you choose. Sophia having nothing to do with them in any way except to look at the Italian's and to see if they are right. It will cost $2.50 to have them cast & you can sell them as low as you please. Then as there are a few persons who would like to buy them to patronize Sophia, we would like to send them to the Italian when we please. I have one cast for her. I sell it somewhere below $10. Dr. Johnson insisted on paying her $10. I think I would like to have one on hand always at my room to sell for Sophia.

My hope to see you . . .

Yours truly

Elizabeth P. Peabody

(E. Peabody, personal communication, 1841)

After her visit at the Perkins Institution, Lydia completed her travels with a stopover in Lexington. She was delighted to be back, so much so that her face naturally fell into a pose of pleasantness and relaxation. Her return, much like her first day of admittance, was marked by rainy weather. Lydia reflected that everything looked the same as it had been on that first day she entered the school. Whereas not much seemed to change in Lexington, she reflected that it was not so in Dedham, where she resided with her family. Dedham seemed to be marked by more activity, perhaps because the town was larger.

Peirce was glad to see Lydia, and spent some time sharing stories about the ventures of some of the other normal school graduates. Eliza Pennell, one of Horace Mann's nieces who attended the school with Lydia, had taken on a school that held a number of very large boys (L. Stow, personal communication, journal entry, November 10, 1841). In the nineteenth century a belief endured that female teachers were unable to discipline older boys who often disrupted the classroom (Bernard & Vinovskis, 1977, p. 337). Male teachers, by contrast, were assumed to possess characteristics not only of intellectual superiority, but also the emotional restraint and physical dominance necessary to effectively educate adolescent males. This belief was in marked contrast to the emerging ideology that suggested female teachers would draw from gentleness, moral superiority and maternal love in their work (Preston, 1993, p. 532). In his interactions with his students, all women, Peirce exhibited paternalistic views. He clearly was amused about Eliza's work and asked Lydia how she dared undertake such a venture. Over the next several days, Lydia attended lectures, assisted at the model school and visited some of her acquaintances in the area. On more than one occasion she thought that Peirce looked tired. "No wonder," she thought. He worked all the time in an effort to move forward a successful normal school movement, and had encountered painful controversy during the process (L. Stow, personal communication, journal entry, November 13, 1841). Yet, he strived to prepare competent and qualified teachers to work in the common schools. She knew, however, that he was trying to do more than his strength would permit. At this time, she likely did not know that Peirce, due to his frail health, had requested of Horace Mann a leave from his position. Mann had asked him to reconsider for the sake of the normal school movement.

When it was time for Lydia to leave the normal school, she wondered if it would be the last time that she would sit within its walls. She recorded in her journal, "I shall have the happiness of looking upon the hours spent here as being the most profitable and pleasant of any that have gone by" (L. Stow, personal communication, journal entry, November 15, 1841).

Mary Swift

Shortly after completing the normal school program, Mary took a position at the Perkins Institution housed in a renovated hotel in South Boston. Unlike Lydia's initial teaching experiences in the common schools, Mary's focused on working with the blind and deaf. Five stories in height and topped with multiple smoke stacks, the former hotel boasted wrap-around porches on the first two levels, a once-upon-a-time majestic entrance, numerous windows, and a roof deck. It was located near Fort Independence in South Boston, a granite structure in the shape of a pentagon, which had been used for harbor defense of the city (Clarke, 2010, p. 111). Two miles away was the Marlboro Hotel, the first public house in Boston. Samuel Jenks, Peirce's brother-in-law from Nantucket, visited Perkins on February 9, 1840, and described the facility to his daughter.

> The Institution now occupies the very large and splendid building, very near the fort, just back of where we lived when you was an infant....The building was erected by an association for a Hotel, at a cost of one hundred thousand dollars. The company failed, and the persons who came in possession exchanged the estate for that which the blind formerly occupied in Pearl Street in the city. It was a capital bargain for the Institution. It contains spacious and splendid parlors and halls, the floors all of marble, *tessellated*, that is, laid in square pieces of about a foot each, diamond wise. (S. Jenks, personal communication, February 9, 1840)

At the new location in South Boston, there was ample space for classrooms and workshops. Rooms were available for student residence with males and females able to have quarters in separate areas of the building. Since the new location also was close to the sea, fresh salt air added to the

Figure 5.2   Perkins Institution in South Boston, Massachusetts.

overall appeal of the vicinity (Trustees of the Perkins Institution for the Blind, 1844, p. 25).

Lydia Drew, who became acquainted with Mary while they studied together in Lexington, recommended her to Dr. Howe for employment at Perkins. In February of 1840 she wrote to Dr. Howe:

> Lexington February 18th 1840
>
> My Dear Friend,
>
> I have a leisure moment and I will improve it in answering your kind letter which I received yesterday and will endeavor to reply to some of its "direct questions." I like to write to you, particularly when I stand in need of some of your counsel.
>
> You ask if one of my young friends might not be induced to go to the Institution on trial, and mention two whom you should select for Miss French and Miss Bancroft. No such young ladies are in school but the lady from Nantucket is Miss Swift and the other lady is Miss Stodder of Boston. As to the former—she is now quite ill; and her father has forbidden her to attend to her studies. By over work her nervous system has become completely prostrated at the end of the term she will go home, and will probably not commence teaching at present. I do not know but that Miss Stodder would like to go, but I could not tell; she is a beautiful reader, by far the best in our school.

I do not know how well she would please you, she is a good girl, but rather thoughtless. She is young however, and will probably improve in this respect. I wish you could get Miss Swift. She is the *right one.*

(L. Drew, personal communication, February 18, 1840)

In March of 1840, less than a month later, Ms. Drew again wrote to Dr. Howe, urging that Mary Swift be the teacher to join the Perkins Institution.

Lexington March 6th 1840

My Dear Friend,

I should have answered your kind letter earlier, but I hoped to be able to answer all your inquiries. For your kind advice, please to accept my gratitude. I hope I shall be enabled to act in this matter as will be for the best. I appreciate the kind interest you have ever manifested for me, and thank you for it....With regard to Miss Stodder, I think she would like the situation of a teacher in your Institution and I think she would give satisfaction of her scholarship, you know already of her excellent heart and amiable disposition. I can have no doubt and I think it would be her wish to please you. I wish however you could be so fortunate to have Miss Swift, for she is far superior to any one I ever saw, but the poor girl will not be able to teach for some time.

(L. Drew, personal communication, March 6, 1840)

Mary did not initially accept Dr. Howe's subsequent invitation to join the Perkins Institution. Since her health was fragile, her father had deemed it best for her to return home from Lexington and not start teaching until she had fully recuperated, to which Mary consented. However, when Mary's health seemed restored, her father wrote to Dr. Howe that he would be willing to let his daughter assume a position at the Institution (P. Swift, personal communication, April 10, 1840).

Dr. Howe, Mary's new mentor, had come to direct the Perkins Institution through a circuitous path. He had grown up in Boston, the son of Joseph and Patty Gridley Howe. His father was a ship owner and manufacturer (Trent, 2012, p. 37). When he was a youth, he attended Boston Latin School and thereafter Brown University. He then enrolled in medical school at Harvard College, completing his degree in 1824. Following those experiences, and a broken romance, his life path took an unexpected turn and he traveled to Greece during the Greek Revolution. In 1821, the Greeks had started to revolt against Turkish rule (Trent, 2012, pp. 29–50). Within a few years, Egyptian forces joined with the Turks, so the Greeks faced a war against Turkish-Egyptian forces. Thomas Jefferson had invited

Americans to support the holy cause of the Greeks, one which Howe answered when he was 23 years old, when he joined the Greek army as a commissioned surgeon. In one hospital in Nauplion, he provided services for ten months (Trent, 2012, p. 36). He then served as a ship's doctor on the Karteria, which he found to be a slow moving vessel in constant need of repairs. While in Greece, he experienced the hardships of an ordinary Greek soldier. Howe also experienced war in another, conflicted manner when he killed a man in battle. Throughout this period in his life, Howe sent letters to Horace Mann, his former classmate from Brown University, and Edward Everett, who would later become Governor of Massachusetts, about the Greek cause. Due to his exceptional work during the war, the King of Greece awarded him the title of Chevalier of the Order of St. Savior (Trent, 2012, pp. 29–50).

Howe returned to the United States in 1827 and set about raising money for the Greek army, with which he met success. He then went to Paris to continue his medical studies and returned again in 1831 to the United States. By this time, he was not enthusiastic about undertaking a career as a medical doctor. However, when he was asked by Dr. John Fisher, his friend, and some other trustees to direct the establishment of the New England Asylum for the Blind in Boston, he agreed with interest and enthusiasm. Dr. Fisher, when a medical student, had traveled to Paris to visit the first school for the blind and was impressed with the teaching and learning that he witnessed. Howe, in turn, before starting his work with the New England Asylum, went to Europe to learn more about working with those who could not see (Howe, 1876).

When Howe returned to Boston he began to work with blind children at his father's house. The location soon moved to Pearl Street where Thomas Perkins initially provided his mansion and grounds for the use of the institution. Thereafter Perkins sold his mansion and donated the proceeds for the use of a facility located in a former hotel in South Boston. The New England Asylum thus became the Perkins Institution. At this time in his life, Howe had not only gained fame for his work in the Greek Revolution, but was considered a confident and persuasive man (Howe, 1876). He also was very handsome.

When Mary Swift settled in at the Institution, living in a room on-site, she initially worked with Joseph Smith, a blind boy, whom she prepared for Harvard College. As a woman she was unable to attend Harvard. However, Mary not only had a strong background in an English curriculum, but she had studied classics with Cyrus Peirce while she was a student at his private school on Nantucket as well as at the normal school. She was equipped to help Smith (Lamson, 1881). Soon after her arrival, Mary also began work with Lucy Reed, a deaf and blind child who resided at the Perkins Institution. The learning and training that Mary undertook at Perkins was intense and valuable. She gained much. However, she also found that she questioned some of the practices and wondered how they could be improved. For example, Mary questioned the preparation that Lucy Reed received at the Perkins Institution. Though some progress had been made during Lucy's sixth month stay, Mary felt it was not as great as it could have been. Lucy was taught using the raised alphabet system that had been used to initially communicate with other students such as Laura Dewey Bridgman (Lamson, 1881, p. 370). Tags with raised letters were placed on objects, and then introduced to blind and deaf students. This teaching method, devised and utilized by Dr. Howe, was how the blind and deaf students at the Perkins Institution were expected to develop language skills. Mary believed, however, that an introduction to raised letters at the beginning of educational training was useless for an individual who was deaf and blind, and resulted in unnecessary complications. She believed that no one would "teach a little child to read until it had learned to talk, so the deaf and blind child should only be taught to spell the names of objects on the fingers, and not to read the raised letters at the same time"(Lamson, 1881, p. 370). When Lucy's parents withdrew Lucy from Perkins, Mary was sad to see her depart.

As time passed, Mary shared some of her teaching ideas with Dr. Howe and was pleased when he summoned her one day in September 1841 and told her that a new deaf and blind child had arrived at the Institution and that she could begin to work with him drawing upon her own teaching methods. Oliver Caswell, Mary's new student, was 12 years old. He had lost his sight and hearing at the age of three years and four months when he contracted scarlet fever. Mary, 18 years old at the time, would later recall that when she met her new student, she brought him into a room where they would not be disturbed. She seated herself on a sofa with Oliver at her side. He wished to know who Mary was so she gave him the opportunity to touch her hair, feel her face, dress, chain, breastpin and ring. She was patient during his exploration. After a time, he rested quietly beside her. Mary then led him to a door and placed his hand on the key which was in the lock. He made a turning motion and looked at Mary with an expression that clearly suggested that he knew the purpose of a key. Mary then placed his hand on the key again and lifting it moved his fingers in the positions for the letters k-e-y. She repeated this several times. She then tapped his hand which meant that she wanted him to repeat her motions. He repeated them. Next, Mary drew Oliver's attention to a mug. He raised the mug to his lips to indicate that he knew what it was used for. Mary then moved his hands so his fingers spelled m-u-g. After three efforts, he was successful in signing "mug." Mary was pleased. She noticed that Oliver, a thin boy with light hair, was quite obedient in nature (Lamson, 1881, pp. 369–373).

Mary gave Oliver the pin from her dress. He made a motion of sticking it into his coat, suggesting that he knew the purpose of the pin. She then lifted his hand and spelled p-i-n. He tapped Mary's hand indicating that he wanted her to repeat the motions. However, before Mary could do this, she felt that Oliver was filled with earnestness. She would not forget that moment. She remembered that he pulled her to a table and tapping her fingers he indicated that he wanted her to spell table. A look of radiance appeared on his face. It filled Mary with satisfaction. She felt that Oliver had interpreted, in a matter of a half an hour, information that had taken Lucy Reed three months to absorb (Lamson, 1881, pp. 369–373). Mary's memory of this event, which was recorded over 30 years after it occurred, likely is embellished though she probably did experience some initial success in communicating with Oliver. Oliver remained at the Perkins Institution and worked closely with Mary.

Since her start at the Perkins Institution, Mary also worked with other students, one of whom was Laura Dewey Bridgman, whom she had first met while she was a student at the normal school. Laura, who was in her early teen years in 1840, was a thin child of average height with thick light brown hair which she wore pulled back from her face. It was said that she resembled her mother. At first, Howe had requested Mary to spend one hour a day in conversation with her (Lamson, 1881, p. 50). Eventually, the time increased to two hours a day. When Mary started to interact with her, she noticed that Laura had developed over 60 different vocal sounds that were used to identify the people with whom she interacted. If she were asked to demonstrate some of these sounds, Laura could immediately and quickly offer 27 or more of them (Lamson, 1881, p. 61). These vocal sounds appeared to develop naturally. No one had instructed Laura to associate specific vocal sounds with certain individuals. Laura also was familiar with the manual alphabet for the deaf, finger talk, having been exposed to this while studying with Howe and Lydia Drew.

Mary often observed Laura when she was unaware of her presence. She saw that Laura talked to herself using finger talk. A sense of lonely self-communion was displayed during those times, as Dr. Howe would describe it (Lamson, 1881, p. 12). Laura would speak to herself with one hand and reply with the other. Sometimes she purposely misspelled a word with one hand and then would tap it with her other, indicating that the word needed to be corrected.

Laura had a sense of humor and could be mischievous. If she felt her behavior went too far she also could be remorseful. She liked to examine clothing and ribbons. Laura also loved the other children at the Perkins Institution. When Laura walked through a passage way with her hands spread out before her, she would greet whom she met with a sign of recognition. Dr. Howe recorded, "If it be a girl of her own age, and especially if one of her favorites, there is instantly a bright smile of recognition and a twining of arms, a grasping of hands and a swift telegraphing upon the tiny fingers, whose rapid evolutions convey the thoughts and feelings from the outpost of one mind to those of the other. There are questions and answers, exchanges of joy or sorrows, there are kissings and partings, just as between little children with all their senses" (Lamson, 1881, p. 13).

Howe had very specific ideas about how he wanted the education of Laura to progress, specifically with regard to her religious instruction. Mary understood that his wishes were to be strictly followed. Howe, a Unitarian, believed that a child such as Laura provided him with a chance to conduct a profound experiment. Since Laura had been sealed off from communication with much of the outside world, he felt that her thoughts and feelings could only be understood as the expression of pure human nature. Laura, in other words, represented the innate potential of all children. Howe did not want Laura exposed to any religious instruction that did not arise from a strong innate moral foundation. Howe believed his experiment would provide opposition to Calvinistic views of the innate depravity of human nature. Howe also drew his ideas from the teachings of philosopher John Locke, an influential Enlightenment thinker (Freeberg, 2001, pp. 31–39). Locke did not believe that humans are born with innate ideas. Rather, Locke believed that the mind is a blank slate and that it is through experience that knowledge and self-reflection develops. These ideas Howe questioned as well, which made his experiment with Laura Dewey Bridgman not only weighty but of great public interest. Howe's experiment connected to the social and educational reforms and debates of the time.

During her schooling, Howe required that Laura not be formally exposed to religious teachings. Though he introduced her to the concept of God as her studies unfolded, he required that any type of conversation that could lead to religious subjects be avoided by the teachers. Howe's experiment naturally resulted in outrage from orthodox leaders in the community, who were concerned with the fate of Laura's soul. Others supported the work of Howe, while Laura was not aware of the experiment at all.

Mary recognized that, in her work with Laura, she was again in the public eye just as she had been while a student at the normal school. This time she was in the limelight as Laura Bridgman's teacher. The experiment with Laura was widely followed, as had been the start of the normal school movement. However, unlike her progressive education in Lexington under the tutelage of Cyrus Peirce, Howe's requirements of Laura were difficult for Mary to follow. She disagreed with some of them. Mary was used to the inclusion of religion in the curriculum; it had figured predominantly in her normal school studies. To exclude religion, Mary felt, made her own interactions with Laura limited or in some cases untruthful. One day, for example, Laura asked Mary, "Who made water?" Mary told Laura that she needed to ask Dr. Howe for the answer (Lamson, 1881, p. 51). On another day, Laura asked Mary if hearts ever stopped. Since Laura didn't have a clear understanding of death as a physiological phenomenon, Mary did not know how she could explain it, or the idea of a limited existence or an after-life. Howe also had asked that any conversations regarding death with Laura be referred to him. Though Laura had touched the corpse of a child named Adeline when she was six, as well as experienced the death of a pupil named Orrin while at the Perkins, she did not understand the reality of death (Lamson, 1881, pp. 116–117). In response to her question about hearts, Mary simply told Laura that they did not stop.

Though avoiding all types of conversation that could lead to religious discussion was difficult, Mary enjoyed her work with Laura. There was a period when Laura learned the concept of color. For weeks that followed that discovery, Laura often asked Mary the color of certain items. On one occasion, she asked Mary to tell her what Mary's hair color was. Mary replied that it was dark brown, whereas Laura's hair was light brown. Laura then made the assumption that when one became older, one's hair became a darker color. She told Mary that when she grew tall, she too would have dark hair (Lamson, 1881, p. 59). On another occasion, Laura asked Mary where meat came from. She was particularly interested to know about the turkey that she was eating one afternoon. Mary told Laura that meat came from animals. For the next several weeks, Laura refused to eat meat (Lamson, 1881, p. 51). This worried Mary as she wanted Laura to maintain strong health.

Other times, Mary used her time with Laura to help her understand the correct use of grammar. On February 16, 1842, she recorded in her journal, "Having noticed that Laura was growing careless upon the use of verbs, devoted the time to a conversation on 'do' and 'does,' which she uses indiscriminately. As an example of the use of 'do,' she said, 'I do go to bed' and when corrected, asked why it was not as well to omit 'go' as 'do'" (Lamson, 1881, p. 101). They also studied mathematics using Colburn's *Mental Arithmetic* (Lamson, 1881, p. 208). Mary learned to read to Laura by sitting on her left, with a book in her left hand. Using her right hand she would use the manual alphabet for the deaf and spell the words from the book. Laura placed her right hand lightly over Mary's and read the words which Mary spelled (Lamson, 1881, p. 199). Since Mary grew to talk more with her hands than with her mouth, her conversations with Laura were so rapid that no eye could read the words that were exchanged (Lamson, 1881, p. 199).

At times, in the late afternoons, Mary would walk with Laura to the point of the sea, located near the Perkins Institution, where they would stand quietly. Their hands joined together, they would engage in conversation through finger talk. As the water lapped closely to their feet, Mary would explain to Laura why she felt movement on the ground. Other times, she talked with Laura about seaweed or about shells that became attached to rocks. Mary had grown up on an island surrounded by the sea; the terrain was familiar to her. Collections of many different types of sea moss, carefully pressed into books, were some of Mary's most prized treasures (M. S. Lamson, n.d.). Mary knew that the sea was both serene and precarious. Many Nantucket women had become widows when husbands were lost at sea while whaling (Philbrick, 2001). Laura's questions were numerous while they stood at the water's edge. They entailed lengthy and carefully thought out explanations. It could be difficult to explain certain ideas and concepts to her (Lamson, 1881, p. 111). Mary found that an hour with Laura at the seaside went quickly (Lamson, 1881, p. 113).

Louisa Harris

When Louisa completed her normal school studies she returned home to Roxbury and lived with her family. She accepted a teaching position at a primary school, Number 4, on Washington Street in the same town for an annual pay of approximately two hundred dollars (Roxbury School Committee, 1848, p. 15). Wages for female teachers in city areas were generally higher than in rural areas. The low wages that women teachers generally received, however, had been brought to the public's attention, notably in a report by Secretary of Education Horace Mann (Roxbury School Committee, 1848, p. 15). In some cases, women who worked in the factories earned greater wages because they worked more days than teachers who taught only winter or summer schools. Sometimes women factory workers earned six to seven times the annual salary of a woman teacher (Roxbury School Committee, 1848, p. 16).

In 1841 the city of Roxbury operated a Latin School, a free school that provided a course of classical instruction and prepared students for admission to college (Roxbury School Committee, 1848, p. 3). Four grammar schools, as well as twenty-five primary schools, also operated within that city.

The grammar schools were for older children and some were segregated by sex. The Washington School on Washington Street and the Central School near Jamaica Plain were for boys. The Dudley School on Bartlett and Kenilworth Streets were for girls, whereas the Westerly School in West Roxbury was for both sexes. The primary schools, however, typically were not segregated by sex. (Roxbury School Committee, 1848, p. 3). Children between the ages of four and eight typically attended primary schools, which prepared them for grammar school. Some boys, who "from neglect of their parents or other cause, have received little or no primary school instruction" were sent on to Intermediate Schools (Roxbury School Committee, 1848, p. 3). Louisa Harris' assignment to a primary school was typical in nineteenth century America, in which women were commonly assigned to teach younger children (Bernard & Vinovskis, 1977, p. 337).

Reading, writing, and arithmetic were focal points of common school study. Moral education and religious training also were emphasized in the schools in Roxbury. It was the opinion of the Roxbury school committee that teachers, without touching upon the points that divided Christian religious sects, could provide Bible reading in the school house. Though Sunday schools were considered proper places to provide religious instruction, it also was believed that a child who had daily examples shared from the Bible would better be able to resist the temptations of growing up in a city (Roxbury School Committee, 1848, p. 5). Vocal music also was taught, as well as some physical education. However, work still needed to be undertaken in the area of physical education.

Many of the primary school houses in Roxbury were in need of great repair. The air, due to improper ventilation, was impure and the furniture was uncomfortable. Most of the desks were poorly designed, and the construction of the slab seats also resulted in the swinging of legs of the occupants (Enoch, 2008, p. 279). Louisa's school house was considered one of those in greatest need of repairs. The building was small and overcrowded. Due to the size of her school and the number of scholars who attended, the school committee felt that within ten minutes after the door closed at the commencement of a school day, that the children would breathe injurious air (Roxbury School Committee, 1848, p. 5). Many felt that the school house was not fit for occupancy and should be abandoned. Disagreements between the wishes of the school committee and that of the city council, however, resulted in delaying the repair and rebuilding of some schools. In a letter to the Hon. H. A. S. Dearborn, Mayor of Roxbury, the school committee would eventually write,

Primary school No. 4, which is the nearest to Parker Street has 70 children belonging to it. The building is a miserable, low, crazy one, which in its best days could not accommodate more than 30. It is no longer fit for occupancy. The Committee unanimously resolved to abandon it as soon as the new one could be erected. (Roxbury School Committee, 1848, p. 8)

Over 2,000 children attended the common schools in Roxbury. It was typical for the teachers of these children to have their teaching examined by members, men, of the school committee. Mr. Leavens, one of the local school committee members, visited Louisa's school on April 25, 1842. He had not suggested that she was in need of any improvement to her instructional methods, so Louisa took it for granted that he was satisfied. She was annoyed, however, that during his visit he had made remarks to the students that she thought were unnecessary and foolish. It was difficult at times to have examiners at the schools. These officials, not teachers themselves, believed that there should be perfect order and that the children should be motionless, even the youngest ones. Louisa knew that this was not a fair expectation, of the teacher or the children. She thought that the only way to keep children perfectly still was with the detestable use of the rod. She believed that she had more awareness of teaching than her examiner did. After Mr. Leavens' visit to her school, she stopped at Sarah Wyman's school, also in Roxbury, and found the Reverend Fay there, discoursing with Sarah's pupils (L. Harris, personal communication, journal entry, April 25, 1842).

Louisa was especially close to Sarah, one of her former normal school peers. Each morning Louisa rose and set off for her school, sometimes with a copy of *Graham's Magazine,* an American monthly magazine of literature, art and fashion, in hand, and met Sarah for part of the walk (L. Harris, personal communication, journal entry, February 28, 1842). In February of 1842, Louisa found in the magazine an article about Harper's Ferry in Virginia, considered one of the most picturesque places in America with surrounding views of the Blue Ridge and Potomac which she likely enjoyed with Sarah (Graham, Poe, & Batchelder, 1842). On occasion, Louisa forgot the key to her school and she had to retrace her steps. On March 19, 1842, Louisa met Sarah as she hurried to school, and they discovered that they both had forgotten their keys which in the nineteenth century were long pieces of chiseled steel (L. Harris, personal communication, journal entry, March 19, 1842). Louisa and Sarah enjoyed walking together; their paths parted at a specific location and from there they set out to their own schools.

It was not unusual for Louisa to have scholars from the Dudley and Washington Street schools in Roxbury visit her school. At times she let them take part in exercises, though she already had forty-four or more students at her school daily. If the weather was particularly poor, attendance was as well, with perhaps only thirty-five students (L. Harris, personal communication, journal entry, March 11, 1842). On occasion the students and their teacher would prepare a public exhibition. Students, teachers, family and community members would assemble and sing a song demonstrative of a patriotic spirit. Then the students would reveal their proficiency in the areas of reading, mathematics, composition and philosophy. Sometimes two of the one-room schools that were located near each other would join together and collaborate in an exhibition. Horace Mann, referred to as Uncle Horace by the children, at times attended these public exhibitions and at the end of the exercises addressed the assembly with what was often considered a happy style (L. Harris, personal communication, journal entry, March 10, 1842). His remarks at times contained references to the role of women in society. On March 10, 1842, Louisa Harris wrote that Horace Mann had "in the course of his remarks (which were addressed principally to the female pupils) ... said that actions were morals with men but with females manners were morals" (L. Harris, personal communication, journal entry, March 10, 1842).

Louisa worked with the families of her students in a collaborative manner. In 1842, for example, one boy in her class stayed out of school on occasion. In response, Louisa let the boy's mother enlist some of the other pupils to find him. On March 19, 1842, she wrote, "The mother of a truant lad had enlisted several of my boys at recess to join in the pursuit which she had commenced" (L. Harris, personal communication, journal entry, March 19, 1842). (Unfortunately on that occasion, two boys who were recruited to search for the third boy did not return to school either.) Other times Louisa would visit a sick child at home, demonstrating care for her students (L. Harris, personal communication, journal entry, July 29, 1843). Sometimes she would simply sit and watch her students as they took a break from their studies and played in the fields adjacent to her school. On March 3, 1842, she wrote in her journal that "the children seemed so happy in the fields this noon singing their favorite songs, that I really enjoyed their sport though only a looker on" (L. Harris, personal communication, journal entry, March 3, 1842). Louisa looked older than her actual age; when she was 19 she had been described by some as resembling a 30 year old. Her deportment often came across as reserved, which some may have thought supported her success with teaching (L. Harris, personal communication, journal entry, July 30, 1843).

Though Louisa taught five and a half days each week, there were occasions when school dames, a term used to refer to women who taught in schools, were "permitted to run at large and amuse themselves as they please" (L. Harris, personal communication, journal entry, November 13, 1842). One such occasion was when the Governor of Massachusetts was elected on November 14, 1842 (L. Harris, personal communication, journal entry, November 14, 1842). The practice of having election-day off was an experience Louisa had first encountered at the normal school. At that time on November 9, 1840, Peirce had told them that he "wished to exercise the right of suffrage which he considered to be the duty of every man" (L. Harris, personal communication, journal entry, November 9, 1840). The right of suffrage meant the right to vote, which was only available to men in 1839. Until the passage of the nineteenth amendment in 1920 in the United States, women's suffrage was a gradual process which first resulted in non-uniform changes at the local and state levels (Dubois, 1998). Although Louisa was pleased to have the day off in 1842, she had a toothache which bothered her. She used the free time to spin yarn to knit a pair of comfortable stockings (L. Harris, personal communication, journal entry, November 14, 1842).

On other occasions, Louisa enjoyed time with her family. At night, they assembled together and if her brother Warren produced a newspaper which contained a sermon, her mother would eagerly seize it as she enjoyed this type of writing. All present then prepared for serious discourse (L. Harris, personal communication, journal entry, March 8, 1842). Louisa was close to her family, and was satisfied when all numbers were present. She likewise experienced deep regret and devastation in 1842 when she lost one of her brothers, Michael, to the sea. The exact circumstances of his death are unclear. In her journal, she wrote "The sea, the lone blue sea hath one, whose generous heart and buoyant spirit, I will always remember and love, though he return no more" (L. Harris, personal communication, journal entry, November 31, 1842).

Louisa periodically opened her old journal from her normal school days. She would read the passages and turn the scenes over and over in her mind (L. Harris, personal communication, journal entry, March 16, 1842). It is likely that the normal school students expected they would revisit their journals. On one occasion, Mary Swift had written a poem for Susan Johnson, a normal school peer, at the beginning of her new journal.

> Thy page now are pure, my book,
> At spot, they eye can see,
> But when the year again rolls around,
> Then I shall turn to thee.
> And as I read, thy thoughts will flee,
> To those I've loved so well,
> But thou will seem a messenger,

Of by gone days to tell.
Of Days of joy, and those of pain,
Of happiness and woe,
That light up the face of smiles,
This caused the time to flow.
The intersections of our teacher too,
Will find a place in thee,
That though mayist be not only friend,
But also guide to me.
May no reproach of idle hours,
Or misspent time to thee,
May conscience say thou hast done wel
And all that though couldn't do

(M. Swift, personal communication, circa 1840).

Writing poetry provided women with an opportunity to explore themselves and their encounters with others and with the world. It allowed them to build solidarity. It could function as a form of community action. Through poetry nineteenth century women, such as the normal school students, could express opinions and direct social and political concerns. They also could address educational pursuits, or lack thereof. For some women, poetry allowed them to step into a more recognized, public sphere.

Louisa continued to write new journal accounts, though her interest was feeble at times. She wrote letters regularly to her normal school peers, often to Lydia Stow. Other times, Louisa and Sarah Wyman walked to South Boston where they would visit with some of their normal school sisters, Mary Swift and Eliza Rogers, who worked at the Perkins Institution (L. Harris, personal communication, journal entry, April 22, 1842). When a normal school sister, such as Addie Ireson (who belonged to the first class of students and had commenced teaching in the common schools in Cambridge), would visit Louisa, they would meet up with Sarah and spend the night together, quietly discussing and sharing their news until 1 a.m. On August 16, 1842, there was a larger meeting of the normal school students during which Louisa and the others learned that Mr. Peirce would step down as principal of the normal school and would be succeeded by the Reverend Samuel May (L. Harris, personal communication, journal entry, August 16, 1842). Louisa increasingly knew that she could not envision a time when her friendships with her normal school sisters would lessen into mere formalities (April 22, 1842).

6

Challenges Encountered in Teaching and Developing Paths

Inevitably the normalites encountered challenges in their teaching. These challenges were not ones that ended the sense of commitment that Lydia Stow, Mary Swift, and Louisa Harris held towards education and to reform. Rather, these encounters were ones that strengthened their resolve. They were transformative. The challenges in various ways prepared them for future roles as activists and quiet agitators.

Lydia Stow

In 1842, Lydia began her second teaching position in a new school in South Dedham. She had been reluctant to take the job, as there were between fifty and sixty scholars, a very large number to handle, and most of them were under the age of twelve. When a Mr. Morse interviewed her for the job she told him that it would be an aggravation to take such a school. He, however, told her that he needed an answer right away. Out of necessity she assumed the teaching position, a four month summer school in May 1842. She had

Normalites, pages 75–93

not been able to find work in other schools, though many of her family members had made inquiries for her. She had put in an application at the East Street School where she taught formerly, but learned that the school had hired one teacher during previous summers and the job was likely to go to her. She tried a school in Newton, Massachusetts but they wanted an older experienced teacher. She inquired at a school in Walpole, Massachusetts from which a normal school peer, Rebecca Pennell, had recently left. However, the school committee had corresponded to Cyrus Peirce directly and he had recommended another normal school student (L. Stow, personal communication, journal entry, April 9, 1842). At one point, Lydia's Uncle Enos shared news that another teacher had been employed at yet another school at which she had inquired and Lydia internalized that "of course, she was not wanted." She felt that the tide of fortune had turned against her in regard to getting a school (L. Stow, personal communication, journal entry, April 9, 1842). Her purse was low on funds and she needed to make a living. With a feeling that a mountain rested on her shoulders, and after two good cries, she accepted the position in South Dedham and started teaching a few days later on a Thursday. Her maternal aunt Elizabeth Smith, the former Elizabeth Foord, travelled with her to South Dedham, introduced her to Dr. Briggs at whose home she was able to secure boarding and then left her alone at the school house. Her aunt had taught for two years in the Village School in Dedham in 1819 and knew the complications and difficulties of teaching (Slafter, 1905, p. 111). But her aunt did not stay to assist her niece with the transition.

There were 38 students present on Lydia's first day in South Dedham. The number of students in the small one-room building quickly rose to 63 in the days and weeks that followed. She hoped that when a private school in town opened in June, that her numbers would decrease. This was not to be the case. Her work at this school was perplexing and draining, and she often felt that she might give up in despair. She wrote in her journal, "I contemplated the state of things but thinking who always watches and guides his children has given me strength as my day is and I hope to in time by un-carried diligence to accomplish a portion of the work to be done!!"

Since there were so many students, she was reluctantly provided by the school committee with an assistant, a Miss Bullard, to help her. Lydia, for the most part, got along with her assistant and appreciated her help without which she felt she could not have continued. The employment of an assistant, however, had been met with resistance by some members of the school committee, which resulted in protest and conflict. A petition was circulated by some community members demanding that the school be closed. Lydia's plans and modes of instruction were evaluated and considered unsatisfactory by some, though not by all. A vote was called with regard to whether the school should close with the end result of eight to six that it should continue. Prior to learning the results of the vote, however, Lydia did not know if she would be allowed to enter the school building again. Some members of Lydia's extended family thought that she should have resigned from the position rather than risk a damaged reputation. Her grandmother Foord suggested that Lydia talk with the Reverend Alvan Lamson who also was involved with school matters.

The pleasures that Lydia once connected with teaching unfortunately had met their first major challenge due to her treatment by the school committee. She felt unappreciated, distrustful, and unsupported. (L. Stow, personal communication, journal entry, June 20, 1842). She recognized that her limited experience in teaching shaped her abilities and performance. She also likely realized that nineteenth century common schools operated in a "vortex of political issues" (Conway, 2005, p. 140). Schools were affected by battles related to patronage rights, maintenance of buildings and appointments of teachers (Conway, 2005, p. 140). Financial burdens of schools were debated, at times bitterly. Women teachers, such as Lydia, recognized these issues, and realized that they often were unable to fully participate in the political process that shaped schools.

Though Lydia had managed to retain her assistant, the days were long and often hot. Despite her initial rejection of the idea, she succumbed to using corporal punishment with a ferule, a flat piece of wood used to hit the hands of misbehaving children. Even as she engaged in the practice, Lydia found it revolting to inflict the blows. Though repulsive, she reflected in her journal that she did not know what other course to take. One example of its use involved an 11 year old boy. She wrote "he was very angry and so furious that it was as much as Miss B and myself could do to master him" (L. Stow, personal communication, journal entry, June 20, 1842). She noted that after the use of corporal punishment, he was quiet. Lydia spoke with the child's uncle and made plans to send him home if in the future he did not behave.

Cyrus Peirce continued to keep a close eye over his former students, of whom he expected much in their roles as exemplars of the normal school movement. When he found out that Lydia had used corporal punishment in her school, he wrote her a three-page letter condemning the unfavorable practice. Corporal punishment was a tactic that Lydia had thought she would never use. After she had left her first school at East Street in Dedham, she visited the school which was then under the direction of a male teacher during winter session. She learned from the students that corporal punishment was commonly utilized in keeping order. Lydia recorded in her journal that, "such learning has more evil than of good in any opinion" (L. Stow, personal communication, journal entry, February 21, 1842). Yet, she had succumbed to the use of the ferule in South Dedham. In Peirce's letter to Lydia, he beseeched her to let patience have "her perfect work and try faithfully all other methods first or at least such as reasoning, persuasion and the like." He wrote, "think what our Saviour would have done. Go and do thou likewise. I hear of one and another of my children departing from the faith and if you are added to the number my heart will bleed to death and think when all is over how much better it will be to. . . . have subdued without stripes" (L. Stow, personal communication, journal entry, June 20, 1842).

However, Lydia did not know what to do in order to gain control in her large and difficult classroom, and knew that keeping her job—not to mention teaching lessons to her students—depended on being able to maintain order and discipline. In letters from normal school peers, she learned that others also had resorted to the rod. Sarah Locke, a former normal school student who was now teaching in a Lexington common school, had resorted to physical punishment. The child on whom she used this discipline, interestingly, was one who had been asked to leave the model school in Lexington that was overseen by Peirce (L. Stow, personal communication, journal entry, June 20, 1842).

Lydia continued with her school, and over time her developing skills and the settling in of routines helped to make the situation manageable and productive. She developed attachments to the children and was sad when she learned that one of them had suffered a terrible blow to her head from the kick of a horse. Her skull was shattered, yet the child lived. Lydia shared her love of nature with her pupils. Some of her students were interested in flowers and Lydia felt gratified when they brought her some wild flowers that she had never seen before. During the weeks that remained in the summer school, Lydia visited with parents, at times accompanied by Miss Bullard. As they walked down dusty and hot roads, perspiring along the way, they stopped to pick berries to eat. Lydia was delighted when rain brought relief to the heat that dominated the days. Improvements in the school were noticeable. Buoyed by her progress, Lydia was taken by surprise when she was abruptly told one day that her school would close within the week, more than a month earlier than expected. Unbeknownst to her, repairs to the building had been scheduled for that time by the district. Instead of accepting this directive, Lydia requested that the closing be delayed so she could continue to meet the educational commitment she had made to her students. Her sense of advocacy for what she believed in was starting to emerge, as was her courage and willingness to confront conflicting forces. Whether as a result of her protests or other reasons, the school remained open until August 3rd.

The end of summer school culminated with an examination of the children by the school committee. Parents also attended the oral examination. Both Lydia and Miss Bullard were nervous about the examination, but carried it through (L. Stow, personal communication, journal entry, June 20, 1842).

They knew that how well the children performed during the examination was a reflection on their teaching. No records exist which reveal the outcomes of the examination.

Following the end of her second teaching position, Lydia learned that the normalites had been asked to meet with Cyrus Peirce for a small celebration of the normal school movement. They would wear badges of perforated paper wrought with blue silk with the motto "Live to the Truth." Lydia recorded in her journal, "Not a happy meeting will this be!!" (L. Stow, personal communication, journal entry, June 20, 1842). She knew that Peirce would have words for her regarding her performance, which he indeed did (L. Stow, personal communication, journal entry, August 15, 1842). Lydia's meeting with Peirce on that occasion likely was clouded with the stress of having disappointed, perhaps failed, her prized teacher. Lydia may have recognized that Peirce would hold similar conversations with other normalites who did not meet his standards as common school teachers, yet it did not soften her sense of apprehension.

While teaching Lydia had secured accommodations in a residence close to her school in South Dedham, yet she remained in contact with her family and saw them each weekend. She was able to hear summaries of lectures delivered by community members in different churches in Dedham. One lecture was about repentance and Lydia resolved that she too would live differently and hoped that she would have the strength to atone for any wrongdoings she had committed (L. Stow, personal communication, journal entry, March 26, 1842). Different from religious conversion, Lydia believed that repentance entailed a regeneration of one's outward life and a newness of heart. This likely was a period of quiet transformation which took place during Lydia's life.

Mary Swift

In 1841, Mary had returned to live with her family and to regain her health. The long work days at the Perkins Institution had brought about fatigue, and once again Mary's father wanted her to rest and recover. Her family had relocated to Philadelphia where her father worked as a doctor. Philadelphia was a seaport city of merchants, ship owners, ship builders and mariners (Weigley, 1982). The energy of the business leaders also was drawn to the coal and iron found in Northeastern Pennsylvania (Weigley, 1982). With many red brick houses trimmed in white, Philadelphia was in a period of alteration to becoming an industrial city. It is likely that Mary's family chose its move to Philadelphia carefully and with recognition that Quakers were welcomed in the area. The Philadelphia Quaker community was firmly established. Its roots went back to William Penn who had obtained a province of large acreage in the seventeenth century intended for the mass emigration of Quakers from England.

In the seventeenth century, this area was referred to as Penn's Woods. In the nineteenth century, the city of Philadelphia was called "Quaker City" by some.

Philadelphia was new, interesting terrain for Mary. She felt certain, however, that she wanted to return to the Perkins Institution once her health permitted it. At the time, there were 67 pupils studying at Perkins. Thirty-seven were beneficiaries of Massachusetts, whose room, board and tuition were paid for by the state. Fifteen were beneficiaries of other states, and the remaining eight either paid their own way or paid nothing at all. Most of the children were over 14 years of age when they entered (Trustees of the Perkins Institution, 1841, p. 3).

Mary wished to continue her work with Laura Bridgman. Her father, Dr. Swift, again wrote on Mary's behalf to Samuel Howe and Swift agreed to let Mary return. In his letter to Howe, Swift reflected on Mary's extremely conscientious nature and consequently asked for a raise in her salary. He further requested, alluding to Mary's sensitive nature, that she not be required to take part in any exhibition at the capital.

> We are aware of Mary's sensitiveness, even in infancy we could never tell her she had done wrong without exciting inordinate grief hence I have one hundred times said 'little Mary had better not do so.' She would swallow a few times, barely get along without a cry, and never repeat the act. This fine feeling became morbid for the first time at Lexington—her studies were wholly suspended for some weeks by my requiring and then more moderately resumed and to avoid her excitement of leave taking at the end of the term she was unexpectedly to herself taken from the school some days before its close. Her health seems fully reestablished on a few months she resided at home before going to S. Boston, and although at that Institution her peculiar temperament and predispositions were known and watched over with all the care and success that skill and friendship could give, from which now as always, I wish to acknowledge my ineptness we were concerned to witness something more than her ordinary mobility at the several interviews we had with her during the first year of her residence where but as it was her wish to remain. . . . We therefore the more willingly assure to her longer continuance if her health bother circumstances should justify it. Should there be as last year a public exhibition of the pupils at the capital we should wholly object to her taking part in it though she may consent. We should advise her not to enter into a further engagement without an increase of salary. She was offered $400 but a few months since at Nantucket as an assistant in the high school, her board would have been had for $2 per week. Besides several other eligible offers, which I allude to merely as showing her services are estimated elsewhere. I had supposed also that for the present year something would have been added to her salary though no special contract was made to that effect. I am aware that the decision rests with another power but do not doubt what thee opinion in this matter would rightly have a strong if not a controlling influence. (P. Swift, personal communication, November 7, 1841)

Swift's letter reveals how strongly he believed in his paternal duty to protect his daughter and oversee her choices, which undoubtedly must have had an influence on Mary's own self-perception. The letter also provides evidence of the teaching opportunities that Mary had been offered elsewhere.

Work at the Perkins Institution continued to be demanding for Mary upon her return in 1841. Each day the first bell was rung at 5 a.m. At 6 a.m. roll was called for the male pupils. The female pupils engaged in bed making at this time. At 6:30 a.m. students assembled for prayers, after which they worked in shops such as wood working until 8 a.m. From 9 a.m. to 4 p.m. school was in session, with scheduled breaks for lunch and recess. All pupils were asked to exercise in the fresh air each day. From 7 p.m. to 8 p.m. students assembled to listen to a reading or another designated activity. At 8 p.m. prayers were recited and students retired. At 10 p.m., all staff retired (Trustees of the Perkins Institution, 1841, p. 3). On Sundays, all pupils were required to attend church; parents were allowed to select the churches that their children attended. The majority went to the Park Street Church, the same church that Howe approached for support in printing Bibles with raised letters for his students. At a meeting of the clergymen in 1833, Dr. Howe explained his pupils' need for such Bibles and was met with an immediate and voluntary collection of funds for the American Bible Society. Following that meeting Dr. Howe also raised a thousand dollars from residents of Nantucket and New Bedford for the purchase of a press. It was then that he approached the American Bible Society in 1835 for funds so he could pour into the minds of the blind the "light of the Gospel" (Howe & Hall, 1903, pp. 370–371).

Laura Bridgman's fame caused many to want to meet her. On January 29, 1842, the internationally recognized English writer and social critic, Charles Dickens, met with Laura and her teachers. Dickens had traveled to America in order to record his observations, which resulted in his *Notes on America* (Dickens, 1842). In his book, Dickens noted that the Perkins Institution was located in a cheerful, healthy spot and that the structure was airy, spacious, handsome, and clean. He could see the sea from the building and saw the waves bubbling to the surface which he found pleasant (Dickens, 1842, p. 69).

Howe was away during Dickens' visit. However, since Laura was of great interest to Dickens, he and his wife spent several hours with her, during which Mary Swift helped to translate their conversation. Laura, who was thirteen at the time, wore her hair braided on that day and was attired in a simple, neat dress; she held a doll in her hand, and her usual green ribbon covered her eyes. Though often a cheerful child, Laura also could be shy. When given Mr. Dickens' hand as an introduction, Laura rejected it. However, when given the hand of his wife, she accepted it, kissed her and examined her dress with her hands (Lamson, 1881, p. 99). In Dickens' own notes, he recorded that Laura's interactions with her teacher were animated on this day. In Mary's journal, however, the event was recorded in a matter-of-fact manner, which leaves one to wonder how Mary felt about meeting Dickens, whose fame in America was established.

Mary was used to translating for Laura, though the translation she provided was often somewhat different from what visitors thought took place. Visitors typically communicated words of kindness and flattery to Laura. During the process of translation, however, Mary and staff shared the words of kindness, but refrained from restating the flattery. Although Mary knew that Laura's visitors meant well and were sincere in their admiration of Laura's remarkable accomplishments, Mary felt that people did not realize how easily a child in her unusual position could become proud, selfish and disagreeable. Mary as well as Laura's other teachers wanted to preserve her right to be a modest, simple-hearted child. When Laura participated in public exhibits, it was explained to her that she was one among other blind children seated at their desks around the room and that the ladies and gentlemen had come to see how blind children were taught. Laura did not know that her share of attention was far greater than those of other pupils (Lamson, 1881, pp. 99–100).

As a result of Laura's wide recognition a number of notable individuals also wished to serve as Laura's teachers. On one occasion, Elizabeth Peabody wrote to Howe and requested that she become the replacement for Laura's first teacher, Lydia Drew.

July 26, 1842

Dr. Howe

Dear sir,

I understand you are searching for a person to take the place of Miss Drew. I do not know what her duties are—or her compensation—but I know that if the duties involve a case of Laura Bridgman I should of all things like thee—and as my business is not sufficiently successful to make it any object to remain in it—I should like to leave the place—Render my doubts about phrenology—or something of that kind unfits me for the place in your opinion—Can we not converse about it please?

Yours respectfully,

E. P. Peabody

(E. Peabody, personal communication, July 26, 1842)

Dr. Howe's response to this letter is unknown.

Mary became used to the public recognition and resultant responsibilities that surrounded her work with Laura, a child who gained world-wide attention by learning to communicate with the outside world, a world which had once been unreachable to her. Indeed, Howe once boasted that Laura was one of the most famous women in the world, second only to Queen Victoria (Freeberg, 2001, p. 2). Her story and circumstances had turned the Perkins Institution into a popular tourist attraction (Freeberg, 2001, p. 92). As her fame grew Laura was often asked for autographs, which Laura would spend substantial time penning. Her reputation would bring political dignitaries, medical professionals, religious leaders and famous literary sources to her doorstep. There were countless newspaper and magazine articles written about her (Freeberg, 2001, p. 2). Charles Sumner, a prominent Massachusetts lawyer and close friend of Henry Wadsworth Longfellow, was a frequent visitor to the Perkins Institution and Laura in particular (Lamson, 1881, p. 134).

In 1841, Lydia Sigourney, a notable New England poet, met Laura and wrote a poem about her (Lamson, 1881, p. 82). Mary and her normal school peers had read some of Sigourney's writings while they were students in Lexington, including *Mrs. Sigourney's Letters to Young Ladies*, published in 1837, which they considered to be an excellent book (L. Stow, personal communication, journal entry, January 18, 1840). In 1837, the Methodist Review had stated that the book focused on "the acquisition of knowledge, industry, domestic employments, health and dress, manners and accomplishments, and the culture of the moral, social, and religious duties. Beside a preface, and an appeal to the guardians of female education, it contains sixteen letters addressed to young ladies, the object of which is to elevate the literary, moral and religious character of the sex" (Methodist Episcopal Church, 1837, p. 52).

Mrs. Sigourney was considered one of the most popular nineteenth century poets in the United States as well as in Britain. Her prose and poems were published in numerous newspapers and magazines (Kelly, 2008, pp. 11–12). In her poem about Laura, Sigourney reflected on Laura's circumstances, as well as on the controversy that surrounded Howe's experiment with Laura's introduction to religion and God.

Laura Bridgman, the Deaf, Dumb, and Blind Girl at the Institution for the Blind in Boston

Where is the light that to the eye
Heaven's holy message gave,
Tinging the retina with rays
From sky and earth and wave?

Where is the sound that to the soul
Mysterious passage wrought
And strangely made the moving lip
A harp-string for the thought?
All fled! All lost! Not even the rose
An odor leave behind,
That, like a broken reed, might trace
The tablet of the mind.
That mind! It struggles with its fate,
The anxious conflict, see.
As if through Bastille hours it sought
Communion with the free.
Yet still its prison robe it wears
Without a prisoner's pain,
For happy childhood's beaming sun
Glows in each bounding vein.
And bless'd Philosophy is near,
In Christian armor bright,
To scan the subtlest clew that leads
To intellectual light.
Say, lurks there not some ray of heaven
Amid the bosom's night,
Some echo from a better land,
To make thy smile so bright?
The lonely lump in Greenland cell,
Deep 'nearth a world of snow,
Doth cheer the loving household group
Though none beside may know;
And, sweet one, doth our Father's hand
Place in thy casket dim
A radiant and peculiar lump,
To guide thy steps to Him?

(as cited in Lamson, 1881, pp. 82–83)

On another occasion George Combe, a Scottish writer on phrenology, visited with Laura in 1842 (Lamson, 1881, p. 136). Combe had been a student of the phrenologist Spurzheim, whose grave at Mount Auburn Mary and her fellow normalites had visited with Cyrus Peirce. Prior to his death, Spurzheim also had been a close acquaintance of Howe. Mary had read Combe's book, *Constitution of Man*, when she was a normal school student. Around the time that the normal school movement commenced, George Combe also had become a friend of Horace Mann. The two had developed an active correspondence in which they discussed Combe's books, as well as U.S. politics. Their friendship grew strong enough that in 1846 Horace Mann named his son after Combe.

Interest in Laura Dewey Bridgman was central to the communication between Combe and Howe. On November 30, 1842, George Combe wrote to Howe from Edinburgh.

> My Dear Doctor Howe,
>
> Our friend Mr. Mann will have informed you how completely I have been knocked up, for six months, by over-exertion in Germany.... My only apology is that the excitement of the study and the climate combined, tendered me unconscious of the extent to which I was draining on my cerebral powers.... In Germany I found frequent... notices in books & periodicals of Laura Bridgman's case.
>
> (G. Combe, personal communication, November 20, 1842)

In this same letter, Combe discussed the observations of a Dr. Carus of Dresden, Germany regarding Laura Dewey Bridgman. Dr. Carus, an individual of notable reputation, was the physician for the King of Saxony (G. Comb, personal communication, November 20, 1842). Laura's circumstances were, indeed, of interest to many.

Combe's visit to the Perkins Institution in 1842 proved to be a pivotal one for both Laura and Mary. During the engagement, lengthy discussion ensued between Howe and Combe about recording as much as possible with regard to Laura's learning experiences, so nothing would be lost that

Figure 6.1   Mary Swift with Laura Dewey Bridgman. Courtesy of Perkins School for the Blind, Watertown, MA..

could be of value to science. As a phrenologist, Combe was naturally intrigued with Laura's circumstances. Phrenology "offered a system for analyzing personal and social problems and prescribing remedies" (Gitter, 2005, p. 93). It could provide "a complete explanation of Laura's intellectual progress" (Gitter, 2005, p. 94). Combe felt that recording detailed and meticulous notes about Laura should commence at once, and offered Howe financial assistance to assist with defraying the costs connected to this venture. Other sponsors came forward and Mary subsequently was assigned the task. Though Laura and Mary had spent lots of time together before that point, after Combe's visit they were joined almost constantly. Leaning on Mary's right hand for guidance, Laura conversed with Mary steadily through finger talk (Lamson, 1881, p. 136).

It was during this time that controversy over Howe's exclusion of Laura from religious instruction became heated. Howe was criticized in well-read publications (Lamson, 1881). Mary was regularly asked to share her thoughts about Howe's experiment by individuals who visited Laura. Their questions lent to moments of uneasiness for Mary. Truthfully, she did not believe in or support Howe's decision to deprive Laura of religious instruction. Mary also knew that Laura, through her interactions with the other children at Perkins, had been exposed to ideas about God and religion. Laura also attended church with her teachers. It was difficult to not address her questions or her curiosity. Mary, after all, had grown up as a Quaker on Nantucket. On the Island, women were active in the discussion of religious matters, where spiritual and intellectual equality of the sexes was emphasized. Nantucket women also were involved in overseeing many of the island's businesses as men often were out at sea on whaling expeditions. Nantucket women needed to make decisions as they arose (Philbrick, 2001). Mary was therefore sensitive to those who believed that avoiding religious instruction with Laura was detrimental to her self-development.

When Howe married his bride, Julia Ward Howe, on April 27, 1843, he and Julia, along with his friend, Horace Mann and Mann's bride, Mary Peabody, traveled to Europe for a year-long trip. Howe and Mann continued to nourish their friendship, resulting in a shared honeymoon of sorts. Mary consequently worried about Laura's reactions to Howe's departure. She felt that Laura was "inclined to conceal her own sadness at parting with Dr. Howe" (Lamson, 1881, p. 170). She noticed that in the evening following his parting with them, Laura was quiet. Mary and Laura had gone to see the steamship that Howe would travel on to Europe, and Laura had been given the opportunity to explore the vessel in preparation for Howe's departure.

While in Europe, the two couples occupied the same lodgings for a period of time (Howe, 1876, p. 26). They set out on visits to public institutions including work houses, schools and prisons. Charles Dickens, who had eventually met Howe when he was in the United States, accompanied them to Westminster Bridewell, a prison located in the Westminster area of London. Dickens' publication of *American Notes* resulted in Dr. Howe becoming well known in England and throughout Europe (Howe, 1876, p. 27). Dickens also had published *A Christmas Carol* in 1843, which was one of the most influential books of the time. The meetings between Dickens and Howe were recognized affairs. While in London, Thomas Carlyle, a Scottish author, also met Howe with whom he discussed Laura Dewey Bridgman. The Duke and Duchess of Sutherland requested an audience with Howe who was asked to explain how he led Laura, an imprisoned soul, from darkness to light (Howe, 1876, p. 27).

While Dr. Howe was in Europe, Mary was Laura's primary care taker. At that time Laura also heard less from her immediate family. In addition, When Laura wrote letters to Howe, she often did not hear back from him, or if she did it was after an extended period. After having written a letter to Howe in January of 1844 and not having heard from him by March, she wrote to him again.

24th March, 1844

My Dear Dr. Howe:

I want to see you very much. I hope that you will come to South Boston in May. I have got a bad cough, for I got cold when I came home, in much snow with Miss Swift, but my cough is a little better. . . . Why do you not write a letter to me often? . . . I think of you often. I send a great deal of love to you and Mrs. Howe. I shall be very happy to see you & her when you come home.

My dear friend, good bye.

Laura Bridgman

(as cited in Lamson, 1881, p. 245)

It was difficult for Laura to not hear from Dr. Howe. Even earlier, her temperament had been described as less patient. In his 1843 report to the Perkins board, Dr. Howe had written about Laura's restless and excited nature and described her spirit as anxious. "Her spirit, apparently impatient of its narrow bounds, is as it were continually pressing against the bars of its cage, and struggling, if not to escape at least to obtain more of the sights and sounds of the outer world" (as cited in Trustees of the Perkins Institution for the Blind, 1843). Restlessness had its benefits, however. Mary found that Laura did well with physical activity. Mary's father believed in the importance of this activity, and the importance of daily exercise also had been promoted while Mary was a student at the normal school. Sometimes Mary would take Laura for long walks, up to six miles at a time. On other occasions, she would take Laura to visit with some of her normal school friends (L. Harris, personal communication, journal entry, September 16, 1843). She enjoyed those reunions. On July 18, 1843, they traveled to visit with Laura's former teacher, Lydia Drew, who had married and was living in Halifax, Maine. At one point during that trip, they stopped to water the horses. Mary used that opportunity to explain how horses know when they want water and how they put their heads in pails to drink (Lamson, 1881, p. 184).

Mary cared deeply for Laura. She enjoyed teaching her and did not mind her numerous questions. Mary wrote in her journal that "it may seem to those accustomed to teach children with all their senses, who acquire knowledge of such things intuitively, that these questions would be tedious to answer, but in justice to my pupil I must say that I doubt if any teacher had a work of such interest" (Lamson, 1881, p. 184). However, Mary was strict with Laura. If Laura acted out, Mary sent her directly to her room. Mary lacked some of the gentleness of Laura's other instructors, and did not tolerate Laura's behavioral digressions.

In her role as both primary caretaker and teacher, Mary also had to cope with the visitors who were always near at hand, requesting to meet Laura or asking for her autograph. The latter proved especially difficult, since the novelty of signing autographs had worn off and Laura had grown tired of writing them. Mary also sensed that a crisis was developing between her and Laura (Lamson, 1881, p. 233). In 1843, Laura turned fourteen and she and Mary had been working together for four years. There were times when interactions resulted in tears for both of them. Mary, perhaps worn out by the effort required by her constant work with Laura, took actions that she would later, with the hindsight of gained wisdom, have cause to regret. It is unclear what these actions were that Mary would later allude to. They may have been connected to Howe's "great experiment" that pre-empted Laura's religious education and her exposure to spiritual doctrine.

While Howe was away, Mary became a regular parishioner of the Park Street Church. Founded in 1809, the Park Street Church was of the Congregational denomination, as was three-quarters of the population of Boston at that time. When its construction was completed, the church was the tallest building in the city. It overshadowed the state house by ten feet (Rosell, 2009). During that time, Mary also became acquainted with Edwin Lamson, a church deacon. Romantic interests emerged and started to grow between them, while at the same time Mary was increasingly drawn to the tenets of the Park Street Church. During this time of transformation in Mary's life, Laura increasingly had questions about God. She wanted to understand what a blessing was and how one prayed. As noted earlier, Laura may have been exposed to some religious terminology while interacting with other students at the Perkins Institution. In January 1843, Laura wrote a letter to Howe about God and asked numerous questions. "Shall we know what to ask God to do? When will He let us go to see him in Heaven? How did God tell people that he lived in Heaven? Why is He our Father?" (Lamson, 1881, p. 229).

Dr. Howe's reply to this letter was received in April 1843. He wrote Laura that when he returned in June he would answer her questions. Howe said that he would briefly share in his letter some ideas with her about God. "He is not a man, nor like man; I cannot see him, nor feel him...but I know he has the spirit of love" (Lamson, 1881, p. 252). In the same letter he also wrote, "Your mind is young and weak, and cannot understand hard things, but by and by it will be stronger, and you will be able to understand hard things, and I and my wife will help Miss Swift to show you all about things that now you do not know. Be patient, then, dear Laura" (Lamson, 1881, p. 252). It was clear that Howe's experiment with regard to Laura's exposure to religion had failed.

In Dr. Howe's 1845 annual report to the Perkins board, he wrote about the breakdown of this experiment with Laura and his disappointment over it. In drafting the report, Howe had received advice and guidance from his friend Horace Mann.

> I might long ago have taught the Scriptures to Laura. She might have learned, as other children do, to repeat line upon line, and precept upon precept; she might have been taught to imitate others in prayer; but her God must have been her own God, and formed out of the materials with which her mind had been stored. It was my wish to give her gradually such ideas of His power and love as would have enabled her to form the highest possible conception of His divine attributes. In doing this, it was necessary to guard as much as I could, against conveying impressions which it would be hard to remove afterwards, and to prevent her forming such notions as would seem unworthy to her more developed reason, lest the renouncement of them might impair her confidence in her own belief. But various causes have combined to prevent what seemed to me the natural and harmonious development of her religious nature; and now, like other children, she must take the consequences of the wise or unwise instruction given by others. I did not long hold the only key to her mind; it would have been unkind and unjust to prevent her using her power of language as fast as she acquired it, in conversation with others, merely to carry out a theory of my own, and she was left to free communication with many persons even before my necessary separation from her of more than a year. During my absence, and perhaps before, some persons more zealous than discreet, and more desirous to make a proselyte than to keep conscientiously their implied promise of not touching upon religious topics, some such persons talked to

her of the Atonement, of the Redeemer, the Lamb of God, and of some very mystical points of mere speculative doctrine. These things were perhaps not farther beyond her comprehension than they were beyond the comprehension of those persons who assumed to talk to her about them; but they perplexed and troubled her, because, unlike such persons she wished that every word should be the symbol of some clear and definite idea. She could not understand metaphorical language; hence the Lamb of God was to her a bona fide animal, and she could not conceive why it should continue so long a lamb, and not grow old like others and be called a sheep. I must be supposed to mention this only as her faithful chronicler, and to do it also in sorrow. If the poor child spoke inadvertently on such topics, it was without consciousness of it, and she was made to do so by indiscreet persons, not by any communications of mine or of her teacher; we shall never speak to her of Jesus Christ but in such a way as to impart a portion. (as cited in Trustees of the Perkins Institution for the Blind, 1841)

After Howe's publicly written reaction to Laura's exposure to religious doctrine, he was again criticized for his views and experiment with Laura. One of Howe's most vocal critics was A. W. McClure, editor of *The Christian Observatory: A Religious and Literary Magazine.* In 1847, an article appeared in the magazine, written by McClure, about Howe's work with Laura Bridgman.

Dr. Howe, like other gentlemen of that class, will, we have no doubt, avow a great reverence for many things in the Bible. But in all his reports we can see no trace that he regards its biography, its theology, its devotional models, its commands, promises, threatenings or invitations; its views of man or God, of time or eternity, as at all important to education. He contradicts the Word of God, and teaches children so. Dr. Howe teaches the children and the public that they are pure by nature; pure as Eve. "Truth is plainer and more agreeable to children than falsehood; and right than wrong. Children are inclined to tell the truth." The different traits of Laura's character have unfolded themselves successively, as pure and spotless as the petals of a rose; and in every action, uninfluenced by extraneous influence, she gravitates towards the right, as naturally as a stone falls to the ground. She seems to be one of those who have the law graven upon their hearts; who do not see the right intellectually, but perceive it intuitively; and who, if made to swerve a moment from the right by any temptation, soon recover themselves by their native elasticity. How does Dr. Howe know, when she does wrong, that it is all from outward influences? What authorizes him to contradict our Lord, who says, that from within, out of the heart of man, proceed evil thoughts? The Scriptures say, "The heart is deceitful above all things; and that men go astray, from the womb, speaking lies; there is none that doeth good, no, not one." But in the face of all this, we are told of children as pure as Eve, as pure as the petals of the rose, inclining to truth and right rather than to falsehood and wrong. (McClure, 1847, p. 137)

Mary, as the primary teacher of Laura, was questioned by Howe and his close associates with regard to Laura's formal exposure to religious doctrine (Lamson, 1881). As she had been when she was a normal school student, Mary was once again placed in the public light, assessed and scrutinized. She would later write that she felt that her enforced reticence about religion with Laura was disastrous. She wrote that "Could Dr. Howe have anticipated her [Laura's] mental development during his absence, he would doubtless have left her under the charge of some person who sympathized with his views" (Lamson, 1881, p. 277).

Louisa Harris

After a short break in 1843, Louisa returned to teaching in a primary summer school in Roxbury. She appeared to maintain strong control of her school and enjoyed her connections with her students. At times, she also was concerned about them. If the heat was strong, she sympathized about their comfort levels in the one-room school (L. Harris, personal communication, journal entry, April 22, 1842). Louisa was pleased when a student who had traveled to New York for a personal reason, returned to her school (L. Harris, personal communication, journal entry, April 29, 1842). She was sad to see her scholars depart for grammar school at the end of the summer session (L. Harris, personal communication, journal entry, May 7, 1842). Although it was a step up for these scholars, nevertheless Louisa knew that she would miss them. When one of her young pupils smiled when he saw the sun appear after it had been absent for a time, she reflected on the effect of his countenance. "The sunshine which such an act spread over the heart and face of a little child, was enough to warm and cheer all within its presence, and excite a feeling of gratitude towards the author" (L. Harris, personal communication, journal entry, January 14, 1843). Louisa enjoyed it when friends visited her and expressed an interest in school affairs (L. Harris, personal communication, journal entry, March 11, 1842). When she, on occasion, let out school early to attend special events, such as a funeral or lecture, she made up the time with her students on another day. She was in tune with them. There were times, however, when teaching felt like a duty (L. Harris, personal communication, journal entry, January 3, 1843). It could be difficult and tiring. She oversaw large numbers of students, often six days a week. Nonetheless, when she was on break, she anticipated the time when she would resume her labors and perform them well (L. Harris, personal communication, journal entry, August 28, 1843).

In 1843, Louisa's brother Warren assumed a residence in Canton, Massachusetts, a town approximately 15 miles from Boston. Shortly thereafter, her parents also relocated to Canton, taking a house of their own located three-quarters of a mile from any human habitation and in the middle of beautiful and wild scenery (L. Harris, personal communication, journal entry, May 29, 1843). When her family left their home in Roxbury, Louisa recorded in her journal that "our family have left the house which has so long been our home and it passes into the hands of strangers. I could not venture forth to school this morning, that I was to return no more that where I had rested so often from my labors and enjoyed my pastimes" (L. Harris, personal communication, journal entry, April 4, 1842). Her father considered his move to Canton to be a permanent one; he expected to live in his new home for the remainder of his days.

After Louisa's parents left Roxbury, she initially spent some time living with her sister Lucy, followed by a boarding arrangement at a Mrs. Marians and then at a Mrs. Withington's (L. Harris, personal communication, journal entry, May 29, 1843). She knew, however, that she would eventually live among strangers in a boarding house. In the nineteenth century, boarding with other families was a common housing arrangement, with between one-third and one-half of urban residents either boarding, or taking in single or multiple boarders (Gamber, 2007, p. 3). People of all classes lived in boarding houses, including married couples, families, the elderly, and single individuals. Some boardinghouse residents, such as Louisa, were single school teachers. In general, the conditions of urban boardinghouses varied significantly. While some were marked by filthy bed linens and intolerable cuisine, others boasted more favorable conditions. One had to select one's boarding house carefully. Occasionally residents who boarded in the same house formed connections and became friends. Some boarders assisted the landlords with household duties and developed familial bonds with their hosts. In other cases, those sharing such a living arrangement found their housemates to be eccentric or disagreeable, and thus kept to themselves (Gamber, 2007). Fortunately, the first boarding house Louisa resided at was one she believed to be elegant and spacious. Regardless of the qualities and attributes of some boardinghouses, these places did not compare to a home of one's own.

Louisa turned 18 in 1842, and was increasingly aware of her public reputation as a teacher. When she took part in activities she thought some might find unbecoming of her age or her profession, she felt some disapprobation (L. Harris, personal communication, journal entry, January 3, 1843). Since these moments brought her happiness, however, she did not regret them. During evening hours Louisa often rested in the solitude of her room. These moments were simultaneously filled with satisfaction and sadness. She wondered what the future would hold for her. She was pleased when time passed and she did not feel her spirits depressed or "dissatisfied with the portion that falleth to me" (L. Harris, personal communication, journal entry, April 13, 1844). Increasingly, Louisa struggled with fluctuations of her emotions. She felt that the weather influenced them. If it was rainy and dull, she would feel down, but if it was sunny, life was more cheerful. "I am myself inclined to doubt whether tis not rather unphilosophical to depend on the weather for spirits, nonetheless I do so to some extent" (L. Harris, personal communication, journal entry, April 19, 1842).

During the summer in 1842 Louisa had company. A cousin of her friend and fellow normalite Sarah Wyman came to stay with her for a few months, and she much enjoyed the companionship. In general, Louisa enjoyed an active social life and interacted with numerous acquaintances and friends. On March 30, 1844, she wrote in her journal, "Received a letter from Sarah B. on Monday . . . Was visited on Wednesday by Lizzy Marian and Ann Marian. Have also had my sister Laura to pass a few days with me, and have passed my night with her at my sister Lucy's. Also called this week at Primary School No. 15 with Sara and Harriet Taber, and passed some time at Sarah W's school yesterday afternoon" (L. Harris, personal communication, journal entry, March 30, 1844). With so many acquaintances and friends, Louisa worried that her love of ease and socializing was increasingly occupying her time and thoughts (L. Harris, personal communication, journal entry, July 28, 1843). A better self, a higher aim, however, was what she desired (L. Harris, personal communication, journal entry, July 29, 1843). In this frame of mind, she recalled the sense of duty that was at the core of her teaching vocation and commitment. In her journal she recorded that she knew that if she neglected these duties, she would never feel lightness of heart (L. Harris, personal communication, journal entry, January 3, 1843).

By 1850, Louisa had taught in Roxbury for ten years. The school committee report that year suggested that Louisa's efforts as a teacher, largely to new immigrant children, were viewed positively (Roxbury School Committee, 1850). The school committee, in their report, likewise drew attention to conflicts in schooling in Roxbury which connected to cultural and economic divisions.

> The order of the school, and personal appearance of the scholars were quite good, considering the class of families to which they belong. The Reading, in spite of foreign accents, was clear and distinct; the voice well modulated and the emphasis properly placed. (Roxbury School Committee, 1850)

PART **III**

Contexts and Transition Periods

7

Family, Friendships, and Social Contexts

By the early 1840s, Lydia Stow, Mary Swift, and Louisa Harris had become young women, with one or two years of teaching experience behind them. They earned an independent living, and lived as single women outside of their family homes, boarding at private residences and at establishments such as at the Perkins Institution. The work for which they had been prepared as normal school students inevitably brought difficulties and challenges, but it also brought rewards. Lydia Stow, Mary Swift, and Louisa Harris shaped the lives of their students, and as so often happens, their students had a deep influence on their teachers as well.

The normalites came of age in a century that was to bring profound social changes to American society. Although women had been granted some degree of intellectual freedom and independence, such as encouragement to enter the teaching profession, women were still denied the privileges of citizenship. Educated and ambitious women such as Lydia, Mary, and Louisa must have experienced conflict, consciously or not, between their intellectual abilities and accomplishments and the limitations imposed on them by a male-dominated academic and political world. In spite of the

Normalites, pages 97–120
Copyright © 2014 by Information Age Publishing

high professional expectations bestowed on them by Cyrus Peirce, their professional and pedagogical decisions were controlled by local school officials, politicians, and headmasters.

Two of these women, Lydia Stow and Mary Swift, would marry and have children, while Louisa Harris did not. Their personal choices were not seen, as they would be today, as independent of their professional choices. Once Lydia and Mary married and had children, they were expected to leave teaching, which they both did. By not marrying, Louisa Harris was free to continue in her profession, but was socially relegated to the category of "spinsterhood," a woman who either from rejection or repression, it was believed, had forsaken the fulfillment of marriage and motherhood. Cyrus Peirce had urged these three women to live to the truth, a commitment they took to heart and by which they instilled in themselves a vision for the future. As they witnessed reform and change in education and in the larger world unfold around them, they considered and responded to the opportunities and possibilities that presented themselves.

Lydia Stow

In the early 1840s, Lydia Stow remained in close contact with her sister Mary Stow and Aunt Sophia Foord, who both taught in schools in Fall River, while Lydia remained and taught in Dedham. Lydia often worried about her sister Mary. In 1842, Mary had to accommodate an addition of 14 older boys, all Irish immigrants, to her school in Fall River. They came directly from the factories and although they were ready to learn, Lydia felt that it must have been a task. She wrote in her journal, "Many would shrink with sorrow at such an undertaking, but truly there is much merit due to that one who engages with such, with a zeal and interest for their real improvement. There is pleasure there . . . in teaching the poor, ignorant outcasts the thought that we may be the instrument of saving them from their misery and degradation ought ever to press us to duty" (L. Stow, personal communication, journal entry, March 28, 1842). Lydia recognized that her sister Mary had very little respite from her work responsibilities and that she was exhausted. She was thin, weighing only 113 pounds, and had health problems. Mary was her only sister and "her nearest and dearest relation on Earth." Lydia worried about her (L. Stowe, personal communication, journal entry, April 11, 1842).

Lydia had been able to visit her sister Mary's and Aunt Sophia's schools during a Christmas visit in 1841. In December, Lydia, her Grandmother Foord, Uncle Enos, and additional family members traveled to Fall River to visit their relatives who resided there. Fall River, located south of Providence and 12 miles west of New Bedford, was a nucleus of manufacturing activity. Noted for its role in textile work, it was the home of numerous red-brick factories that often were five to six stories in height. Smoke stacks belched smoke, while the high windows provided a view to the outside world. The factories had thousands of spindles that were in operation for 12 to 14 hours a day. The city also was home to over 36 stores, a tavern, a brick yard, bank, and at least four churches including a Congregationalist, Baptist, and two Methodist. At the time, there were also a number of public and private schools that served a population of approximately 6,700 (Earl, 1877, p. 68). As Fall River bordered the Mount Hope Bay, parts of the city offered residents wonderful, picturesque water views. These were ones that Lydia enjoyed.

When Lydia arrived in Fall River during that Christmas trip she reconnected with her sister Mary and Aunt Sophia and was pleased to spend extensive time at both their schools. She had visited her Aunt Sophia's school during the previous winter and was amazed to see the progress her scholars had made in one year. Lydia also enjoyed attending her sister Mary's school, which was the 2nd Primary School in the Village. Even though it was a primary school, older students at times attended. Mary maintained great order in her school, a prerequisite for successful teaching. One year after Lydia's visit, the school committee that oversaw Mary's school wrote "Discipline excellent. Progress of the scholars very satisfactory" (Fall River School Committee, 1842, p. 6). Lydia recognized that many of the children in Mary's school were poor, and some came to school in states of disarray. She even considered some of them "backward" and thought one was "ignorant." Lydia knew it was a great responsibility to teach these children. She helped Mary by teaching arithmetic, a subject she had struggled with while she was a normal school student (L. Stowe, personal communication, journal entry, January 13, 1842).

During the visit to Fall River Lydia engaged in broader learning opportunities that presented themselves. She took part in study of botany with a group of Fall River residents. It was a subject she had been exposed to when she was a student at the normal school. Cyrus Peirce's wife, Harriet Peirce, had a keen interest in the subject and taught lessons to the students. Lydia wrote in her journal that Mrs. Peirce told them that "I have been requested to address you at this time in the subject of botany with which request I readily comply as it is a subject on which I love to talk" (L. Stowe, personal communication, journal entry, May 9, 1840). Along with her small group of class members in Fall River Lydia studied plants and roots, although she often forgot the names of the particular specimens. She believed that studying botany offered inquiry into the higher conception of the author of the universe. Botany classes were held in the homes of Mr. Borden and Miss Buffam, members of notable Fall River families (L. Stowe, personal communication, journal entry, January 7, 1842).

During her 1842 visit to Fall River, Lydia and her family also attended a lecture by Bronson Alcott who spoke about intellectual philosophy. She also stopped by her Uncle James Foord's newspaper office as it produced the *Fall River Monitor*. James Foord, a lawyer, also was the editor of the newspaper. Lydia also attended her first Quaker meeting and noted her interest in it. On New Year's Eve, she and her family were awakened by the sound of bells. A factory was burning and it was feared that the fire could spread. Devastating fires were a common occurrence in nineteenth century New England cities, in which buildings, frequently wooden structures, were built close together. Lydia and her family quickly packed their belongings into trunks and prepared to leave. The fire was contained, however, so they were able to stay.

Lydia enjoyed her visit and did not mind that it stretched to three weeks. When she left, she wondered if her sister Mary would be lonely without her. After her return to Dedham, Lydia reflected that everything seemed unbearably quiet, and her family and acquaintances noticed a distinct change in her personality. She was no longer a quiet individual, but one who had become quite assertive. She wrote in her journal, "I fear that the change may be great from the life and animation that we have had. We will endear or bear up under it." She recorded, "It is thought by some that I have grown wild in three weeks. Dedham people are not accustomed to so much. Must go back" (L. Stowe, personal communication, journal entry, January 15, 1842).

At the end of her school's term in South Dedham, Lydia returned to her grandmother's house in Dedham. Her Aunt Esther had taken over the management of the household and boarders were living there, many of whom were rude. When they came to the table to eat, Lydia thought that they acted like pigs. Running a boarding house was difficult work.

In 1843, Lydia permanently relocated to Fall River. Soon after her relocation, she met Robert Adams, the man she would subsequently marry. Born in Scotland in 1816 to William and Janet Adams, Robert had moved with his immediate family to New Brunswick when he was four years old. A few years thereafter they relocated to Pawtucket, Rhode Island. In 1826, when he was ten, Robert began employment in the Samuel Slater's cotton mill. It was modeled after cotton spinning mills that were first established in England (White, 1836). It was the first water-powered cotton spinning mill in North America to utilize the Arkwright system which came from Richard Arkwright of London. Arkwright had developed the spinning frame, also known as the water frame, to produce yarn. Robert had little formal education, but during his young adulthood he learned the book binding business and drew on this skill. In 1842, when he was twenty-six years old, he moved to Fall River where he made drawings and patterns for American Print Works, a mill that produced printed cotton cloth. He then started to develop his emerging book binding business in partnership with his brother, John Adams. They established quarters for their business on the corner of North Main and Bank Streets (Fall River Daily Globe, 1900).

Robert was acquainted with Lydia's Aunt Sophia Foord who, in 1843, relocated to a communitarian community in North Adams, Massachusetts. It was named the Northampton Association of Education and Industry (Clark, 1995, p. 67). In communitarian communities, the connections between the individual and community were emphasized. The Northampton Association of Education and Industry was one of a number of communal efforts that flourished in Massachusetts in the 1840s. Others included Fruitlands, which had been formed by Bronson Alcott and the Brook Farm community in West Roxbury. The Shakers also formed communities with an alternative lifestyle and religious focus. The founder and members of the Northampton Association of Education and Industry sought to build an American society in which the inequalities of class, race and gender would be destroyed. There were 240 members though only half this number resided at the community at any given time (Clarke, 1995, p. 2). One member was Sojourner Truth, born Isabella. Born a slave in the late 1790s in Ulster County, New York, she was sold several times and owned for a substantial period by the Dumont family. During this time she was married to a slave chosen by her master and had five children. Sojourner Truth suffered excessive abuse as a child and young woman. One year prior to emancipation in New York in 1826, she left her husband and some of her children, taking only her baby with her. Her older children were not legally freed during emancipation as it was not an immediate process. Her son, Peter, subsequently was sold illegally to a family in Alabama. Through the court system Sojourner Truth was able to get him back. In 1839, this same son took a job on a whaling ship named the "Zone of Nantucket." When the ship returned, he was not on board and Sojourner Truth never heard from him again. Truth, who had a commanding presence, poured her energies into abolitionism and women's suffrage, using the voice of a preacher. She developed a strong religious faith (Truth, 1997). At a future time, Sojourner Truth would stay at Lydia's home while she lectured in Fall River.

Sophia Foord had considered the move to the Northampton Association carefully. (Though her decision was made in part as a departure from teaching, she was designated a teacher when she joined the community.) Members of the Northampton Association of Education and Industry lived in single and double family homes, as well as on the top floor of a silk mill that also served as a boarding house. They lived simply, drinking no tea or coffee (Clarke, 1995). The community operated a farm. Lydia's Aunt Sophia was pleased with the silk manufacturing project, which she thought was profitable. She also found the views from her room, which overlooked Mt. Tom, the town of Holyoke and the winding Connecticut River, to be exceptional. By the time that Aunt Sophia Foord joined the community in 1843, she had become increasingly involved in the abolitionist and women's suffrage movements.

In May of 1843 Aunt Sophia wrote to Robert Adams and tried to convince him to join the Northampton Association. She wrote, "Again and again have I been desired to request your presence" (Clarke, 1995, p. 67). Sophia Foord also kept in regular contact with her niece Lydia. Lydia, her sister Mary, and Mary's newly betrothed, Henry Woodward had considered a move to the Northampton Association, but Sophia Foord discouraged it. It is unclear why Foord wanted Robert Adams to join the community, yet discouraged her family members. Her Aunt Sophia remained a woman of considerable influence over Lydia, especially since by the end of 1843 both of Lydia's grandmothers had died and she grew closer to her aunts.

The Northampton community was one with which Robert Adams' father also had connections. In a letter to Robert, he had written about the number of hours each day members must work. He wrote, "I have just learned . . . that the North Hampton [sic] people has . . . their rules from the ensuing years that everyone must work 10 hours per day at the same employment or other if well if all they have concluded to try that for one year to see how it will work" (W. Adams, personal communication, February 27, 1843).

While Sophia Foord resided in Northampton in 1843, Lydia initially lived with her Uncle James Foord who had married Hannah Weaver, a wealthy resident of Fall River. His first marriage had been to Dorcas Adams who died in 1840. When Lydia's family met Hannah Weaver, she was a woman in her sixties (L. Stow, personal communication, journal entry, July 1, 1842). James Foord's law practice brought him into very confidential relationships with many Fall River residents. It was believed that he had drawn up more wills than any of his contemporaries. Sometimes when he attended the court in nearby New Bedford, he was gone several days at a time. James Foord, who had been educated at Brown University, was held in high esteem in Fall River. He often wore a top hat, cloak and cane when he traveled. Lydia considered him to be kind. He allowed her privileges that she would not have been allowed in Dedham. Over time, Lydia also grew to love her new Aunt Hannah and accepted what Lydia considered to be her peculiarities. She reasoned that their union might have been love of antiquity for old fashioned people (L. Stowe, personal communication, journal entry, July 2, 1842). The smell of cigars in the Foord house was one aspect, however, that Lydia would have preferred to live without. She often found herself going outdoors for walks during which she inhaled clean air and purified herself (L. Stowe, personal communication, journal entry, December 17, 1842). Lydia's sister, Mary, also resided with them prior to her marriage, which meant a great deal to her.

Lydia taught at the private school where her Aunt Sophia had provided instruction before departing to Northampton. No records have been found about the specific details of this school, other than that it was called a seminary. Sometimes Lydia would stop in Robert Adam's book bindery to purchase an item, such as a primer, on her way to school. The book bindery also functioned as a place where community members could purchase books and stationery. On some evenings, she attended the weekly lectures that were offered at the lyceum. Lydia was particularly interested in lectures on anatomy given by a Dr. Lambert. At one lecture he brought a skeleton and explained bone structure. On another night he spoke about the brain and nervous system. Another address at the lyceum was delivered by Henry Giles, a brilliant speaker who talked about the Irish people (L. Stow, personal communication, journal entry, January 1, 1843). Giles was a native of the "Emerald Isle" and felt a deep sympathy for his countrymen. In his lecture he said that they still were an oppressed people, but that they were sure to rise from their state. In the mid 1840s, the potato famine struck Ireland, resulting in disease and starvation. The potato crop, destroyed by a blight, was the staple food of rural families. Large numbers of Irish Catholics subsequently left the island and came to the United States where they faced great discrimination (Bartoletti, 2001). Lydia had become acquainted with Irish immigrants not only while living in Fall River, but in the Dedham area as well.

On October 21, 1841, Lydia, her aunt and cousin traveled to Boston for a shopping expedition. Lydia would later write in her journal that the forests looked "beautifully dyed in Autumn's colors. Who can contemplate the wisdom of the Creator of Nature as displayed in the variety of seasons without more exalted conceptions of his goodness—none I think." They spent the day in the "busy city" and then returned home. Six miles from their final destination, however, they passed an Irishman with a cart. This man did not keep to his due share of the road and their wheels collided. Lydia's aunt and cousin were thrown out of their seats. Lydia managed to keep her seat by holding onto the reigns of the horse. Lydia recalled that the Irish man passed, after which Lydia's aunt called after him that they needed assistance. He stopped to find out what the trouble was and acknowledged that he was at fault. He subsequently obtained a rope so he could assist them (L. Stowe, personal communication, journal entry, October 21, 1841). This family memory may have made Lydia more receptive and tolerant in her attitudes toward Irish immigrants.

School instruction was a significant focus of Lydia's life during her first years in Fall River. There were approximately 14 school districts in the city. Both public and private schools operated. Most of the public schools in Fall River were one-room school houses and, though there was some variety among the structures, many were in need of repair and often did not have blackboards. One school operated inside a print works building on Central Street in which a teacher was hired to instruct employees who also were children. Due to a lack of funds, another school operated in a dwelling house. Since there were no funds available to provide bells in each school, a bell from a Fall River factory was rung each morning, reminding all children of the start of school. The city's three-member school committee hired all the teachers who worked in the district schools (Fall River School Committee, 1842).

School attendance was a concern. Many children did not attend school. Although some early laws regarding the educational requirements of children had been passed in the seventeenth century in the Massachusetts Bay Colony, it would not be until 1852 when the first compulsory school attendance law would be approved. Even then, virtually no attempts were taken to enforce the law (Katz, 1976). In 1842, of the almost two thousand children who did attend the schools in the city, fewer than half attended the common schools. Roman Catholic children often attended religious schools. Catholicism was unfamiliar to Lydia who, out of curiosity, once attended a Catholic service with Robert, her sister Mary, and Henry Woodward. Though interested in the service, Lydia found it too "superstitious" for her. She wrote that the "singing was good though in an unknown tongue" (L. Stowe, personal communication, journal entry, December 17, 1842). She questioned the practices that she saw in the mass. Robert told her, however, that it was a matter of form, as found in other churches such as the Episcopalian religion. Lydia reflected in her journal, "There is as much sincerity in what the Catholics go through as in that of most other sects as they are at present conducted" (L. Stowe, personal communication, journal entry, December 22, 1842).

Towards the end of September 1844, Lydia made one of her periodic visits to her school friends. She traveled to Roxbury and saw Louisa Harris and Sarah Wyman. The three of them then set forth to visit Mary Swift and Eliza Rogers at the Perkins Institution in South Boston (L. Stow, personal communication, journal entry, September 14, 1844). As was always the case, they found that their tongues worked quickly when they came together, eager to fill each other in on their news. At night, they found lodging with the family of a normal school peer. Undressing in front of a burning fire, they considered their prospects while they still held the status of "blessed single-ness." Lydia knew, however, that she would change that state "provided a good offer was made." Although Lydia had known and kept company with Robert for a time before their marriage, she did not immediately discern that she would marry him. Indeed, when her sister Mary prepared to marry Henry Woodward, a man for whom she ached with love, Lydia wrote in her journal that "I know not what my destiny may be." On a return trip home to Dedham while her sister was preparing to marry, Lydia had her fortune told. In her journal, she wrote that it was said that she was "to marry better and sooner than I expected. My husband was to rule my course—was to be finished with honor." Lydia thought that this was, "Quite lucky if it all proves true" (L. Stow, personal communication, journal entry, near February, 1844). As foretold, on October 15, 1844 Lydia married Robert Adams. She was 21 years old and Robert was 24. The week that Lydia married, the *Fall River Monitor* published a column about the annexation of Texas to the Union, and about the practice of slavery in Texas (Clay, 1844). The moral issue of slavery, as well as its potential spread to new states as the country expanded its territory, was of growing concern in some areas.

Once Lydia married Robert, she left the teaching profession. Five days before she married, she sent a letter to Samuel May who had become principal of the Lexington Normal School. She discussed the challenges she had encountered in teaching and the appreciation for the education she had received as a normal school student.

Dedham, Oct. 10th 1844

Mr. May

Dear Sir—

Since having [sic] the Normal School, which is three years and a half, I have been engaged in public and private schools. The first school was in Dedham of twenty five scholars for five months, composed of children of all ages from four to fourteen. A school pleased and easily governed.

The next summer I taught in the same town a school averaging fifty with the same variety of ages and still greater of disposition and attainments. Jealousies among the Committee added to some new methods in teaching and created disaffection in the district. To attend to a thorough and daily reading of all was impossible. A portion read one day and the remaining the next, which proved more satisfactory to teacher than parents. The examining committee expressed their approbation.

For the year & half past I have been teaching a private school in Fall River of twenty scholars, with a mixture of ages as in the other schools. A barrier to success.

The plans and modes of teaching recommended at the Normal School, I have in the past adopted, am satisfied a continuance in school the system would develop more fully and awaken new fields of thought to the child's mind.

In disciplining schools I have not had satisfactory success yet. Experience teaches me that the law of love is the first, most salutary and will bestow much more good than sterner measures, which to often methinks effects only an outward appearance of good order.

It is but little I have done for the progress of any, but for that little I feel that I am much indebted to the influences of the Normal School. Shall ever cherish the principals there inculcated as giving myself and others a true means of developing the physical, moral and intellectual being.

Yours respectfully

L. A. Stow

(L. Stow, personal communication, October 10, 1844)

Honest in her letter, Lydia acknowledged the challenges she encountered in teaching.

Life was difficult in Fall River during this period. On July 2, 1843 a great fire occurred in the city. This time, unlike the episode in 1841, the fire had not been contained and many families suffered. The fire started when two young boys fired a small toy cannon. Some wood shavings were subsequently lit and the fire spread. It was a sweltering day on that July 2nd with a temperature of 90 degrees. It also was extremely windy (Martins & Binette, 2010, p. 116). Since the weather had been dry, the water in the river was low. Little resistance could be offered against the fire which raged for seven hours. The devastation was enormous. At the heart of the city, over 20 acres were completely burned over. Factories, stores, schools, churches, and homes were lost (Earl, 1877, pp. 218–219). Lydia's Uncle Foord, in addition to losing his home, lost his printing office. The *Fall River Monitor* ceased operations for a time. When it resumed, her uncle wrote in the paper:

Through the kindness of friends, we are enabled once more to furnish our readers with the Monitor. Since we last issued our regular paper on Saturday the 1st inst., our entire establishment, type presses, everything belonging to the office (the account books excepted) has been destroyed by the fire—not a dollar saved. (Foord, 1843)

Friends from the Providence newspaper helped the *Fall River Monitor* resume its printing operations. Colonel Bradford Durfee, brother-in-law of James Foord, also allowed the paper to set up temporary operation in his house.

Robert Adams' book binding shop was also lost to the fire. After he re-established his business at a temporary site on Main Street, he advertised the new location in the *Fall River Monitor*.

Bookstore and Bindery

The subscribers would respectfully inform the people of Fall River and vicinity that they have taken a stand opposite the Baptist Temple, formerly occupied by J. Renehan as a tailor's shop, where they have just made additions to their stock of Stationary. Paper hangings, Black books & c. which were saved from the late fire, and also intend carrying on the book binding business as usual. R & J Adams July 15. (Adams, 1843)

Following the fire, a committee on behalf of the people of Fall River appealed for help with food, clothing and money. They noted that the city was in desolation and a deep state of distress. Help came from Boston, Providence, New Bedford, Pawtucket and other cities. Churches sent funds. A women's association in Roxbury helped to raise money for the needy in Fall River. The Perkins Institution engaged their residents in sewing articles of clothing. Mary Swift, Lydia's normalite friend, explained to her pupil, Laura Dewey Bridgman, the nature of the work they undertook and the reasons for it.

In her hour for conversation she [Laura Dewey Bridgman] asked why there was so much work about the room. It belonged to a company of ladies who were assisting the Fall River sufferers, and I thought it a good opportunity to give her a lesson on it. Told her how much the fire burned, and then of the poor people who had no home and clothes. (Lamson, 1881, p. 189)

After the Fall River fire, plundering took place and a night watch was set up to oversee the activity of the city. Disturbances that the night watch encountered, however, typically centered on men who drank and became intoxicated. These events likely were difficult for Lydia and her family and friends.

Lydia's husband was a hard-working and ethical man. He previously received careful advice from his father regarding the business of running a store. His work with the store continued.

Pawtucket, February 27th 1843

Dear Robert and John,

I take the opportunity to send by friend Johnson today that we are well after Isabella has wrote you ... I am glad you have got moved to where you are. You have now a good chance ... if you are careful and attentive. ... when the rest of the people call to work go you to your store although you may hear no takers in the morning yet you may have another work to do. And you will be there if any person shall call.

To John [Robert's brother], I would say be careful to cultivate an cosy [sic] and affable and obliging manner if you expect to success in business.... Yourself nature has not done so much for you in that respect as it has for Robert and.... I speak so because it is my duty as because I love you and must feel pleased at your success and so much depend on your own manner of knowing.

(W. Adams, personal communication, February 27, 1843)

In public, Lydia's husband, Robert, could, if pushed, be aggressive and even pugilistic, particularly if talk centered on politics. However, Lydia knew this was not his common practice. In general, Robert was well liked, which would serve as a foundation for his later work as a school committee member and city alderman. His traits Lydia recognized were related to his sense of ethics and principles. After her marriage, Lydia was surrounded by extended family. Robert was close to his siblings John, Charles, and Isabella, who all lived nearby. Lydia's sister Mary had married Henry Woodward, a physician, in March of 1843 and they too resided nearby, though Henry only lived another year before dying from tuberculosis.

Throughout the remainder of the 1840s, other significant changes occurred in Lydia's extended family. In 1846, Lydia's Aunt Sophia Foord left the Northampton Association and took a position as governess of the Alcott children. Bronson Alcott had tried to set up a private school with Sophia Foord but it did not succeed. Instead Sophia Foord served as the governess of his children. She joined the Alcott household, receiving praise from Abba Alcott, wife of Bronson Alcott (Harding, 1962, p. 225). Eventually, the children of Ralph Waldo Emerson also came under her instruction in the Emerson's barn. A bedroom was built in the barn at which Sophia lodged. Henry David Thoreau was hired to build the chimney so the room would be kept warm (Harding, 1962, p. 225). By 1846, Emerson had become an influential writer and Lydia's Aunt Sophia was in the esteemed position as the governess of his children.

The children found Aunt Sophia Foord to be a wonderful teacher. When they were not engaged in lessons at the barn, they went outdoors for excursions. Louisa May Alcott wrote in a letter to one of her younger friends about a walk they had taken to Flint's Pond.

Now if you won't laugh, I'll tell you something—if you will believe it. Miss F and all of us waded across...a great big pond a mile long and half a mile wide, we went splashing along making the fishes run like mad before our big class, when we got to the other side we had a funny time getting on our shoes and unmentionables, and we came tumbling home all wet and muddy, but we were happy enough, for we came through the woods howling and singing like crazy folks. (Harding, 1962, pp. 225–226)

Foord also took the children out on flower scavenger hunts with Henry David Thoreau as guide. As a result of these interactions, Sophia Foord fell in love with Thoreau and eventually asked him to marry her. He, as history revealed, declined. In an 1847 letter from Thoreau to Emerson, which was later censored, the marriage proposal was discussed.

I have had a tragic correspondence for the most part all on one side, with Miss ____. She did really wish to—I hesitate to write—marry me. That is the way they spell it . . . I sent back as distinct a no as I have learned to pronounce after considerable practice, and I trust that this now has succeeded. (Harding, 1962, p. 225)

Lydia's aunt never married. For a time, she lost her emotional balance and there was some question of whether she attempted suicide. When Aunt Sophia Foord did regain her balance, however, she continued to write to Thoreau (Harding, 1962, pp. 225–226).

At the time Foord became the governess of the Alcott and Emerson children, Lydia and Robert had been married almost two years and continued to live in Fall River. Though no records have been found that attest to Lydia's interactions with the Alcott family during the time when her aunt served as their governess, it is likely that this happened. Prior to Lydia's marriage to Robert, the Alcott family had visited with the Stow family when they resided in Dedham. On February 28, 1842, Lydia wrote in her journal, "Got home before ten found that the family were living without me. The news . . . was that Mr. Bronson Alcott had been here & passed an hour or two and was much liked by Esther and Elizabeth who were the only ones to enjoy his company. If I had only been at home I should have been glad" (L. Stow, personal communication, journal entry, February 28, 1842).

The *United States Federal Census of 1850* reported that, childless, Lydia, and Robert shared a residence with Robert's two brothers, John and Charles. Lydia's sister Mary also joined the household. Later census reports listed Lydia's livelihood as either "wife" or "keeping house." Her sister Mary was listed as having no occupation. During this period, Robert's sister, Isabella, also stayed with them for a time and worked as a clerk (United States Federal Census, 1850).

Mary Swift

On June 22, 1846, surrounded by friends and family, Mary Swift married Edwin Lamson, whom she had met at the Park Street Church in Boston. They formalized their union in her parents' city of Philadelphia. Edwin's father, Captain Samuel Lamson, had died the year before Edwin married Mary, and his mother, Sarah Sleuman Lamson, had been deceased for six years. Prior to her death, Sarah Lamson had endured a severe illness for more than 17 years. Nonetheless, she was described as a woman who exerted a powerful influence on her children and family. Married according to the ways of the Presbyterian Church and the laws of the state of Pennsylvania, Edwin was 35 years old and Mary was 24.

From Salem, Massachusetts, Edwin was the middle child of seven brothers and sisters, two of whom had died during childhood. Edwin was handsome with thick brown hair and beard, a firm jaw and dark, kind brown eyes with a pronounced cleft between them. A successful Boston merchant, he was a partner in the firm of Twombly & Lamson. The firm owned clipper ships that sailed between ports in Boston and San Francisco. Designed by Donald McKay from East Boston, clipper ships were faster than steam ships, easily breaking their travel records (Hunter, 2013, p. 44). Developed with use of increased knowledge about ocean winds and currents, clipper ships were both practical and advantageous. The name "clipper" was derived from the phrase "going at a good clip" (Clark, 1912, p. 57). One of the ships owned by Twombly & Lamson was the *Witch of the Wave*, which weighed 1,498 tons and could make the voyage from Boston to San Francisco in an average of 113 days (Essex Institute, 1906). In addition to Twombly & Lamson, John Bertram, Alfred Peabody and William Glidden were listed as owners of this particular ship. Another ship acquired by the firm was named *John Bertram*. It weighed 1050 tons and had a light and graceful bow with an eagle perched on its extreme. This ship was designed for both California and China trade (Boston Daily Atlas, 1851). In the mid nineteenth century, clipper ships were considered the most beautiful ships that had ever been built. Twombly & Lamson operated their successful business out of 13 Custom House Street in Boston.

Edwin continued to serve as a deacon of the Park Street Church, which Mary too attended. After their wedding, they established a household at 5 Beacon Street in Boston. Edwin bought the house from John Proctor, one of the owners of Proctor & Clark Booksellers. It had been built by Cornelius Coolidge, a well known architect in the Boston area (Guarino, 2011, p. 32). In the mid-nineteenth century, the houses on Beacon Street were serene facades that overlooked the Boston Common. The State House with its lofty dome was located close by, as was Faneuil Hall (Lawrence, 1922). Mary and Edwin were considered part of the high or elite culture of Boston. The elite in Boston were a relatively homogeneous group who were mercantile, of the upper merchant class, and of a federalist orientation (Wolff, 2009, p. 3). The merchants typically made fortunes in foreign trade, as had Mary's husband. Others of the Boston elite were lawyers who practiced commercial law and/or entered into politics (Wolff, 2009, p. 3). Industrialists who acquired wealth in the textile industry also were absorbed into the Boston elite class. In some regards, the Boston upper class was a cohesive group who enjoyed literature, the arts, and intellectual refinement (Wolff, 2009, pp. 3–4). Although Mary had come from an economically secure family from Nantucket, her marriage brought her into a new social class marked by abundant wealth.

Prior to her marriage to Edwin, Mary resigned from the Perkins Institution. It is unclear if she left due to the publicity that surrounded Laura's education, and the experiment that was attached to it, or if it was because she was to marry Edwin. When back in Boston, however, Mary reconnected with her former student Laura Dewey Bridgman, with whom she exchanged visits. Because Mary was able to speak so rapidly through finger talk, Laura compiled long lists of words that she would inquire about with Mary (Lamson, 1881, p. 338). After Mary's first daughter, also named Mary, was born on December 30, 1847 she brought the baby to visit with Laura. She and Edwin were married approximately sixteen months when their first child was born. Mary experienced the rapturous love that so many mothers feel, especially with a first child. A baby, particularly a first child, is accompanied by passion of the mother, who wants to provide protection, while simultaneously share her love.

Laura Bridgman loved being with the baby and to hold her in her arms. Over the months that followed, Laura observed baby Mary's growth and development with great interest. She secured a pair of small shoes as a gift for the baby. In Laura's journal on January 23, 1847, she wrote:

> I was very pleasantly detained by visitors. Mrs. L and little Mary came to spend the P.M. with us. I was so highly delighted to have such pleasant company. I derived so much pleasure from giving so constant attention to my cunning pet. I led her about the work room and our room. I loved to carry the child in my arms about very much. I willing [sic] let her hear my musical box play for a while. When I took it away from her it caused her to cry instantly, because she disliked to give the music up. We went to the shop to put the child on the scales and let the blind boys see her. I was very sorry to have her go home. (as cited in Lamson, 1881, p. 335)

Mary Swift also would have Laura to her house for visits. On these visits, Laura would wander through her house, open closets and draws and carefully touch items. Nothing gave Laura more pleasure than to be left alone and allowed to examine things at leisure. Once Mary had led her through her house, Laura no longer required any assistance in her explorations. She became familiar with the rooms, closets and bureaus. Because Laura was so gentle, Mary felt that it was safe to trust Laura with her most valuable objects (Lamson, 1881, p. 338). While she visited Mary's house, she also spent time with the baby.

When Mary's baby became ill with a fearful fever, Mary felt anguish. She recalled listening to the sounds in the room where the baby was kept. Each day she had trembled with hope that the day would bring relief for her daughter. In the nineteenth century, epidemics of cholera, typhus, and yellow fever claimed the lives of many children. Infections, the products of pathogens that were ever-present in communities, took their toll among infants and young children in particular. Nearly two out of every ten children died before reaching their fifth birthday (Golden, Meckel & Prescott, 2004). The days that followed the onset of the fever did not bring relief for Mary's daughter and she did not recover from the illness. Following her death, Mary sensed their daughter was at rest, but she knew it would be many long years before the wound that she felt so deeply would heal.

Laura Bridgman learned of the death of Mary's daughter and wrote in her journal.

> I had a great many sad thoughts in my mind to-day, my dear friend's only little daughter has died. I used to love & caress her when she was a very little babe very much, as if she was my own child. I used to call her my little pet, etc. (as cited in Lamson, 1881, p. 336)

In a follow-up letter to Mary, Laura wrote that she was surprised and saddened to hear of little Mary's death. She wrote that she was "positive God and His beloved Son, Christ, will educate your child much better than men could in this world" (as cited in Lamson, 1881, p. 336). As is obvious from this letter, Laura had increasingly developed a religious belief system. She said to Mary that she sent her best love to her.

The death of her first child was a tragedy that Mary would later reflect on when she was with her normalite sisters (Lamson, 1903, p. 49). Though the occasion that had first brought them together, as pioneers of a new state normal school movement, was to prepare them for teaching, their relationships were by now firmly bound by much more than their professional interests. They had become a life support to each other.

Mary later gave birth to three children. Helen was born on February 3, 1852. Gardner was born on April 27, 1855 and Kate, nicknamed Daisy, on January 3, 1859 (Nantucket Historical Association, 2013). She and Edwin continued to reside on Beacon Street where a chamber maid assisted Mary with daily activities. Edwin's business continued to prosper and he became a member of the Boston Athenaeum. Membership in the Athenaeum signified one's status in the city; it was a sign of belonging and of civility (Wolff, 2009, p. 57). Edwin also continued to be active in the Park Street Church. Mary and Edwin became life members of the Massachusetts Bible Society. Their lives increasingly connected to religious affairs through which they came to know prominent ministers and theologians. During parts of 1856 and 1857, for example, Reverend Charles Finney and his wife stayed at their house. An opponent of old Presbyterian theology, Finney was known for his innovations in religious meetings. Mary's husband, Edwin, had the uttermost regard for Finney, who became the president of Oberlin College in 1835. Oberlin was founded in 1833 by Presbyterian ministers. Though Finney was perceived to be a moderate abolitionist, Oberlin started to admit both women and African American students to the college, the same year during which Finney assumed the presidency (Hambrick-Stowe, 1996, p. 171). When in Boston at the home of Mary and Edwin in 1856 and 1857, Finney preached almost every day, often at the Park Street Church. He became associated with revivalism, a movement that was connected with the rise of spiritualism, religious excitement and at times missionary zeal. Mary and Edwin also became followers of revivalism.

Louisa Harris

On October 23, 1844, Louisa Harris wrote in her journal that it was an "anniversary of my entrance at the Normal School at Lexington, an era from which date the birth of friendships from which I have derived the purest satisfactions" (L. Harris, personal communication, journal entry, October 23, 1844). Visits with her normal school friends continued to bring her enjoyment during the four years that had passed since they had completed their studies. She felt that the normalites were as close at that time as when they had been in school together. On May 28, 1842, she reflected on some of their meetings in her journal.

> I went up to Sarah W's and we reached the Lowell Depot in Boston.... Messengers were dispatched for Hannah R. who came soon after in breathless haste ... Thursday we rode down to Eliza's where we found her ready with the horse and chaise to carry us to Lowell which proved a delightful ride.... We crossed the bridge over the Merrimack to Dracut where we found Miss

> Kimball, an old schoolmate who seemed much the same as ever.... Friday morning we were obliged to bring our delightful visit to a close. (L. Harris, personal communication, journal entry, May 28, 1842)

When Louisa visited her favorite brother, Elbridge, in Bangor, Maine in August of 1844, Sarah Wyman from the normal school made the journey with her (L. Harris, personal communication, journal entry, August 31, 1844). Elbridge at that time served as the director of a 13-mile railroad track which ran from Bangor to Milford (The Maine Register and Business Directory, 1856). Louisa considered Elbridge's Maine residence to be her Eastern home (L. Harris, personal communication, journal entry, August 2, 1842). Her sister Jane also lived in Bangor. (L. Harris, personal communication, journal entry, July 28, 1843). Though travel to Bangor from the Boston area took a full 24 hours by boat and Louisa was inclined to seasickness, she was more than willing to undertake the journey (L. Harris, personal communication, journal entry, August 2, 1842).

Prior to her marriage, Mary Swift needed to cancel a visit with Louisa on April 7, 1844 because exhibitions with Laura Dewey Bridgman kept her busy. It was a cancellation that Louisa met with disappointment. On December 23, 1844, two days prior to Christmas, Louisa and Sarah Wyman, traveled to see Mary Swift and Eliza Rogers at the Perkins Institution. In her journal she recorded, "Wednesday being Christmas, Sarah W. and myself visited our S. Boston friends, Mary Swift, Eliza Rogers ... the former being absent to leave the institution, where they have taught so successfully, and where we have so frequently enjoyed our pleasant interviews with them. Not among the least regretted of Times' changes, shall I class the departure of two rare and valued friends from our vicinity" (L. Harris, personal communication, journal entry, December 23, 1844). Whenever Louisa did not receive a promised letter from one of her normal school friends, she recorded her disappointment. She recognized how important these connections were to her.

In October 1846, Louisa visited with Rebecca Pennell, niece of Horace Mann. Rebecca was then teaching in the coeducational Westfield Normal School, which was the second state normal school formerly located in Barre, Massachusetts (L. Harris, personal communication, journal entry, October, 1846). It was a prestigious position where Pennell worked with a small number of faculty members under the leadership of Principal David Rowe. The coeducational environment at Westfield was one where teachers, regardless of gender, were seen as "molders of community—as shapers of moral and civic consensus—in and out of the classroom" (Rothermel, 2002, p. 39). At Westfield the idea of teacher as nurturer ran alongside the idea of teacher as intellectual. Students undertook advanced work in subjects such as philosophy, natural sciences, and rhetoric. These were subjects that Pennell had studied when she was a student at the normal school in Lexington. Peers and others thought highly of her work (Kolodny, 2010).

Louisa's father, who now lived with her brother Elbridge in Maine, had grown increasingly ill and Louisa was worried about him. The incessant anxiety concerning her father also tired her (L. Harris, personal communication, journal entry, July 15, 1855). Louisa continued to write in her journal, "believing that it was good and right to search the soul's chambers and bring forth some evidence that all was not dead or slumbering there" (L. Harris, personal communication, journal entry, September 12, 1852). Louisa believed that she would be stronger if she could find the time to write in her journal, though she scarcely found time alone in the place at which she boarded. She recognized that her emotions often changed throughout the days and seasons. "In the morning . . . I feel grand all over. And my soul seems swelling up fresh and ardent to meet the goodly sunshine and mingle with the healthful breezes. At night an earthquake would scarcely thrill me. And I feel that I have not realized the visions of the golden morning hour. And so I am weaving my web of life. What shall the figures be, when it is woven?" (L. Harris, personal communication, journal entry, September 14, 1852). Louisa continued to battle with her emotional states and tried to avoid the periods of melancholy that beset her at times.

As Louisa was well aware, a number of her normal school peers had entered into the "voyage matrimonial." When Eliza Pennell married in 1843, she shared a piece of wedding cake with Louisa. Louisa recorded in her journal that Eliza "quit this life [i.e., a school teachers] . . . for the married" (L. Harris, personal communication, journal entry, December 23, 1843). On April 7, 1844, Louisa, Rebecca and Eliza met for a visit, along with Sara Wyman. They traveled by stage from Boston to Medford and were joined by three men, as yet unknown to them, during the ride. As they traveled, the women reflected on their normal school days and Louisa recognized that their spirits were so buoyant that she felt exhausted from their frequent laughter. Their interactions with the men, who were joined by a cousin, continued as they met them again at an area greenhouse and then later on the stage ride back to Boston. Louisa was surprised to find the "prudent and judicious Rebecca not only lending a willing ear to the incessant small talk of the cousin, but lavishing her wit and smiles as freely as though she felt assured she had found the very looks and eyes, prides tried to hear all her sighs." Louisa wrote, "I turned towards E. and S. when we too commenced a brisk conversation, wondering what unwanted spirit had possessed itself of our friend Rebecca" (L. Harris, personal communication, journal entry,

April 7, 1844). The cousin turned out to be Timothy Bigelow, his brother being the author of *Bigelow's Plants of Boston*. Louisa was surprised that Rebecca took part so freely in the social exchange, demonstrating both interest and invitation into courtship. She was flirting. A year later, on May 7, 1845, Louisa stayed at Sarah Wyman's with Eliza Rogers and Mary Swift, noting in her journal that it "probably was the last night that the latter ever will spend with us" (L. Harris, personal communication, journal entry, May 7, 1845). Mary at that time was preparing to marry Edwin Lamson, as noted earlier. Louisa wrote in her journal, "As the fact becomes more apparent that the favorite few, with whom we yet meet, in all the confidence and gladness which characterized the confidence of our schoolgirl days are one by one going forth to pursue new interests, everything connected with them becomes dearer and more valued" (L. Harris, personal communication, journal entry, May 7, 1845). This weighed on Louisa's mind. The pressure of new duties and cares once the normal school students married, not to mention the primacy of their relationships with husbands and children, Louisa knew, would result in fewer visits between them. They would not walk together as closely as they had in the past (L. Harris, personal communication, journal entry, November 3, 1844). The truth was fast becoming impressed on her mind that the ranks in which she had so happily walked would be broken. Their paths would diverge and there would be some parting of the ways. For Louisa, the possibility of remaining single weighed on her mind.

Some of the women with whom Louisa boarded also married and she felt a loss at their departure. In 1844 she had become close to a woman named Susan. They socialized together, went to see friends and purchased ice cream. Louisa was melancholy when she learned that Susan would leave the boarding house to marry. In her journal she wrote:

> This week has witnessed an important change in our household. Susan having set forward on Wednesday evening on the voyage matrimonial...has actually married this week; and although still a member of the family, is no longer my chum, with whom I can discourse "at even" upon the events of the day and anticipate those of the morrow...As I retire *alone* to my chamber I feel that a beautiful spirit, which diffused light a beauty around, has forsaken it. She is certainly the bright light of our household, and embodiment of all that is good and graceful; one to whom nature has been lavish of her gifts, which have not been abused. An active, inquiring mind, and a warm, loving heart, enshrined in a most graceful, attractive dwelling...that the angel of peace and love may ever hover around her home. (L. Harris, personal communication, journal entry, January 27, 1844)

Louisa Harris had received offers to marry. In April of 1842, she wrote in her journal that she received "the promise of an old bachelor, including house, barn, and appertaining there to" (L. Harris, personal communication, journal entry, April 4, 1842). She also had expressed interest in a 45 year old bachelor who excited her, but whose heart was drawn to another. This particular man had a lot of material possessions. Half-heartedly, she wrote in her journal, "What a glorious chance for some spinster. I almost said aloud. I thought of the bachelor, and sighed deeply that he would enjoy all those things alone. He was so pretty too!" Though Louisa recorded these thoughts in her journal, it was in a light manner. In her journal she wrote that the bachelor was not interested in tall women, and she was a tall woman (L. Harris, personal communication, journal entry, November 28, 1842). With a sense of humor, she wrote that perhaps she could take her head off. On another occasion, after spending a short time with a Deacon Jones, Louisa returned to her chambers and wrote in her journal that she finally had gained some recognition of her beau ideal (L. Harris, personal communication, journal entry, December 23, 1843). However, for reasons unrecorded, a courtship did not develop between them.

Sarah Wyman, one of her closest friends from the normal school, became engaged in October of 1852 and married the following May 2nd. Of the normal school members from her class, most had married by that time. The normalities who had not married, however, continued to support themselves through teaching. Addie Ireson was one who continued to teach, building a career in the Cambridge schools. Hannah Damon, another single normal school sister, also was teaching. Rebecca Pennell likewise was still single, which likely shaped her lifework.

In 1852, Horace Mann accepted the role of president of the newly founded coeducational Antioch College in Yellow Springs, Ohio. Antioch College had been conceived at a convention of the Christian denomination that was held in Marion, New York in 1850. It was a nonsectarian institution, yet careful attention was paid to the religious education of the students. It also was coeducational with a mission to provide both men and women with a similar education. Land, as well as building funds, was provided. (Yellow Springs Bicentennial Committee, 2005, pp. 17–20). Initially Mann was unsure about accepting the post, cautioned by friends such as Catharine Beecher who were wary of the quality of the students the college would attract. Mann, however, had lost a gubernatorial election in Massachusetts and was searching for a new career.

Once Mann accepted the role of president of Antioch, he appointed Rebecca Pennell and her brother, Calvin, as professors. Calvin, whom Louisa had met when he visited the normal school on November 10, 1841, was reluctant to accept the position. In a letter to his sister Rebecca, he wrote, "I consider it a great sacrifice. We certainly should be obliged to be on 'salt pork' and wear cow hide shoes. When anyone speaks of his going, they say, well, I suppose he will have a much handsome salary. I say nothing. You know a new institution like that is of slow growth and probably it would not increase for some time" (C. Pennell, personal communication, October 17, 1852). Rebecca, however, was willing to accept the new adventure.

On April 10, 1853, before Rebecca left for Antioch, Louisa visited her at the Mann residence. Rebecca at that time resided with her Uncle Horace, his wife Mary Peabody Mann and their family. Following her departure from Westfield, Pennell had assumed a similar position at the Lexington Normal School in 1849, which by then had relocated to West Newton, Massachusetts (Kolodny, 2010). Rebecca's parents both had died at this time and she increasingly turned to Mann as a father figure. Though the living arrangement was convenient for Rebecca, tensions existed and often surfaced between her and Mary Peabody Mann. When Louisa met with Rebecca, they discussed her future work at Antioch, and briefly entertained the idea of Louisa relocating to Yellow Springs herself. Louisa recorded the following notes in her journal:

> Since my last entry I have been out to W. Newton with Adie and Hannah D. to visit our friend and classmate Rebecca Pennell who has been honored with a professorship in Antioch College. Mr. Mann who is President invited us to join the institution which I for one would very gladly do if such a thing was practical for me. How I would like to put off the pedagogue for a season and become a pupil again. I build air castles to that effect sometimes but I am confident they can never become substantial fabrics. (L. Harris, personal communication, journal entry, April 10, 1853)

Though 13 years had passed since they had completed their normal school studies, the normalites continued to meet and support each other. Pennell, on arriving at Antioch in 1853, subsequently became the first woman college professor on the faculty at the institution, and likely the first woman professor in the United States. At age 31, she taught physical geography, natural history, civil history, didactics, and drawing. Her selection of courses expanded over time to include subjects such as botany and zoology. She had been given the same pay as her male colleagues, though other women who joined the faculty after her, did not receive equal wages. Later, Rebecca's sister Eliza also arrived at Antioch along with her husband; her husband serving as assistant treasurer of the college. At Antioch, Rebecca eventually met Amos Dean, treasurer of college, and married him at the age of thirty-four (Stern, 1962, p. 147).

Louisa continued to be an avid reader following her normal school studies. She did not like to sew during the evenings, a common pastime for women. Instead, she often read when she was not teaching. While at the normal school she had encountered a variety of books. Her peer, Lydia Stow had recorded in her journal that the normal school held 77 volumes dealing with both education and other interests. Along with such works as *American Education, Home Education, Coldwell on Physical Education* and *Barbington on Education,* there were other books which included the *Life of Schiller, Bigelow's Theology, Lincoln's Botany, Cheever's Studies in Poetry* and *Aikin's British Poets* (L. Stow, personal communication, journal entry, October 1840). These books caught the notice of the normalites. At times when Louisa read books of special interest, she would transcribe portions of them into her journals for future reflection. When she read selections from Charles Dickens' *A Christmas Carol,* she wrote in her journal that she was delighted with it and had tried to read as much as she could before her morning school duties called her. "An old miser, in worldliness, who can see nothing about him to inspire happiness, but growls at those who can, is visited by a spirit who conducts him to scenes of earlier times when he beholds himself as he was before he had become the cold and hardened wretch. The spirit leads him to see that love and charity are his business." On another occasion Louisa carefully reflected on aspects of *Practical Education* by Maria Edgeworth (L. Harris, personal communication, journal entry, April 8, 1842). In this book a variety of topics, including the discipline of children, were discussed. Edgeworth believed that the dread of shame was more effective than the dread of bodily pain. Alone in her boarding chambers, Louisa read Ms. Stow's *Sunny Memories* and Ms. Bremer's *Homes in the New World* (L. Harris, personal communication, journal entry, April 1, 1855). She read the *Life of Columbus* (L. Harris, personal communication, journal entry, March 1, 1842). Another time she read about rural funerals and the process of placing flowers over grave stones (L. Harris, personal communication, journal entry, March 3, 1842). She reflected that there was a dismal process going on within the grave where "dust can return to its kindred dust" (L. Harris, personal communication, journal entry, March 3, 1842). In her journal she recorded a lengthy analysis of this particular book. When she read the *Legend of Sleepy Hollow* she felt a personal connection to Ichabod Crane. She thought it was probably due to the appearance of the character, suggesting that Louisa may not have been happy with her appearance (L. Harris, personal communication, journal entry, March 13, 1842). At times, if Louisa found a poem that spoke to her, she also wrote it down in her journal so she would have a record of it.

Writing also became a growing interest to Louisa (L. Harris, personal communication, journal entry, November 14, 1844). She briefly considered exercising her literary ambitions, but eventually came to the philosophical conclusion that she was meant to focus on her primary school work. She viewed this to be a laudable and praiseworthy ambition despite some moments of dissatisfaction. Though Louisa did not move into professional writing, it brought her joy and her journal proved to be her outlet. From time to time her diligence waned to be thereafter rekindled.

> I commenced this record of thoughts and events as a relaxation from care, a companion in loneliness, a confident of my joys and sorrows and something which in future time might give form and substance to the "shadowy past." That it has to some extent answered its purpose I feel confident. Often when the spirits, whisperings have only been sad and mournful, when the past has seemed only a vanished dream, the present a land of weariness, and the future a way of care and toilsome duty from which the spirit shrinks in its weariness, have I found . . . voices of encouragement and consolation, inspiring new hopes and, revealing glimpses of joy and beauty which in my gratitude I had shouldered in my somber hues. . . . Yes in such moments to commune with my own heart, to find new strength there, to feel that good 'angels' do often minister in the form of reverent, lofty thoughts, to give expression freely and confidingly to each earnest purpose and heartfelt emotion, to feel that to myself I can return, upon myself rely, and yet be not without companionship, has surely been no slight privilege. . . . Ay, Life's journal . . . May I keep it well and faithfully, write it in characters of light; remembering that He who transmitted it to my keeping will know whether it has proved a blank, or worse than blank or been filled as his inspirations teach. (L. Harris, personal communication, journal entry, unspecified date, 1844)

Louisa continued to board around. In 1850, the Federal Census listed her as living in an establishment with the Reed family, several single individuals, and the Reverend Silas Curtis and his wife Patricia. She called this residence her Linden Park home. Boarding, though an unsettled life of sorts, allowed Louisa to meet new people. Although marriage had not proven to be her destiny, she had no lack of opportunity for socializing with others.

8

Abolitionism, the Underground Railroad, and the Civil War

In addition to the personal and professional changes that impacted the normalites as they entered adulthood in the middle of the nineteenth century, these young women also were profoundly affected by political upheaval taking place during that time period. The issue of slavery had an intensely wide ranging impact in the nineteenth century. Thousands of Black men and women suffered brutal circumstances connected to enslavement. Slavery, in turn, informed public discourse, legislation, and the actions of individuals. A compromise between the free and slave states could not be reached. Americans from both the North and the South were willing to fight as survival of society was considered at stake. The Civil War subsequently took place between 1861 and 1865.

Leading up to and during the period of the Civil War, the work of the abolitionists was viewed from a variety of perspectives. Some supported the work of abolitionists, while others viewed them as radicals and revolutionaries. *The Liberator*, a widely read abolitionist newspaper edited by William

Lloyd Garrison, was produced weekly in Boston from 1831 to 1865 and advocated for complete and immediate emancipation of all slaves. The American Anti-Slavery Society, formed in 1833 by William Lloyd Garrison and Arthur Tappan, eventually held over 250,000 members. The normalities, due to family, social and political networks, as well as their own values and sympathies, naturally were part of the antislavery movement.

Frederick Douglass was a key speaker at Anti-Slavery Society meetings. Born a slave in Maryland in February 1818 to Harriet Bailey, Douglass' father was thought to be the manager of a plantation. As a child, Douglass was sent to Baltimore as a "houseboy" to Hugh Auld, a shipbuilder. During this time, Auld's wife taught him some of the alphabet. Douglass also learned to read from White children in the area and by observing the writing of the men for whom he worked. In 1838, Douglass escaped from slavery using papers as a free seaman. He traveled to New York where he married Anna Murray, a free Black woman whom he met while he worked for Hugh Auld. The couple thereafter moved on to New Bedford, Massachusetts, a community in close proximity to Lydia Stow's Fall River. Douglass soon began speaking at abolitionist meetings and writing about slavery (Douglass, 1845).

In 1835, Angelina and Sarah Grimke, the daughters of an elite slaveholding Quaker family in Charlestown, South Carolina, also left their community and became lecturers for the American Anti-Slavery Society. They lectured in this role until 1839. The Grimke family's wealth had been gained through a plantation the sisters had never visited, which was run by a hired overseer. The Grimke family household in South Carolina was run by slaves, many who had relatives on the plantation. In their lectures, the Grimke sisters described the horrors of slavery (Sklar, 2000, pp. 2–3). Their message was powerful and widely received. Maria Weston Chapman, who was on the executive committee of the national Anti-Slavery Society, wrote to the Female Anti-Slavery Societies throughout New England in 1837 about the work of the Grimke sisters. In her letters, she implored the members to "help THESE women, who have labored thus in the Gospel and thereby help us to manifest gratitude for the important aid they are affording to Anti-slavery enterprise. Help them to exalt the national character of our women...that they might pursue their Christian course unimpeded by sneers or ridicule, ecclesiastical mandates or publick [sic] outrage" (Sklar, 2000, p. 113). Chapman's message undoubtedly reached Lydia Stow, who had attended meetings.

Leaders of the normal school movement were opponents of slavery. Horace Mann was an ardent abolitionist. In 1852, he delivered a speech to the House of Representatives on the "Institution of Slavery" (Mann, 1852). Samuel May also delivered an oration titled *Liberty or Slavery, the Only Question in New York in 1856* (May, 1856). When Cyrus Peirce left his post at the Lexington Normal School to recover his health in 1842, he too turned increasingly to working for the abolitionist cause. In an 1843 letter to one of his students from Nantucket, Electa Lincoln, who had enrolled at the Lexington School, he described the loss he felt upon leaving the normal school.

> I cannot make you understand, dear Electa, how disappointed and sorrowful way made in being obliged to give up my school here for which I wrote to Lexington for assistants. I felt very desirous to test practically my own principles of school—government in the presence of this community and thus to convince, if possible, the unbelieving and questioning among our teachers. I wished also to set before them through good practical demonstration of the beneficial influence of normal training and, in this way to enhance or create more properly an interest in behalf of normal school. But sorry as I was at first, that my health would not allow me to go on, my grief was greatly increased when I learned that I had been thus defeated in the enjoyment of the society and cooperation of two sweet girls and very endeared and worthy pupils. (C. Peirce, personal communication, 1843)

Cyrus Peirce nonetheless wrote that he had found a way to "Live to the Truth," while he was away from the normal school. That way led to antislavery efforts. After Peirce left Lexington, he traveled to Washington as the bearer of one of the two great Latimer Petitions, which he carried in a large cylindrical box.

George Latimer was the son of Mitchell Latimer, a White man. His mother, Margaret Olmsted, was a slave. In 1842, George Latimer and his pregnant wife fled from Virginia to eventually settle in Boston. A fugitive slave, Latimer was arrested when a former employee of his owner identified him. His arrest resulted in a violent uproar in Boston (Hudson, 2006). Frederick Douglass subsequently wrote to William Lloyd Garrison about slavery in the city of Boston.

> Slavery, our enemy, has landed in our very midst, and commenced its bloody work. Just look at it; here is George Latimer a man—a brother—a father, stamped with the likeness of the eternal God, and redeemed by the blood of Jesus Christ, out-lawed, hunted down like a wild beast, and ferociously dragged through the streets of Boston, and incarcerated within the walls of Levitt-st. jail. And all this is done in Boston—liberty-loving, slavery-hating Boston—intellectual, moral and religious Boston. (Douglass, 2000, p. 6)

The Latimer case inspired antislavery activists to draw up two petitions that would introduce legislation forbidding the Commonwealth of Massachusetts from compliance with slave laws enacted by other states. The "Great Massachusetts petition" was signed by close to 65,000 citizens in Massachusetts. It weighed almost 150 pounds as the petition was wrapped around a metal reel. It was presented to the legislature demanding three things: (a) that a law be passed, forbidding all persons who hold office under the government of Massachusetts from aiding in or abetting the arrest or detention of any person who may be claimed as a fugitive from slavery; (b) that a law be passed forbidding the use of the jails or other public property of the state for the detention of any such person before described; (c) that such amendments to the Constitution of the United States be proposed by the legislature of Massachusetts to the other states of the Union, as may have the effect of forever separating the people of Massachusetts from all connection with slavery (Laurie, 2005, pp. 116–117). The second petition was the "Great Petition to Congress," which Cyrus Peirce subsequently carried to Washington. Tended to with care by Peirce throughout the journey, the petition also was wound on a large reel. When Peirce arrived in Washington, it was placed on John Quincy Adams' desk in the Capitol building, which was still in the process of being constructed. Though John Quincy Adams was no longer President of the United States of America, having served from 1825 to 1829, he remained involved in Congressional affairs serving as the U.S. Representative from Massachusetts (Nagel, 1997). Peirce wrote to Electa Lincoln that "How that sight of that big roll did make those Philistines of the South rage and foam and stamp . . . They threatened . . . and looked daggers. Sometimes at me for bringing it there, but more gently at Mr. A. for having the audacity to present it" (C. Peirce, personal communication, 1843). As this correspondence suggests, the normal school students had front row seats to the unfolding of abolitionist fervor and political ferment.

Lydia Stow

Lydia Stow became one of the most active abolitionists of the normalites. This was not surprising. She had attended abolitionist meetings as a child and young adult and her relatives were active in the movement. In her quiet, speculative manner, Lydia also had been assessing the scene, reflecting on the injustices that lay at the heart of slavery. When Lydia Stow completed her normal school studies and returned to Dedham, she resumed participation in nearby antislavery meetings. On October 13, 1841, Frederick Douglass visited the meeting in Dedham and Lydia reflected that she was much interested in his discussion (L. Stow, personal communication, journal entry, October 13, 1841). When Lydia heard him in 1841, he had transitioned to working full-time as an abolitionist lecturer and was touring with William Lloyd Garrison. Garrison and Douglass called for an immediate end to all slavery. Douglass was 23 years old and Lydia was 18 when they first met. In the future they would become close acquaintances. The day after Lydia heard Douglass speak, her aunts Sophia and Esther Foord went to meet with him. Lydia continued to attend lectures during this time that centered on "prejudice against color." In her journal she wrote that Black people are beings "made of the same flesh and blood as ourselves receiving the scorn and contempt of many who have a different hue of skin" (L. Stow, personal communication, journal entry, October 13, 1841). Her commitment to abolitionism increased as her awareness of the injustices which surrounded slavery grew.

After Lydia relocated to Fall River and married Robert Adams in 1844, she developed a new set of friends. Mary Rice Livermore, the wife of Daniel Livermore, a Universalist minister who served churches in Fall River, was one of the new acquaintances who she met in 1845. She would become a life-long intimate companion of Lydia's (Phillips, 1945). Mary Livermore had been raised in a strict Calvinist family, and the teachings of that denomination troubled her. When she met Daniel Livermore at a Universalist church service she asked him for some literature. He provided her with books from his library and subsequently met with her for further discussion. This led to their love and marriage. Mary Livermore, a former teacher, had been a tutor on a plantation in Virginia where she witnessed the cruelty of slavery. Lydia likely recognized the connected affinities that she and Mary Livermore shared and which led to the formation of their friendship.

Along with Robert, Lydia increasingly became involved with abolitionist activities in the Fall River area. In November of 1845, she wrote to Maria Chapman in Boston, an executive committee member of the national Anti-Slavery Society who was an acquaintance of her Aunt Sophia, about an antislavery event. She signed the letter, "I am yours for humanity."

Fall River, Nov. 3rd 45

Mrs. Chapman,

Dear Madam

Last week I received your note of the 7th. Since then I have met our few Anti-Slavery Friends. We should be happy to have a table at the Christmas Fair but shall be unable to do so. We will prepare a few articles, which we will send trusting the little may manifest a *will* to do more if it was in our power. With our best wishes for your success in laboring so devotedly on behalf of our fellow bondmen. I am yours for Humanity.

Lydia A. S. Adams

(L. Adams, personal communication, November 3, 1845)

The fair referenced in the letter was one of a series of fundraising events that had been developed for the purpose of raising money for antislavery societies. At the fairs, hand-made and luxury items were sold. In Boston, the Fairs became social events during the Christmas season (Rodriguez, 2007). During that same month in 1845, Lydia's husband wrote to Ralph Waldo Emerson and requested a lecture at which he would speak with the "ladies," presumably about slavery. This topic was referenced in Emerson's reply of regret.

Concord, 1, Nov. 1845

Robert Adams, Esq.

Dear Sir,

Forgive me for my delay in replying to your letter which in some confusion of my papers was mislaid and which after much seeking I have just recovered. I think it will not be in my power to comply with the request of the ladies, your friends. My time is necessarily devoted to certain studies which are very jealous and allow a few and rare departures from their demands. I shall be glad to esteem the invitation you send me as a door left open for me in case anything good and reasonable should come into my thoughts, on that subject of slavery, but, at present, sad as it is, I have nothing to say of it.

Yours respectfully,

R.W. Emerson

(Emerson, Rusk & Tilton, 1939, pp. 60–61)

Lydia's husband was not as well-known as some of the more prominent antislavery activists during that time period, but he played a significant role in abolitionist circles as a conductor of the Underground Railroad. In 1850, he received a letter from Wendell Phillips, a graduate of Harvard Law School and member of the Anti-Slavery Society for which he made frequent speeches. The letter, brief in scope, noted that George Thompson, a British abolitionist, would be coming to Fall River the next Friday. Phillips continued to say that Mr. Thompson was a stranger and would need a conductor. He told Robert that he had no tickets left and that he must get them printed (W. Phillips, personal communication, circa 1850). The language of the letter likely contained a hidden message that related to the Underground Railroad. Other letters that Robert received during this period appear also to have included similar code language. In July of 1845, Robert received one such letter from his sister, Isabella.

Pawtucket July 19, 45

Dear Brother,

We received your letter of the 14th . . . Were sorry to hear of your misfortune but hope by this, you are healed and enjoying the great privilege of locomotion. Your invitation to the great Anti-Slavery time is duly appreciated and will no doubt be accepted by some friends in this quarter.... You will probably see some of us at the *time.*

Love to all your household...

Farewell in haste,

Isabella

(I. Adams, personal communication, July 19, 1845)

The *time* that Isabella emphasized likely referred to a significant antislavery event. In other letters from Isabella, the presence of his wife Lydia, referred to as Lydia Ann, was requested.

Code words, such as the ones used in Wendell Phillips' letter, were typical of the operations of the Underground Railroad, the secret routes by which slaves escaped to Northern states or Canada to a place of freedom and safety (Blight, 2006, p. 2). Participation in the Underground Railroad required courage on the part of the slave as the odds were often against success. In his interactions with fugitive slaves, Robert grew to understand these fears as well as the hopes which went with them.

As a conductor, Robert worked closely with the Buffum and Chace families who resided in Fall River for a short time before relocating to Valley Falls, Rhode Island. By nightfall and in a closed carriage, Robert brought slaves to residences where citizens had agreed to house them in secrecy until they could be transported to their next destination. Fall River served as a refuge for slaves who were able to escape by sea from southern ports to New Bedford and towns on Cape Cod. Temporary refuge in Fall River, a town further inland from the exposed seaport areas, was considered to be a safe place for concealment. From Fall River the escaped slaves were sent to Canada by way of Valley Falls and Worcester. In Fall River, slaves were sheltered by Nathaniel Borden and his wife, Sarah, the sister of Elizabeth Buffum Chace. The Chace family was also where Sophia Foord had served as governess upon leaving the Alcott and Emerson households. Foord, no doubt, played an integral role in these activities (Salitan & Perera, 1994, p. 105).

On one occasion Robert helped disguise a man in a woman's Quaker costume with his face hidden by a thick veil. This individual had escaped from Virginia with his wife and child. He and his family found lodging in New Bedford and employment for 11 months. However, since this man was a blacksmith by trade, he was sought after by his master who had traced him to New Bedford. African Americans in town learned of this discovery, and alerted local abolitionists so the man could be hurried off. Later his wife and child joined him at his new location (Salitan & Perera, 1994, p. 105).

On another night, Robert arrived at the Buffum Chace household with two young Black men in their twenties. They were from Portsmouth, Virginia and had secured secret passage on a trading vessel that was headed for Wareham, Massachusetts. They each had a wife and child whom they would not have left, yet they learned that they were to be sold and separated from them (Salitan & Perera, 1994, p. 106). On a third occasion Robert brought a woman and three children to the Buffum Chace household. The woman escaped from Maryland with her family and was working in Fall River as a laundress. Her son, who was 17, worked in a stable. They learned that a slave catcher had been searching the stable where the son worked and fearful, decided to move north to Canada. In addition to serving as a conductor of the Underground Railroad, the Adams house became a central meeting place for other efforts that supported the cause of abolitionism. Frederick Douglass, a close confidante of Robert, often attended the meetings (Boston Transcript, 1900). As Robert's wife, these activities became a focus of Lydia's life as well.

The abolitionist activities of Lydia and her husband undoubtedly created tension in their social lives. Personal safety was sacrificed as abolitionism could be dangerous work. The Fugitive Slave Law, enacted in September 1850, authorized federal commissioners, not state judges, to process escaped slaves. It obliged every citizen to assist in capturing runaway slaves. If individuals protected fugitive slaves they risked severe penalties with fines as high as $1,000 and imprisonment for six months. Pushed through the U.S. Senate with the strong support of members such as Daniel Webster, the Fugitive Slave Law had been called by the New York Evening Post, "An Act for the Encouragement of Kidnapping" (May, 1861, p. 3). Samuel May, who eventually wrote a book on the subject recorded that in New Bedford, Pennsylvania on October 1, 1850, two fugitives from Virginia were attacked and one was mortally wounded and another dangerously. On October 25th in Boston, an attempt to seize William and Ellen Craft was undertaken. They fled the city and escaped to England (May, 1861, pp. 11–12).

Complicating the situation was the fact that New England mill towns such as Fall River and New Bedford relied heavily on the production of cotton obtained from the south, which was made possible by the direct shipping routes between southern and northern ports along the eastern coast. Cotton was used extensively in the manufacture of clothing, and thus its availability was a key factor in local economic growth and prosperity. Though prominent Fall River citizens were involved in abolitionist activities, they often compromised their own economic futures by doing so.

Mixed signals were encountered in Fall River regarding abolitionist work. This would continue throughout the Civil War period.

Following the War, Lydia and Robert would remain connected to abolitionist friends. In 1870, Sojourner Truth, for example, stayed with Lydia and her husband for a brief time. Robert arranged for Sojourner Truth to hold several speaking engagements at area churches. One announcement in the Fall River paper read:

> Sojourner Truth—the colored American Sybil—is spending a few days in our city, and will gladly welcome any of her old or new friends at the house of Robert Adams, Esq., on Rock Street. She bears her four-score years with ease, showing no signs of decay, but conversing on all familiar topics with a clearness of apprehension that would hardly be expected of one who has passed through the varied unpleasant experiences which have fallen to her lot. Give her a call, and enjoy a half an hour with a ripe understanding, and don't forget to purchase her photograph. (Titus, 1881, pp. 200–201)

Other announcements provided a schedule for the church meetings. A hand written note recorded by Mary Swift also seems to suggest that Lydia Stow was involved in the efforts of the Sanitary Commission (M. S. Lamson, personal communication, unknown date). The Sanitary Commission was a private relief agency created by federal legislation in 1861. Volunteers for the Commission collected donations, worked as nurses, and provided supplies to soldiers.

In 1888, Lydia's husband wrote to Frederick Douglass to send birthday wishes and received a response from him in return. Douglass had relocated to Washington, DC in 1877 with his wife Anna, who died in 1882. Douglass thereafter married Helen Pitts, a White feminist. Throughout all of the years since Douglass had met Robert and Lydia, he had come to spend time with them—almost every year.

Cedar Hill

Anacostia, D.C.

March 23, 1888

My dear Friend Robert Adams:

I hope it is not too late to thank you for your kind and thoughtful birthday letter. I have happily received a good many of such letters but none which touched me more deeply than yours. Do you know that yours was the first eyes that beamed kindly upon me in Fall River. Seven and forty years ago my dear old friend. I shall never forget that look of sympathy you then gave me. I was then only three years from slavery. I had not fully realized the possibility that a white man could recognize a colored man as a man and a brother but I saw such recognition in your face and have ever since in...and in storm feel I am in your friendship. Helen joins me in kind remembrances to you and Mrs. Adams. We are both glad to have your photograph to look upon.

Always your friend,

Frederick Douglass

(Douglass, personal communication, March 23, 1888)

Mary Swift

Mary Swift's life also was shaped by antislavery and abolitionist activities and the Civil War, though her experiences differed from Lydia's. Mary's youngest sister, Elizabeth, called Lizzie, lived with her family in Baltimore, a deeply divided city. It was unclear what Maryland would do with regard to slavery and the Civil War. Baltimore rested in a realm of tension. Mary was visiting her sister in Baltimore when tensions reached their breaking point in 1861.

Mary had left via steamer from Woods Hole on April 12, 1861 in route to Baltimore to see her sister Lizzie. During the voyage the sea was turbulent and the boat rolled in crashing waves throughout the passage. The ship captain's wife was sick throughout the trip and the captain himself admitted that he felt anxious. Mary wished she had her children with her. They, however, had stayed in Boston with Edwin and celebrated a stormy, snowy Easter without her. Edwin wrote that Mary's son, Gardner, was particularly fussy and vocal during the absence of his mama. As the boat ride continued the tensions with the South were discussed persistently among the passengers. In one letter to Edwin that Mary would send after the ship docked, she wrote, "I have found the feelings of the passengers is that the end will be, that the South will have her way and will take in the middle and westward sides into the new confederacy and N. England will be left over. Hope I shall hear something more hopeful when I get to Baltimore" (M. S. Lamson, personal communication, April 12, 1861). Troops were being mobilized.

After arriving in Baltimore, Mary quickly realized that it was an unfortunate place to visit at that time and wished that she had not set out on the journey. Both pro- and antislavery citizens of Baltimore believed that the city was on the brink of ruin. Fighting between northern and southern troops had started at the edge of city. Mary learned that the city was to be attacked from five different directions. She saw that Lizzie's next door neighbors had packed their belongings and were ready to start north on the canal line. However, word was out that boats would no longer be making that trip. The bridges in the city also were being torn up by Baltimore citizens in an effort to protect their city. Mary thought that the policy the "Baltimoreans" had adopted was suicidal. People were running around wildly. No one dared express their sentiments about what was taking place. In a letter to her husband Edwin, Mary wrote that her sister's husband, John, "was in a depot not far from the store where the troops went through yesterday and saw the mob pelting the soldiers in the cars. He said without thinking, 'if I was there with a musket I should certainly fire into the crowd,' at once two of the men said 'there's a Black republican,' and their hands were on their revolvers" (M. S. Lamson, personal communication, April 20, 1861). Mary learned that Massachusetts troops were present and involved in the fighting. Lizzie's husband, John, realizing that few options remained, closed his store, put the shutters down and discharged his men who were going to enlist. Mary wanted her sister and family to leave the city. She was fearful for them. Nearly every man that she met in the city carried a gun. It was rumored that seventeen thousand men had left to fight the Union. The men in Baltimore who felt sympathies for the Union dared not speak. Mary felt that since Maryland had not remained neutral, it had invited the war to its doorsteps. Yet, even as fears crept into her mind, her thoughts also were drawn to her children and to a new overcoat which she purchased for Gardner. She wondered if her husband Edwin would like it (M. S. Lamson, personal communication, April 20, 1861).

News traveled that men from the Massachusetts troops had been injured in Baltimore, and Mary tried to investigate. When she subsequently saw a list of those who were killed and injured, she was relieved that none of the names were familiar to her. Lizzie's husband, John, also made inquiries with regard to Massachusetts troops. For reasons now unknown, Mary was especially anxious to hear news of a Massachusetts solider named William Henry. In a letter to Edwin, Mary wrote that her broth-in-law, John, "went first to the Catholic Infirmary where they reported to be taken—found two insensible and likely to die any moment from being hit on the head by bricks and one hurt in the leg who was Michael Greene from Lawrence. He could talk and told John he talked with William Henry in the cars and that was the last he saw of him" (M. S. Lamson, personal communication, April 29, 1861).

Mary, her sister, and sister's family escaped to Philadelphia where her parents resided. They left Baltimore in haste and with fear, even leaving dirty dishes in the kitchen sink. When they arrived in Philadelphia, Mary was exhausted. Her mother, Dorcas Gardner Swift, had been fraught with worry and had lost much weight during the weeks that had passed. Her father, Paul Swift, too was anxious. At that time, Paul Swift had left his medical career for a professorship at Haverford College, a Quaker Institution that had been established in 1833 by the Society of Friends. There Paul Swift gained a reputation for his enthusiasm in teaching Chemistry and other branches of Natural Sciences (Haverford Alumni Association, 1892, p. 245). He also taught English, Moral and Political Sciences. His blunt nature with his students became part of his legend and his use of epithets seemed unlimited (Haverford Alumni Association, 1892, p. 316). He often told his students, "But wisdom is justified of her children." Paul Swift, clearly intelligent, also could be compulsive and if he found broken furniture in the classroom, such as a chair, he quickly hurled it out the nearest window (Haverford Alumni Association, 1892, p. 316). As Haverford was a Quaker college, the faculty and college community opposed violence (Haverford Alumni Association, 1892, p. 241). Many Quakers were opposed to abolitionist activities because they believed fighting and hostility should not be wedded to movements (Jordan, 2004, pp. 588–608).

Once she arrived in Philadelphia, Mary wrote to Edwin. He was worried because he had not received an earlier letter she sent. One can only imagine that Mary too was distraught at having been in a city in the midst of war while away from her three children.

Figure 8.1   Haverford College, Haverford, Pennsylvania. Courtesy of Haverford College Library, Quaker and Special Collections, Haverford, PA.

Figure 8.2   Dr. Paul Swift. Courtesy of Haverford College Library, Quaker and Special Collections, Haverford, PA.

Figure 8.3   Dorcas Gardner Swift. Courtesy of the Nantucket Historical Association, CDV1497, Nantucket, MA.

After Mary had left Baltimore, she learned that Senator Charles Sumner of Massachusetts had been in Baltimore at the time of the attack. The *New York Tribune* read:

> Senator Sumner of Massachusetts unexpecting of danger stopped in Baltimore the night before the Massachusetts men were there, put up at Baltimore's Hotel....Walked directly out to visit a friend....Very soon the house was surrounded by fierce, vociferous thousands, crying, 'Bring him out'...Threatening to tear down the house. They were assured that there was no such person in the house. At 81/2 Mr. Sumner returned, was taken in a side door, unrecognized and shown to his room. Here he was speedily waited on by the landlord and the manager, who each entreated him to leave to save his own life...He refused since he could not get out of the city and had no right to expose a private dwelling to danger....He left at 5 a.m. a private carriage taking him from the private door, so that he should not be seen. (The New York Tribune, date unknown)

Sumner's views about slavery and the Civil War had put his own life in jeopardy on previous occasions. In May of 1856, for example, he delivered a five-hour oration entitled "The Crime Against Kansas" in Washington at the Capitol. The speech was an indictment against those who supported the spread of slavery. After the speech, Preston Brooks, a member of the House of Representatives from South Carolina, retaliated by striking Sumner on his head with a heavy walking stick while Sumner sat at his desk in the Senate Chamber. Brooks was a relative of a slaveholder whom Sumner had specifically criticized. Sumner's recovery was slow and he was only able to appear in the Senate intermittently during the three years that followed (Senate Historical Office, no date, pp. 3–4).

In 1861, the same year that Mary found herself in the midst of the fighting in Baltimore, Julia Ward Howe, the wife of Samuel Gridley Howe who had been Mary's mentor at the Perkins Institution, wrote *The Battle Hymn of the Republic,* which became the marching hymn for the Union forces. The hymn was written while Dr. and Mrs. Howe were in Washington to meet with President Lincoln, as a result of their work with the Sanitary Commission. The song had originally been composed about John Brown, an antislavery activist who had tried to free slaves by leading a raid on Harper's Ferry in Virginia in October 1859. Financed and backed by a small group of men known as the secret six, including Samuel Gridley Howe, Brown had not succeeded with the attempt and was captured and executed a few months later. The incident became widely known and helped to spark the Civil War. Following Brown's execution, "John Brown's Body" became a war song (Reynolds, 2006). Julia Ward Howe was encouraged to write lyrics in place of "John Brown's Body." In Washington D.C., at the Willard Hotel,

Howe found that the words of the song came to her while she slept. Her lyrics were published in the *Atlantic Monthly*. "Mine eyes have seen the glory of the coming of the Lord," wrote Julia Ward Howe, who became from then on a famous woman (Howe, 1900, pp. 273–275). Mary Swift had met and talked with this woman while she was a teacher at the Perkins Institution.

The events that unfolded in Baltimore had shaped Mary deeply. She tried, through charitable efforts, to support the work of the Union soldiers. At times, she involved her own children in these efforts, having them periodically send some items and a letter to the soldiers. On February 6, 1863, a letter was sent from her youngest daughter Kate, nicknamed Daisy. Since Kate could not yet write, Mary served as scribe.

My dear friend,

My name is Daisy & I am a little girl five years old. I can not write, so I asked my mama to and she is writing just what I tell her to. I love the soldiers and I wanted to sew something for them so I sewed a good while and I made this bag all myself for you. I want you to write me a letter & tell me if you like all the things. I put in a sheet of paper & a stamped envelope for you to write me but if you have a little girl at home that you want the paper to write to her, you can have if for that for she will want a letter from her papa.

I send my love and a kiss,

Daisy Lamson

(K. Lamson, personal communication, February 6, 1863)

In April of 1864, little Kate received a letter back from a soldier from Camp Bariston Station in Virginia.

My Dear Little Kate,

While in the chaplain tent this morning I saw a large box of something. I did not know what but he informed that it was full of comfort bags sent by the Ladies and little girls of the City of Boston of which he told me to take my choice. I made the choice and after opening I found it was from Little Kate to whom I am happy to address. I am nineteen years in the Army of the Potomac and about three months ago re-enlisted for three years longer. I have seen a great many, have fought battles and expect to see more as we are waiting everyday to have the cannons in our front but Dear Little Kate I thank God that I am prepared to meet whatever is my doom. I am a reformed man. I profess religion and should it be my doom to fall it is in defense of that good old flag also the homes of you little girls who is doing so much for our comfort where I expect to meet you all is in Heaven where sin and sorrow never comes and battles never fought. Then Kate we shall never part . . . the kind letter and good advice which (you gave me) came from a little girl only five years old. I must say I like the letter best.

I must close hoping this may find you well.

I remain

Your friend truly

Henry C. Stone

(H. Stone, personal communication, April 24, 1863)

The same year that Kate received a letter from a soldier, Mary's former normal school peer and colleague from the Perkins Institution, Eliza Rogers, went to work for the Freedmen's Bureau, a government agency that was established to provide aid to freed slaves. A recognized achievement of the Freedman's Bureau was its work in the field of education. Former slaves were eager to learn to read and write and teachers were needed. In 1864 Eliza was assigned a station in Benedict, Maryland, to teach Black soldiers in General William Birney's regiments while they prepared for service. The travel to Maryland, by sea, was difficult for Eliza as it was winter. On arriving at the camp, Eliza, along with a small group of women with whom she traveled, saw white tents and squads of soldiers. Eliza began her school at once. It was her first glimpse into the life of slavery. On visiting a nearby farm she saw slave children dressed in rags. She saw that their living conditions were equivalent to residing in a shed with no window (Rutledge, 1912, p. 5).

Thousands of teachers, over half of them women, served as agents of the Freedman's Bureau in the 1860s (Small, 1979, p. 381). Anna Gardner from Mary's home town, Nantucket, also had joined the Bureau. Many of these teachers taught for a season or two. Some of the Southerners saw the Yankee schoolmarms as arrogant, opinionated meddlers (Small, 1979, p. 383). Mary, no doubt, was aware of Eliza's work with the Freedman's Bureau, as they had stayed in regular contact since their normal school studies.

Louisa Harris

There are few records from which to base assumptions about how Louisa was shaped by abolitionism and the Civil War in contrast to her peers, Lydia Stow and Mary Swift. Louisa continued to keep her journal throughout the nineteenth century, including during this period. At one point Louisa received news that a friend lost her brother in battle near Port Hudson while leading his troops. Louisa wrote that the memory of that death "will bear no sting, growing brighter and holier...that such precious blood must quicken and fertilize that tree of freedom that is to shelter and protect and be for the healing of the nations." When President Abraham Lincoln was assassinated in April 1865, Louisa wrote that "never did the nation before descend from such jubilant heights of joy to such a depth of sorrow" (L. Harris, personal communication, journal entry, April, 1865). She noted that the days that followed Lincoln's assassination were draped in dark and sorrowing emblems.

Without context, the lives of nineteenth century women teachers often are reduced to mere numbers. They taught for a certain number of years, often married and then left the education profession. Their lives are not considered in a holistic sense; the intermingling of their public and private circumstances remains unattended. The stories of Lydia Stow, Mary Swift and Louisa Harris, however, illustrate that the roots of formal teacher education in the United States, which began in the normal schools of Massachusetts, are deeply entwined with nineteen century social contexts and reform movements. The normalites' early decisions to take part in the movement had a profound impact on their sense of self, their impact on society, and their friendships and social networks that lasted a lifetime.

PART IV

Transformations of Normalites, Life Work,
and Living to the Truth

9

Louisa Harris and the Life of a Single Teacher

Louisa Harris began work at the Young Ladies Seminary and Boarding School in Somerville, Massachusetts in February of 1860. She was 37 years old, and had been recruited for the position for some time by Miss Sarah Cushman, the principal (L. Harris, personal communication, journal entry, February, 1860). The school's advertising described the goals for this private school for young women.

> It is to be their study, their work, and, with Divine help, their fulfillment, to educate the whole nature, since no part of it can be neglected without detriment to all the rest. Therefore would they advance the growth and development of the entire structure: physically, because the inner life demands it; morally, because peace and happiness depend upon it; intellectually, because the highest wisdom can only be attained through the culture of the mental as well as the moral powers. For these reasons, they have sought to establish their School and Home on such a basis as to combine truthful accomplishments with healthful knowledge—thus preparing the pupil to

Normalites, pages 141–149

meet the varied instances of life—controlling their influences rather than being controlled by them. (Cushman, 1859)

To be taught at the school were subjects such as English, ancient and modern languages, natural sciences, music, painting, drawing, and physical exercise. The eight references listed in the advertisement for the school, all men, included ministers and lawyers (Cushman, 1859).

Upon assuming the position, Louisa lived at Miss Cushman's boarding house, where ten students also resided. Two additional scholars were day students. Louisa did not interact often with Miss Cushman, who typically was engaged in a whirl of activity, often in Boston. Louisa thought that there was something about her that seemed showy and not genuine (L. Harris, personal communication, journal entry, February, 1860).

After starting her new position, Louisa traveled to visit Mary Swift and Mary Haskell, another friend from her normal school days. She also visited Hannah Damon and Addie Ireson, two more "normalites." All of these women lived in the Boston area. Louisa continued to enjoy these visits exceedingly. Together, the women aired their spirits and Louisa found that her laughter could almost reach hysterics. After the visits she felt a sense of loss and loneliness because these were the individuals who had come to mean so much to her (L. Harris, personal communication, journal entry, February 1860).

Overall, Louisa did not regret her move to Somerville. Initially, she was happy in her work there and did not feel the sense of exhaustion and weariness that had claimed her after a day of teaching in Roxbury. She had come to feel increasingly depleted by her work in the common schools (L. Harris, personal communication, journal entry, February, 1860). There were so many students and the working conditions were difficult. She believed that a fearful pattern was starting to mold her. She did not feel completely happy with her social life in Somerville, but this was not a new occurrence for her. In her journal she wrote, "I miss companionship and do not find myself attracted to anything below stairs" at Miss Cushman's boarding house. She knew she could, instead, find her satisfaction among the witty and wise and entertaining souls speaking from the books on her table or in the shallow and dilapidated scraps of paper buried among her treasures. She also found new time and energy to dig out some of her old writings. In her journal entries, Louisa continued to record that her emotions rose and fell from one extreme to the other. She also began to think that she would become a misanthrope, and mused that perhaps she would write a poem or a paradise lost (L. Harris, personal communication, journal entry, February, 1860). In reflecting on a "paradise lost," Louisa probably considered the work of John Milton, an English poet.

Louisa liked Miss L. A. Dudley, the assistant principal at Miss Cushman's, whom she found to be intellectual and self-sustained. She thought that she would always be on excellent terms with her, but initially thought there would be nothing more (L. Harris, personal communication, journal entry, February, 1860). While writing in her journal, however, Louisa admitted that she felt a strange attachment to her. She wrote, "Although I have no doubt I shall always be on excellent terms with her—am quite sure there will be no romantic attachment. (There is now at this wishing a very strong one)" (L. Harris, personal communication, journal entry, February 1860). Over time, Louisa and Miss Dudley discovered a shared interest in books and often spent time together poring over the contents of those books.

There was another boarder, Miss S, who Louisa disliked exceedingly. Her father was a notable doctor from Troy, New York. Louisa thought Miss S's demeanor was most disagreeable. Miss S was thought to travel in high circles; however, she could not find this in her interactions with her though Louisa knew she was familiar with the conventionalities. Over time, however, Louisa grew fond of her too. The housekeeper at Miss Cushman's was from Norway, a woman of high pretense and intelligence and of great importance to the family. Louisa felt that Dickens himself "would make a great deal of her." In spite of the interest she gradually assumed in some of the other inhabitants of the boarding house, Louisa found that she most often preferred to retire to her own attic bedroom window. Her room contained a nice kerosene lamp and she had put a comforter on her bed. In her room she opened her books and read and mused about her life and her future.

Miss Cushman was prone to financial crisis and this worried Louisa, particularly after she had settled into her work and domicile. The continuation of the school often seemed precarious. As time passed, Louisa increasingly disliked the character of Miss Cushman. She attempted to resign on at least one occasion, but Louisa wrote in her journal that Miss Cushman in her skillful way persuaded her to stay. At the close of the term of her first year at this school, Louisa took some time off and taught the children of a Dr. Humphrey who lived on Springfield Street in Boston. During the period that Louisa taught Dr. Humphrey's children, he reciprocated by teaching her Latin. Louisa felt friendship towards Dr. Humphrey's wife whom she thought was quite lovable.

Although Louisa had not intended to return to Miss Cushman's school, she did start a second year. While at the school, Louisa took lessons in Spanish and Italian. The financial crisis of the school that Louisa anticipated then came to pass, and Miss Cushman's school was dissolved (L. Harris, personal communication, journal entry, June, 1861). When the school closed in 1861, Louisa and former assistant principal Miss Dudley made arrangements to take the pupils for the next term at Ashland Place in Boston, a temporary situation that lasted until July of 1862. In many ways, Louisa enjoyed teaching in the private school realm. There were a few aspects to the work that displeased her, however. One of these was that a sort of espionage was demanded over the young ladies who attended. Louisa and Miss Dudley were supposed to monitor their students' activities and make sure their actions were socially acceptable. Louisa found this to be narrowing and humiliating (L. Harris, personal communication, journal entry, June, 1861). During this time, Louisa continued to teach a few hours a week for Dr. Humphrey who in turn continued to teach her Latin.

When her work with Miss Cushman's former students fully came to a close, Louisa took a position in Lenox in western Massachusetts for a short period in 1862. Her responsibility was to teach the three children in the house of the Brevoorts, an esteemed and socially elite family. She described her household company as all "members of the Sacred Legion of the Somebodies." Though Louisa battled with her emotions, she also had developed a sense of humor about life circumstances. The views in Lenox, Massachusetts were lovely and Louisa thought they would have satisfied an artist's longing for splendor. The mountains were a constant sight. The varieties of green moss, ferns, ground cover and trees, painted a picture of beauty. The silent lakes which she saw in the distance, backed by quiet peaks, could still a heart and calm one's being. The house where Louisa stayed was an old fashioned gable-roofed dwelling with an interior that had an air of easy elegance. When Louisa rode to Lee, a village approximately five miles away, she passed a modest house where Ward Beecher had his star papers. Miss Fanny Kimble's cottage was situated in a broad, grassy field surrounded by rude, primitive fences (L. Harris, personal communication, journal entry, July, 1862). The house of Miss Sedgwick, an author who wrote *Hope Leslie*, *Clarence*, and other novels, was almost hidden with shrubbery. Located not too far away also was a common red house where Nathaniel Hawthorne wrote *The Scarlet Letter*. Hawthorne's house commanded a lovely view of a lake named Mountain Mirror. Louisa loved to inhale the air in western Massachusetts, but wondered if the Brevoorts were aware of the riches that they were missing, which she had become used to in Boston. Though some found beauty in the splendor of the mountains, others found them to be objects which get in the way of where one hoped to go.

As a newcomer to the family, Louisa monitored her discourse and was not free with her words. Her interactions with the family were measured by polite, agreeable conversation. She got along comfortably, but there was not one soul within miles who knew her well. Never before in her life had she moved such a distance away to live among strangers. She supposed that all new experiences had some value. If she were rich, however, she noted wryly that she would not be so apt to test those novelties. It was during those moments that Louisa felt that she did not have much of a part in the household activity. Though there were many visitors to the house, Louisa felt that their interests were remote from hers and besides, she was "the help." She longed for familiar faces, for her friends. In her journal she wrote that there was a "certain, cool, calm, philosophical kind of happiness about it, if there are none of those joyous thrills that stir us among genial and beloved friends" (L. Harris, personal communication, journal entry, July, 1862). It was at this household where Louisa came to know that she longed to return to work in the common schools. In the end, the world of the private school was not hers. Her work as a tutor in Lenox, Massachusetts, as well as her experiences with Miss Cushman's school, steered her occupational path back towards public school work.

> I am not sorry I left school when I did. I have benefitted in numerous ways. And I sure feel in better condition to teach then when I left R [Roxbury]. But pleasant as much as my teaching in private schools has been—I not only feel assured I have no fitness for the anxiety and outside effort they require. But also that there is a looseness and un-satisfaction in the methods of teaching forced upon one—of which I have become a little disgusted and which prevents my efforts to obtain a school home in one. Won't it be just about picking season when I return? And couldn't I do something in that line. (L. Harris, personal communication, journal entry , August 21, 1862)

Following her work with private schools, Louisa resumed teaching in the common schools in the Roxbury area. For a time, she boarded at a Mrs. Wiley's. Her sister Laura lived near her, likely with their mother. Louisa's father had died following illness. Though Louisa was pleased with the boarding arrangement at Mrs. Wiley's, the rent was raised and it was more than she could afford. She had to find other quarters. Sarah Wyman's parents took her in at that time, providing lodging for the fall and winter seasons. In 1864 she wrote in her journal, "My school life has not been painful or very wearisome, neither is it so pleasurable or inspiring as I think one's daily work ought to be . . . I seek in books and study the satisfactions I do not find in pupils" (L. Harris, personal communication, journal entry, January 4, 1864). Louisa continued to visit with her friend Miss Dudley during school vacations and they would pore over books together. Absorbed in books, they lost track of time and of the outside world (L. Harris, personal communication, journal entry, January 4, 1864).

Interested in intellectual discourse, Louisa also attended nearby lectures. She found these activities enjoyable. She had heard many distinguished speakers since her normal school days. In one lecture, delivered by John Park, matrimony was discussed. In her journal, Louisa wrote, "that much abused but highly important relation—Matrimony, for the protection which the law affords to the rights of married families" was explored (L. Harris, personal communication, journal entry, December 23, 1843). During this time, marriage no longer was undertaken primarily as an economic arrangement. Ideas of companionable marriages, based on love, increasingly took hold. As matrimony became to be seen less as an economic mandate for women, the number of single women also rose. Some single women reflected that they were better able to dedicate themselves to the needs of others by remaining single (Wayne, 2007, pp. 4–6). In her journal, Louisa did not appear too keen on marriage.

Mr. Henry Giles of Ireland was another lecturer whom Louisa went to hear speak on several occasions. He spoke of Irish history, emigration, wit and humor. Giles also reflected on the struggles in Ireland. When Louisa heard him provide an address on April 10, 1844, she recorded in her journal that the lecture was "delivered by Rev. Henry Giles, with whose eloquence I was so much charmed a few winters since at the Lyceum and of whom I have made some mention in a former journal" (L. Harris, personal communication, journal entry, April 11, 1844).

Theodore Parker, a Unitarian minister and member of the Transcendentalist Club, was another lecturer of particular interest to Louisa (L. Harris, personal communication, journal entry, December 14, 1842). Parker was from Lexington, where he had attended a district school and thereafter the Lexington Academy, which was established in 1822. When the Lexington Academy subsequently closed, the building was turned into the normal school, the very one that Louisa attended (Kollen, 2004, p. 44). Though it was at different times and under different auspices, Louisa and Theodore Parker both were educated under the twelve foot high ceilings that graced the upper level of the building. They both had peered out of the wooden framed, glass-paned windows that provided views of the Lexington Common and surrounding area.

In his lectures, Parker rejected the authority of the Bible and of Jesus, which made him a controversial figure. Some viewed him as a saint, whereas others thought of him as a fanatic or infidel (Grodzins, 2002). Regardless of how one viewed the man, there was no questioning his prominence. He was pastor to the largest church in Boston. Almost three thousand people went weekly to hear him preach. Individuals such as William Lloyd Garrison regularly attended his services. Horace Mann frequently turned to Parker for counsel. Another 50,000 people listened to him on a yearly basis as he lectured in lyceums (Grodzins, 2002, p. ix). His followers also included Wendell Phillips and Charles Sumner. Parker also had baptized Samuel Gridley Howe's first child while they were both in Europe (Grodzins, 2002, p. ix). This was the time when Mary Swift was left as the primary care taker of Laura Dewey Bridgman, while Dr. Howe and Julia Ward Howe were on their honeymoon. Dr. Howe felt gratified that his daughter was baptized by Parker.

Louisa attended several lectures that were part of a series offered by Theodore Parker. One focused on theology and religion. During that lecture, Parker suggested these terms were often confounded. Louisa recorded in her journal, "The former he defined to be our thoughts about the latter. Religion has a feeling or sentiment, while theology meant only our intellectual thoughts about that sentiment" (L. Harris, personal communication, journal entry, December 28, 1842). Theodore Parker offered reflections on the "animosity which theologians of one sect cherished towards those of another . . . the bitterest of all animosities, often following . . . even to the grave" (L. Harris, personal communication, journal entry, December 28, 1842). He suggested that it was not in religion that we differed, because we all had the same religion. Rather, it was in theology that we differed. Louisa wrote in her journal that his "heretical views were boldly, and very beautifully expressed" (L. Harris, personal communication, journal entry, January 4, 1843). In that same lecture, he discussed the idea that the Bible was not every part true. "He said he could find one who never read the great truths of the Bible, more than he did, he said he would go far to sit down at his feet and learn from him." Louisa thought that the deepest words that man ever spoke "were registered there" at this time. She felt that his words were so convincing and his love for truth and reverence for everything holy so deep, that she would assent to all he said. "I could not but feel gratified to find that so profound a searcher after truth, deems reasonable the doubts which manage the pious teachings of my youth would arise" (L. Harris, personal communication, journal entry, January, 1843). In a letter that Louisa sent to Lydia Stow, she reflected on Parker's integrity and wholesomeness. In response, Lydia Stow recorded in her journal that the martyrs and heretics of one age, are the saints of the next. Lydia too had heard Parker preach. She felt that he was such a pure man he must infuse purity of heart into all who hear him (L. Stow, personal communication, journal entry, April 10, 1842).

The mid-nineteenth century in general was a time of significant religious fervor, reform and at times agitation. There was turmoil between the Unitarians and the Congregationalists. The Catholic Church was establishing a greater presence, in large part due to the Catholicism of immigrant groups. By 1875, Mary Baker Eddy also had written *Science and Health With Key to Scriptures*, a foundational text for Christian Scientists, a growing association (Eddy, 1889). Not only between religions, but also within religions, controversies would unfold. Early activist and supporter of the Christian Science religion, William Bertram, for example, a man with blue eyes who often wore a diamond tie tack that would later be made into a ring for his daughter, would temporarily defect from the Christian Science association and become a medical doctor. Though this created tensions, he and his family would not cease their ties with Christian Science for the next few generations. As a resident of the Boston area, Louisa undoubtedly was aware of the increasingly ecumenical landscape and was influenced by the changes and controversies.

When Louisa was approximately 42 years old, on the 18th of November in 1865, she was called to her mother's bedside after receiving word that she was not well. Louisa thought her mother was suffering from a severe cold, noticing that she trembled when she breathed. She did not realize, however, that her mother was "almost home." At one point, Louisa's mother asked her to read from the Bible. She wanted to hear the Epistles of John and told Louisa that there was nothing like the Bible and she did not care to read other books anymore. Though her mother's mind was perfectly clear, the nights that followed were restless. Miss Dudley stopped by to call on Louisa during her mother's illness, during which time Louisa left her mother briefly. When she returned, she fanned her, gave her a little wine and helped her stand up as her mother requested. Her mother then rested in Louisa's arms while her breath left her; it was a painless and peaceful death. Louisa knew that her mother was aged and weary, but felt that the severing of the ties that bound them was bitter (L. Harris, personal communication, journal entry, November 18, 1865).

In 1866, following her mother's death, Louisa became a head assistant at the Adams School in Belmont Square in East Boston. The school was overseen by a master, initially Robert Metcalf, a submaster and three to four head assistants. The head assistants usually were women. In addition, eight assistants, all women, often were employed at the school (School Committee of the City of Boston, 1870). The city of Boston, at this time, operated five high schools and almost thirty different school districts. The Adams School was one of many serving a city population of approximately 267,000 (Fay, 1901, p. 22).

At least through the early 1870s, the schools in Boston continued to be overseen by ward school committees, all of the members of which were men. In addition there were specific branches of the city school committee that oversaw the rules and regulations of the schools, the curriculum and textbooks, and the salaries of the school teachers. All members of these committees too were men. In 1870, the city was considering the establishment of an "experimental" kindergarten based on Friedrich Frobel's ideas. The formal abolishment of corporal punishment also was being tackled and pushed forward. Members of the school committee debated whether there should be some statute in Massachusetts providing for the protection of children against excessive punishment in school. The school committee acknowledged, however, that they did not know what form of discipline should be used in its place (School Committee of the City of Boston, 1870).

It was in these contexts that Louisa Harris continued in the role of head assistant at the Adams School until September of 1873, when she retired for a season of rest. Her normal school studies had prepared her for a life of teaching. By then, she had taught for over 30 years and likely worked with over a thousand students during that time, many in one-room school structures (Massachusetts Teachers Association, 1873, p. 418).

In the mid-1800s, Louisa relocated to Dedham where she boarded on Myrtle Street with a Mrs. Murdock. In her late seventies, she turned to other pursuits that brought her joy. She wrote poetry and short narratives. At this later point in her life, her identity moved toward one of an "authoress." She always had enjoyed reading and writing. In 1884, she wrote a poem that was read at the 150th anniversary of the First Church of Christ, North Congregational in Cape Elizabeth, Maine (Williamson, 1896, p. 231). In 1900, Louisa drafted "The Art of Forgetting," which was published in *The Christian Register*. The message of the narrative suggested that one should not dwell on unhappy moments, but rather think about one's purpose in life. She suggested that if one focused on one's intentions, it would yield sunlight into the soul. In writing this essay, it appeared that Louisa had made peace with the unhappy moments in her life's journey and had moved toward acceptance. Louisa wrote:

> There are dark and painful chapters in all lives, whose events are so inwoven with their very fibre that no effort will banish them; and then, seen through Memory's mellowing glass, must have their lesson. But the wise and healthy nature does not dwell on the painful details of past misery or seek to keep alive the dark and bitter aspect of any bygone trouble.... Memory must often be quenched in the stronger light of purpose if we could bring health and sunlight into our souls. (Harris, 1900, pp. 652–653)

10

Lydia Stow, First Woman School Board Member in Fall River and Founder of the Fall River Women's Union

By the latter half of the nineteenth century, Fall River had become an increasingly prosperous city, fueled by its growth as a hub of the textile industry. Streetcar lines were laid on Main Street (Martins & Binette, 2010, p. 167). The population grew rapidly due to the influx of immigrants including Irish, French Canadian, and Portuguese. Dwellings which held multiple families were erected (Martins & Binette, 2010, p. 167). As a result of population growth, the appearance of the city was marked by an increase in houses and buildings, crammed together in close physical proximity.

Robert Adams' bookstore continued to prosper during this time. After the great Fall River fire of 1843, he found new quarters on South Main Street and from there moved to Borden block. Though Adams' store had started as a bookbinding business, it grew into a stationery and book selling enterprise. On one occasion schoolbooks were purchased from Adams'

Normalites, pages 151–163
Copyright © 2014 by Information Age Publishing
All rights of reproduction in any form reserved.

store by Samuel Longfellow, a Unitarian minister in Boston who also was a chairman of the Boston school committee. Samuel Longfellow, brother of the poet Henry Wadsworth Longfellow, ordered the books for children who could not afford them (The American Stationer, 1922, p. 40).

Lydia and Robert's first and only child Edward was born on June 16, 1856, 12 years after they married. A child changes the life of a couple, particularly for a couple that has waited a time for one. Records do not suggest that any children were born before Edward. It is likely that it either took time for Lydia to become pregnant or to keep a pregnancy. However, when Lydia assumed the role of mother she was ready for it. Lydia's sister Mary also was active with supporting her with this new responsibility. She continued to live with Lydia and Robert following her husband's death.

When Edward was 17, he was sent to a boarding school in West Newton, a place that he described as "a very pleasant and quiet village; quiet with the exception of the cars which are passing every few minutes; the stores are not very numerous, hardly enough I should think for such a village" (E. Adams, personal communication, journal entry, September 17, 1873). The school itself, a coeducational boarding school, was one that was sought out by wealthy families, whose children, as Edward had deduced, "have many advantages for learning" (E. Adams, personal communication, journal entry, May 6, 1874). Edward, an average size boy of 121 pounds, was initially "rather blue," being away from home. Nonetheless, he delved into his school work, studying French, English literature and book-keeping (E. Adams, personal communication, journal entry, September 19–22, 1873). One of Edward's teachers told the students that "home sickness…was good for you, although the tears often come to your eyes, you need not be ashamed of it" (September 24, 1873). While at school Edward took walks in the surrounding countryside, attended the local Unitarian Church, and played ball during free time. A cousin named Wheeler joined him in studying at the West Newton school and they often would spend time together. Edward also looked forward to the steady flow of letters he received from home.

Lydia, on occasion, visited her son at school, often with her sister Mary. (E. Adams, personal communication, journal entry, February 5, 1874). Sometimes, Lydia would meet him at school and they would travel together to visit aunts in Dedham, likely her aunts Esther and Sophia Foord (E. Adams, personal communication, journal entry, February 9, 1874). At times, his aunts and Dedham cousins traveled to West Newton to see him (E. Adams, personal communication, journal entry, October 16, 1873). When Edward made trips home from school, he took in the scenery of Fall River, on one occasion noting that it was dull "as nearly all the mills have shut down to half time" (E. Adams, personal communication, journal entry, November 3, 1873). Industrialization increasingly shaped the work in Fall River. During school

Figure 10.1   Lydia Stow. Courtesy of the Independent Association of Framingham State Alumni, Framingham, MA.

breaks, Edward worked in the store with his father and enjoyed time with his mother and aunt. Like his mother, Edward kept a journal of his studies, which primarily served as a recording of his school work and daily activities.

While Edward was away at school, Lydia's attention increasingly focused on her work in the community. In 1872, Lydia became the first woman school committee member in Fall River. At this point in the nineteenth century, Massachusetts began to reserve some school board positions for women (Sklar, 1995, p. 65). Schools boards, first established during the colonial era, initially took all school-based decisions to town meeting. In the eighteenth and nineteenth centuries, school boards were dominated by professionals, always men until the 1870s. Primary tasks of local school boards included the hiring and firing of teachers, school construction and repairs and curriculum matters (Provenzo, 2008, pp. 278–279).

Along with eight other school committee members, all male, as well as a male superintendent, Lydia helped set policies for the schools in the city of Fall River in 1872. Her husband had previously served as a school committee member, so it is likely that he provided her with some guidance. The schools in Fall River were categorized into primary, intermediate, grammar and high school. Due to the thriving mill industries, unprecedented growth took place in Fall River during the period between 1840 and 1870 and the city subsequently did not have enough space in the schools for all its children. Five thousand, eight hundred and seventy-eight students were registered for school in 1872, yet the city only had 4,686 seats available. The school committee report stated, "Let then ample accommodations be furnished for our whole school population, who are soon to become important factors in the community; so that each child may receive the blessings of a common school education" (School Committee of the City of Fall River, 1872). The largest numbers of students attended or were eligible for the primary schools. Older children often went to work in factories (Martins & Binette, 2010, p. 52). Struggling families needed the financial support of their older children to exist (Phillips, 1945, p. 77). Fall River also had developed factory schools, which children attended after the mills had closed for the day (Phillips, 1945, pp. 77–78). The average per pupil expenditure at this time was estimated to be $14.78 annually (School Committee of the City of Fall River, 1872, p. 8).

Lydia, along with a Mr. Holmes and a Mr. Aldrich, served as the subcommittee of the third school division in Fall River. They had oversight of schools on Maple, June, and Brownell Streets, Town Avenue, Turnpike, Stafford Street, Slade's Ferry, Lower New Boston, Steep Brook, and North Schools. In addition, they oversaw the Alms-House school. Some of these schools were in great need (School Committee of the City of Fall River, 1875). The condi-

Figure 10.2   Maple Street School in Fall River, Massachusetts. Courtesy of the Fall River Historical Society, Fall River, MA.

tions of schools varied according to the neighborhood at which they were located. Neighborhoods in turn varied according to social class. Schools "Up the Hill" in the wealthier area of Fall River were, in general, written about more favorably in school committee reports (Martins & Binette, 2010, p. 56).

During Lydia's tenure with the school committee, the group became intent on establishing an evening school through which students over age 20 could receive an education. Lydia and other school committee members knew it would be difficult for these individuals to attend the common schools with children who were 15 years or younger, but participation in an evening school would provide a possibility for them to receive an education. It would raise people in the social scale and keep them from the idleness that might accompany evening time. The first evening school was held in the Anawan School and lasted for five weeks (School Committee of the City of Fall River, 1875).

The work of school committees had been discussed when Lydia was a student at the normal school in Lexington. On January 2, 1840, she wrote in her journal about school committee work. Among other things she specifically reflected on the role of the school committee in administering examinations to prospective teachers. "The question for discussion was 'ought school examinations to be confined to the committee?' The discussion was not very animated. It was decided two in the affirmative, 18 in the negative" (L. Stow, personal communication, journal entry, January 2, 1840). There was an aspect of uncertainty which teachers encountered with the school committee. If one was well regarded by the committee, one could be favorably assessed. The contrary likely could take place. The assessment of the teaching ability of the teacher was not the only factor which led to performance decisions made by the school committee. The vote recorded in Stow's journal entry attests to the disapprobation normalities felt toward the school committee's oversight of their work, especially since committee members' subjective feelings about a teacher's pedagogical approaches or other matters could and did prejudice their decisions. Although no references have been found in her correspondence, Lydia's ill treatment by the school committee in her second teaching position was likely in her mind as she ran for and worked on the Fall River School Committee.

On February 6, 1874, Edward, Lydia's son, wrote in his journal that his mother had spent a few hours at his school in the morning and then traveled into Boston. He further wrote that "A vote has been passed that the ladies recently elected on the Boston School Committee cannot hold office; it is calling up a great deal of discussion" (E. Adams, personal communication, journal entry, February 6, 1874). Women continued to encounter constraints in their work in the education profession in the later part of the nineteenth century. During this time, school committee work continued to be a point of focus for Lydia, as noticed by Edward. On May 12, 1874, he recorded in his journal, "There seems to be a great deal of talk at home concerning the School Committee and Mr. A. K. Slade, the Principal of the High School who is to leave at the end of the term. At the High School graduation last Friday, Mr. S. made a very ungentlemanly speech" (E. Adams, personal communication, journal entry, May 12, 1874). The content of this "ungentlemanly" speech is unknown, so one can only conjecture how it concerned the school committee. Though some information has been preserved about Lydia's school committee work through annual reports, there remain unanswered questions as to whether she experienced any discrimination as the first woman on the school committee in Fall River.

In addition to Lydia's work with the school committee, she increasingly turned her energy towards the work of the Fall River Women's Union. She had become one of the founding members of the Women's Union in 1873. The Union was open to all women regardless of race, religion or class (Fall River Women's Union, 1895, pp. 9–10). It offered a variety of educational and social services to women, particularly to the women of the mills. The latter part of the nineteenth century had witnessed a burgeoning of benevolent organizations and women's associations, as well as the birth of the Women's Suffrage Movement. In 1850, when the Worcester Convention took place, Lydia's Aunt Sophia Foord attended and was registered as a member (National American Woman Suffrage Association Collection, 1851). Sojourner Truth also was present and spoke on the platform. Sojourner Truth, who had remained connected to Lydia and her family since Sophia Foord's stay at the Northampton Association, had become a notable speaker and activist. At the convention, topics such as the wages of women, who were compelled to work for less than half a man could earn, were considered (National American Woman Suffrage Association Collection, 1851).

These circumstances and events were likely an impetus in Lydia starting the Fall River Women's Union. They solidified for her in the early 1870s when a group of women in Fall River realized the need for the working women and girls in the city to engage in recreation and other activities that could lead to self-improvement. An initial meeting was held with Mrs. Jennie Collins of Boston, a pioneer in the area of social work, on October 30, 1873 (Fall River Women's Union, 1895, pp. 9–10). A former factory worker and an abolitionist, Jennie Collins was a public speaker by 1868 who presented the working woman's point of view. As a member of the New England Labor Reform League, she also helped establish the Boston Working Women's League, which aimed to give women a means to become independent proprietors. In addition, Collins established Buffin's Bower in Boston, which provided assistance to young women who were without work and in need. It was an organization to which she was said to give her whole life and time. Buffin's Bower was considered, by some, as a place where the weakest and least competent went (Leach, 1980, p. 165).

A second meeting with Mrs. Collins took place in Fall River on December 15, 1873, at the Troy Cotton and Woolen Manufacturing Company. Lydia was present and elected to serve as one of the three vice presidents of the organization, later called the Fall River Women's Union. Though there were problems initially and disappointments related to organizing for the needs of working women and girls, effort and commitment encouraged the group to persevere. They were "far-sighted and public-spirited women" (Hutt, 1924, p. 437). The first action of the group was to establish a reading room where working women and girls could come together for enjoyment and assistance. Thomas Borden, owner of the Troy Manufacturing Company in the city, provided the use of Room 18 in the Troy Building (Fall River Women's Union, 1895, pp. 9–10). Built over the Quequechan River, the mill contained over fifty thousand spindles and over one thousand looms that were used to produce cotton weaves.

As the work of the Women's Union unfolded, additional services did as well. In 1879, the Union established a sewing school. Both interest and attendance in the sewing school grew. In 1883, the treasurer of the Union Manufacturing Company, Thomas E. Brayton, provided the use of rooms over the offices for the sewing school and additional endeavors. Classes for

Figure 10.3   Troy Factory in Fall River, Massachusetts.

millinery, dress-making, crocheting, and gymnastics were established (Fall River Women's Union, 1895, pp. 9–10). Saturday sewing classes also were held in the Anawan School in Fall River.

When the sewing classes were in session the rooms were full. Often there was a wait list of twenty or more young women hoping to gain admittance. By 1896, the sewing classes were so large that 60 women had to be turned away due to lack of space and lack of teachers (Fall River Women's Union, 1897, p. 6). Various kinds of garments were constructed in the sewing schools. Underwear, however, was a common item. Because of the high cost of clothing it often was undergarments that families could barely afford to purchase. The sewing classes provided an avenue for women to learn to make these necessities. Lydia was a faithful instructor in these classes, teaching, and moving throughout the room checking on the progress of her students (Fall River Daily Globe, 1904). Lydia likely had started to first work with a needle when she was a young girl. Lydia's family had kept with care a sampler made by her mother, Lydia Foord, when she was a ten year old child. There undoubtedly were many moments when Lydia, who lost her mother when she was only 11, had held the sampler in hands.

Encouraged by the success of the sewing school, Lydia proposed the establishment of a cooking school to the Women's Union officers. Mrs. Geddes of Cambridge was consulted with regard to the method of

Figure 10.4   Sampler Made by Lydia Foord (Lydia Stow Adam's mother). Courtesy of the Fall River Historical Society, Fall River, MA.

Figure 10.5   Girls Club of the Fall River Women's Union. Courtesy of the Fall River Historical Society, Fall River, MA.

teaching in a cooking school. Information was obtained and the cooking school opened the following January. Women who were members of the Women's Union paid five cents admission for each of the cooking classes (Fall River Women's Union, 1882). A boarding residence, thereafter, opened on Pine Street in Fall River. It was a home for women, where they could "obtain meat and comfortable rooms by the day or week at a reasonable price." A Home and Industrial Exchange emerged at this same location where "women's work of every description may be placed for sale and where orders for the same may be received." A Working Girls Club was formed by the end of 1889. Reports from the Women's Union suggested that, by 1891, rooms over the Union Mills Office had been opened two evenings a week for younger women (girls) between the ages of 12 to 15 years (Fall River Women's Union, 1895, pp. 9–10).

Lydia often served as the overseer of the Women's Union meetings in the absence of the president. She served in the role of vice president for the Union for 27 years between the period of 1873 and 1899. In 1887, she was elected to serve as president of the Women's Union for a term. The Women's Union board meetings were full, active proceedings. The Board of Directors numbered almost 40 and there were over 20 life members including Lydia and her husband, Robert. There also were over 130 honorary members. Although the Union had been operating since 1873, it was not officially incorporated until 1889, when Lydia signed the original articles of agreement along with 12 other women.

The Fall River Women's Union grew and included many women members from the city. Lizzie Borden, a member of the large, prominent Fall River Borden family, was involved in the Women's Union as a board of director in 1891 for a brief period (Martins & Binette, 2010, p. 255). When the notorious Borden murders took place in 1892 during which Lizzie Borden's father and step-mother were killed by hatchet, the city of Fall River was thrown into a spin of notoriety. Newspaper accounts of the murders could be read throughout New England. One of Lydia's early and close friends from Fall River, Mary Livermore, who had become well known for her work in the Sanitary Commission, came to the defense of Lizzie Borden. In turn, Lydia's son, Edward, and Mary Livermore met and held a quiet and confidential conversation. The focus of this conversation remains unknown (Phillips, 1945, pp. 39–40). Lydia likely was aware of that conversation, as she was Livermore's close friend.

Overtime, the needs of the elderly also became an increasing concern of Lydia and her husband, Robert. Lydia's Aunt Sophia Foord died on April 1, 1885, after a lengthy illness (Dedham Historical Society, 1885). Undoubtedly, Lydia had interacted with her aunt during this illness and felt sadness at her loss. Sophia Foord was 82 years old when she died. She had been cared for primarily by her sister, Lydia's Aunt Esther. Louisa May Alcott, her aunt's former student, wrote to Esther Foord, following Aunt Sophia's death.

Early April 1885

My Dear Miss Ford,

I am forbidden to write, having suffered much from writer's cramp & vertigo this winter, but I will certainly try to pay my grateful tribute of respect to your sister as soon as possible.

I had hoped to come & see her, but in these busy lives of ours many pleasures get pushed aside by duties that cannot wait. I am very sorry now that it is too late to say good bye if no more.

Father is well for his state, but the right arm is useless & he but dimly remembers much of the past. I shall recall Sophia Foord's name to him when I go home & see if her remembers her.

I do remember, most pleasantly in the old Concord days when she kept school for the Emersons & us. Also during my Dedham experience years later.

I am sorry she was long ill, & glad that eternal health & youth are hers again. I have been much of an invalid since my nursing attempt in war times, so I can sympathize with all who suffer.

My sister Anna desires to be remembered to you, & I am with much sympathy affectionately yours,

L. M. Alcott

(as cited in Myerson, Shealy, Stern, 1995, p. 289)

Louisa May Alcott thereafter wrote a memoriam about Aunt Sophia in the Woman's Journal. It read:

In memoriam of Sophia Foord

The columns of a paper devoted to the records of woman's worth and work seem the proper place for a brief tribute to the memory of an estimable woman lately gone to her rest.

Sophia Foord was one of those who, by an upright life, an earnest sympathy in all great reforms and the influence of a fine character, made the world better while here, and left a sweet memory behind her.

She is one of the most prominent figures in my early Concord days, when she kept school for the little Emersons, Channings, and Alcotts in the poet's barn. Many a wise lesson she gave us there, though kindergartens were as of yet unknown; many a flower hunt with Thoreau for our guide many a Sunday service where my father acted as chaplain and endless revels where old and young play together, while illustrious faces smiled upon the pretty festivals under the pines.

The warmth and vigor of her own nature were most attractive and sincerity made her friendship worth having, and her life desire for high thinking and holy living won for her regard of many admirable persons of which she was too modest to boast.

I regret that I know so little of her later years, but take comfort in the knowledge that a devoted sister cheered her long illness, and that after the refining discipline of pain, age and death, her strong spirit rejoices in the larger life she aspired to know.

L. M. Alcott

(Alcott, 1885)

By 1885, Louisa May Alcott had achieved fame as an author; *Little Women* had been published in 1868 and 1869. At an early point in Louisa May Alcott's writing career, Sophia Foord had acquired a book of poems written by Louisa. The hand-written poems, written in pencil in a small blue book filled with white lined paper that was kept together with a thin piece of string, was one of Sophia's treasures. The inscription to Sophia Foord read:

Dear Miss Foord,

I wish I had something better to give in return for all you have done for me, but as you expressed a wish to see some of my nonsense, I have provided you with a good dose. Now I hope you appreciate the great sacrifice I am making in thus allowing you to see this choice collection of poems which being so exceedingly brilliant will cause to lift your hands in admiration and thus let them tumble into the fire, so that no one may suffer the mortification of not being able to write as fairly.

As your ever loving nonsensical

Louisa

(L. M. Alcott, personal communication, no date)

At Sophia Foord's death, the book was passed on to Lydia. She likely held the book gently in her hands, an item that would be cherished.

Following her aunt's passing, and perhaps motivated by that loss, Lydia and her husband increasingly turned their attention to the needs of the elderly in Fall River. It was another life transition for Lydia, prompted by circumstances that she had come to understand about growing old. Others in Lydia's social circles also were aware of the realities of becoming old. In 1891, a letter to Robert Adams from Frederick Douglass, discussed the death of some old friends of the antislavery society. At the end of that letter, Douglass wrote, "Kindness and best regards to your household. Yours truly to the end. Frederick Douglass" (Douglass, personal communication, November 12, 1891).

In Fall River, the elderly, particularly elderly women, was a population in need of help. Fall River had become a prosperous textile manufacturing community but it was a city divided along class lines. The city's prosperity, however, made possible extensive philanthropy. Some community members contributed large sums of money and hours of service to address and alleviate problems. Once again in a mill, this time in the Cotton Manufacturer's Association, the idea of the Fall River Home for the Aged was generated and an association formed to move the initiative forward. Extensive fundraising followed and sizeable financial contributions were made. A suitable piece of property for the home, however, needed to be furnished, one which was well situated, spacious, and not removed from the center of the city. The Association also wished for the residents to have access to a private garden. Though a Mr. Samuel Watson offered a plot of land on Eastern Avenue in the city, the Association felt that the location was too far removed from the city center. In response, Lydia and her husband Robert offered land that they owned on Highland Avenue. It was a beautiful piece of property on a hill that commanded grand views of the river and mills below. Their son Edward contributed an adjoining plot of land so there would be enough space for a garden. Several years were needed to complete the erection of the building. During that time the facility was housed in temporary locations. Fundraising and construction continued until the Fall River Home for the Aged opened on March 8, 1898. The majestic brick building had three stories with handsome brownstone trim and white woodwork. The gable roof had a deck surrounded by white railings. The dining hall was seventeen by twenty-six feet. Sunlight streamed through its numerous windows. Arched beams graced the hallways which were accented with numerous pieces of antique furniture. An elevator connected the floors of the building and telephones, invented by 1877, were located inside an engineer room. The home also boasted a laundry room, a drying room and an ironing room. It was built to accommodate thirty residents. Fifteen lived at the establishment at the time of its dedication. This building did not have the air of an institution rather it was a home (Adams House, no date). Lydia continued to give of herself at this point in her life.

11

Mary Swift, Advocate of Education for the Deaf and Blind and Founder of the Boston Young Women's Christian Association

Although Mary left teaching as paid employment once she married, she remained actively involved in the field of education and social reform for the remainder of her life. With this work, she juggled the responsibilities of raising three children, attending to their activities, educational pursuits, and overseeing their general well-being. In these endeavors, she also continued to maintain and draw from the connections she formed as a normal school student.

Following her work at the Perkins Institution, Mary maintained communication with Samuel Gridley Howe. On occasion, Howe organized meetings and reunions for those who taught at Perkins to which Mary was invited. If unable to attend, she felt regret (M. S. Lamson, personal communication, July 10, 1861). Though Mary no longer worked as a teacher of the deaf and blind, she found that her guidance and advice were sought because of her experience at

Normalites, pages 165–183
Copyright © 2014 by Information Age Publishing
All rights of reproduction in any form reserved.

Perkins. In 1864, for example, she was approached by Mrs. James Cushing of Boston to help her find an instructor for her child, Fanny, who was deaf. Mrs. Cushing had been told about Mary by the Honorable L. L. Dudley, a member of the Massachusetts legislature. He himself took Mrs. Cushing to meet Mary (DeLand, 1908, p. 35). Mary subsequently recommended Harriet Rogers, the sister of Eliza Rogers with whom Mary had studied with at the normal school. Harriet also had completed her normal school studies following Mary and Eliza. In generating this recommendation, Mary likely conferred with Eliza, who was teaching for the Freedman's Bureau in the 1860s. Through the connections that they formed as normalites, Mary was able to draw on their support and suggest a recommendation for Mrs. Cushing. Harriet took the position for which Mary had recommended her.

In the 1860s, there was growing interest in the oral method of instruction for deaf children. It was considered a controversial method of teaching. Advocates of sign language viewed that method as a natural language for the deaf. Others, however, viewed speech as the first priority. Harriet Rogers obtained information about lip reading, the oral method of instruction, and the modes of instruction utilized at the Institution for the Deaf and Dumb in Berlin, Germany. The school drew from the teachings of Samuel Heinicke who had developed an oral methodology for deaf education. Harriet also received advice about the oral method of instruction from a Mrs. Henry Lippitt who taught speech to her deaf daughter who had lost her hearing due to scarlet fever (DeLand, 1908, p. 35). Overall, however, relatively little was known about this type of instruction in the United States in the mid-1860s. Though Harriet had not taught deaf children prior to Fanny Cushing, she achieved success using the oral mode of instruction.

Harriet ultimately hoped to teach a larger group of students using oral techniques, and contacted Mary Swift Lamson for help. Mary, whose social connections and cache had risen after her marriage, subsequently arranged a meeting at her house on Beacon Street in Boston in 1865 at which Harriet Rogers was introduced to Gardiner Hubbard of Boston, President Thomas Hill of Harvard College, the Reverend Norris Kirk, Samuel Gridley Howe, and others. Harriet brought her pupil, Fanny Cushing, and was able to show the group her pupil's progress. The evidence was convincing and Reverend Kirk drew up a statement that subsequently was publicized in a Boston paper and in others.

Certificate

The subscribers have witnessed the examination of a child nine years old, a deaf-mute under the instruction of Miss Harriet B. Rogers, who entirely substitutes the voice or articulation for the sign language. From the results of this experiment we feel authorized to recommend Miss Rogers and her method, and to encourage her in forming a class.

Thomas Hill
Edward Kirk
John D. Philbrick
Henry M. Dexter
James C. Dunn
Gardiner Hubbard
Lewis B. Munroe

(as cited in DeLand, 1908, pp. 37–38)

An advertisement in the Boston paper read:

Private Instruction for Deaf Mutes

Miss Rogers proposes to take a few deaf mutes as pupils for instruction in articulation and reading from the lips, without the use of signs or the finger-language. The number is limited to seven, two of whom are already engaged. Immediate applications must be sent to Harriet B. Rogers, North Billerica, Mass.

References
Thomas Hill, D.D., President Harvard College
S. G. Howe, M.D., Superintendent Institution for the Blind
Edward N. Kirk, D.D.
John D. Philbrick, Superintendent Public Schools
Henry M. Dexter, D.D.
James C. Dunn, Esq.
Gardiner G. Hubbard, Esq.
Lewis B. Munroe, Professor of Elocution
James Cushing, Esq., 101 Devonshire Street
Mrs. Edwin Lamson, 5 Beacon Street

(as cited in DeLand, 1908, pp. 37–38)

In Massachusetts social circles, this was deemed an exceptionally prestigious endorsement of Harriet Rogers and her work with deaf children using the oral mode of instruction. Mary Swift, referred to as Mrs. Edwin Lamson, was the only woman listed among the esteemed group that she herself had convened (DeLand, 1908, pp. 37–39).

During this same time period, the Massachusetts General Court was petitioned by Samuel Gridley Howe to formally establish a school for the deaf where the oral method would be used. The petition was stifled. Nevertheless Harriet Rogers established a small private school in Chelmsford, Massachusetts. Gardiner Hubbard, who had attended the meeting at Mary's house, had a deaf daughter, Mabel, who subsequently attended Harriet's school (Bruce, 1973, p. 86). Hubbard thereafter became a strong supporter of the school, "the first regularly organized school for the deaf" in the country using the oral method of instruction (DeLand, 1908, p. 39). Hubbard not only provided financial assistance, but also his time to help make the school a success. By 1867, there were eight pupils in attendance (DeLand, 1908, p. 39). The endorsement of Harriet's school in the Boston newspaper brought officials of institutions for the deaf from other states to visit and observe. Since the method was controversial, some visitors thought it was wasteful of time and money. Others, however, highly appreciated the value of the new system of instruction and gradually introduced it in their respective institutions (DeLand, 1908, p. 40). Some of the students in Harriet's school went on to lead noteworthy lives. Pupil Mabel Hubbard, for example, would later marry and serve as an inspiration for Alexander Graham Bell, inventor of the telephone.

Mary continued to be called to serve in roles of guidance, oversight and supervision in educational and social initiatives. In 1871, for example, she was asked to serve on the advisory board to the trustees of the Industrial School for Girls in Lancaster, Massachusetts. The request, written on official stationery from the Commonwealth of Massachusetts, came from Governor William Claflin. The institution had been established to be a home and school for girls who were "vagrants, perversely obstinate or guilty of petty offences, or without proper guardians, and exposed to a life of wretchedness and crime" (Board of the State Industrial School for Girls, 1866, p. 7). The school may have been established as a result of circumstances connected with increased industrialization and connected poverty for specific groups. The school was run as a family school and a refuge, where girls could be properly instructed in useful and appropriate forms of female industry. After girls had been at the institution for a length of time and their dispositions had become known to the matrons, they could be indentured. This seems to have contrasted with the ideals that the institution would not be viewed as a prison. To be indentured was a type of debt bondage. In return for room and board, the girls were expected to provide labor, including the maintenance of a one hundred and forty acre farm owned by the Institution. Girls committed to the school by the state would be kept, disciplined, instructed and employed under the direction of the trustees until bound out or until reaching the age of eighteen. In some instances, the trustees of the institution could hold a girl until the age of 21, and serve as guardian with all related power and authority. Though the trustees for the Institution were all men, the special advisory board on which Mary served, consisted of three women. Mary served along with an Annie Endicott and Mary Claflin, wife of the Governor of Mas-

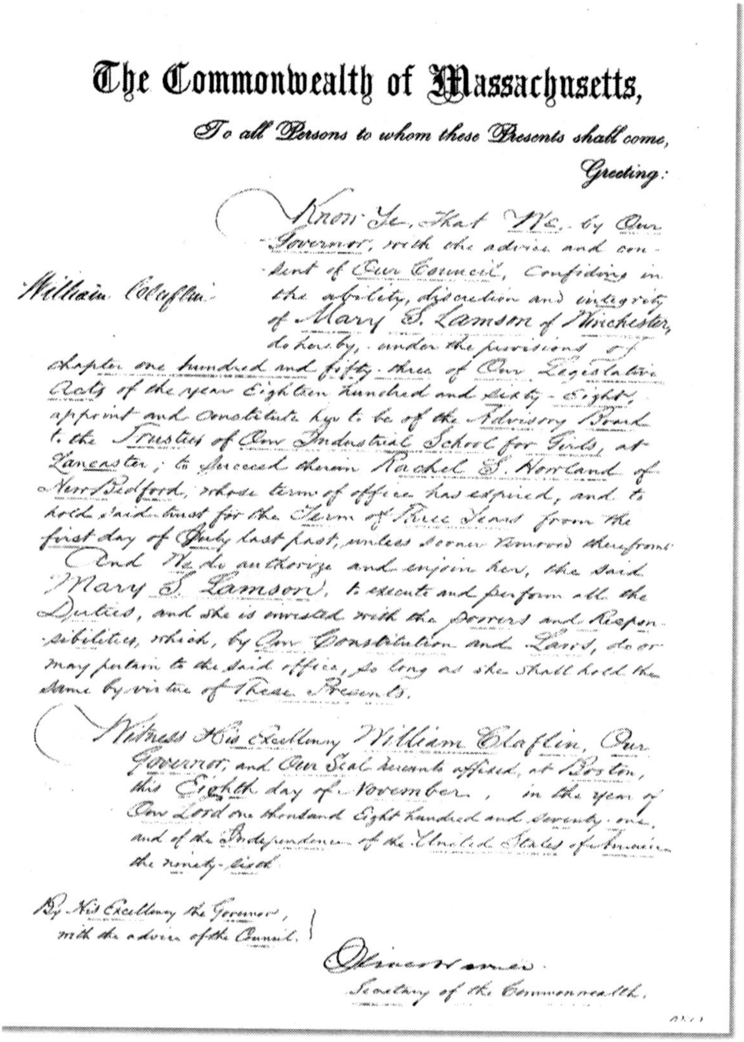

The Commonwealth of Massachusetts,

To all Persons to whom these Presents shall come,

Greeting:

William Claflin

Know Ye, That We, by Our Governor, with the advice and consent of Our Council, confiding in the ability, discretion and integrity of Mary S. Lamson of Winchester, do hereby, under the provisions of chapter one hundred and fifty-three of Our Legislative Acts of the year Eighteen hundred and sixty-eight, appoint and constitute her to be of the Advisory Board to the Trustees of Our Industrial School for Girls, at Lancaster; to succeed therein Rachel S. Howland of New Bedford, whose term of office has expired, and to hold said trust for the Term of Three Years from the first day of July last past, unless sooner removed therefrom.

And We do authorize and enjoin her, the said Mary S. Lamson, to execute and perform all the Duties, and she is invested with the powers and Responsibilities, which, by Our Constitution and Laws, do or may pertain to the said office, so long as she shall hold the same by virtue of These Presents.

Witness His Excellency William Claflin, Our Governor, and Our Seal hereunto affixed, at Boston, this Eighth day of November, in the year of Our Lord one thousand Eight hundred and seventy-one, and of the Independence of the United States of America the ninety-sixth.

By His Excellency the Governor, with the advice of the Council.

Oliver Warner

Secretary of the Commonwealth.

Figure 11.1 Courtesy of the Independent Association of Framingham State Alumni, Framingham, MA.

sachusetts (Board of the State Industrial School for Girls, 1866). The special advisory committee had no formal vote with trustee meetings. Nonetheless, they helped shape policy and yielded considerable influence with the overseers (State Board of Charity of Massachusetts, 1874, p. 9). By 1877, however, Mary's role evolved and she became an official trustee for the Institution (Gifford & Marden, 1876, p. 243).

During this general time Mary also became aware of the efforts that had been undertaken in New York to assist the "working girls" of that city. Members of New York's elite society thought that these young women, who worked in factories or as domestic help, often boarded in the attics of houses whose lower stories were filled with young men. These arrangements at times led to temptation, a loss of virginity, which most of New York's elite considered regrettable. In response, a group of Christian women at New York's Broadway Tabernacle, the church at which the Reverend Charles Finney had begun his preaching, organized themselves to care for the moral and religious welfare of women. They held weekly meetings and founded the first Women's Christian Association, subsequently opening a boarding house for working women in 1860 (Lamson, 1893, pp. 3–4).

Mary Swift Lamson believed that the circumstances and needs in Boston were similar to those in New York. In 1858, a wealthy Bostonian named Lucretia Boyd had reached a similar conclusion, and had prepared a statement on behalf of the hundreds of young women in the city, which she presented to Charles Scudder, who was the President of the Boston Missionary Society. She wrote:

> In the course of my labors in a religious capacity, I have been made acquainted with the wants of a very numerous and respectable class of young women, whom I have desired to benefit religiously, socially, and intellectually; but in the main have failed to do so. Among this important class, who have taken up their abode with us, either transiently or permanently, is a limited number who have been religiously educated, and who have sufficient *inherent strength* and *principle*, to resist the downward tendency of city life. (L. Boyd, personal communication, 1858)

In Boyd's appeal to Scudder, she asked "Cannot something be done by our Benevolent Ladies, that shall remain a permanent Institution? . . . We would speak of the reciprocal, temporal benefit, of such an enterprise, were not the Inspiration of the Hope of turning many to righteousness, paramount to all things else" (L. Boyd, personal communication, 1858). It is unknown if Boyd received a response to this particular letter to Scudder.

At around the same time that Lucretia Boyd had written to Scudder, she had also asked Mary and a few others to consider their duty to the "working girls" in the city. Mary immediately recognized the need to organize. In addition to helping women find adequate shelter, the envisioned association would help them find suitable employment, establish a prayer meeting room, provide social meetings, create a literary department and form a visiting committee. Mary would later write:

In November of 1858 Mrs. Boyd (Lucretia) called on me "to lay before me the condition of the many working girls in this city who were strangers here and had come simply to earn an honest living." She then showed me a memorandum book with pages of names of girls living in her district, which she visited as a Missionary of the Boston City Mission, and comprised Chamber St. and the neighborhood. She spent a couple of hours with me telling of facts that she had learned in the previous year or two, and from these she said she was warranted in saying that nearly one half of the girls on the lists would be led astray unless something could be done to place some additional protection about them. The City Mission was doing what it could but far more was necessary, and then in her peculiarly earnest way she brought the question home to me. "Is it not true that the Christian Women of Boston do something for their sisters who are strangers among them, and can not you start some movement?"

With this she left me and at once commenced my teachings which I could only look upon as providential. Every day it seemed as if someone had been sent to tell me some incident learning on the subject, until at last I was so overpowered with it and yet so physically unable to do anything. I prayed for rest. My youngest child was born and still even in my sick room my teachings continued and as soon as I was able I began to try to find some ladies who would join me in studying up the subject and acting upon the results. (M. S. Lamson, personal communication, November 3, 1884)

The formation of an association for the improvement of Boston's working women was an endeavor that Mary believed would help elevate the conditions of women in the city. She felt that she was called on and divinely guided to do this work. This may have connected with her Quaker upbringing. Ideas to "Live to the Truth" also had influenced her through her interactions with her teacher, Cyrus Peirce. Mary was surprised and dismayed, however, when this first attempt to form such an association met strong opposition from an unexpected quarter. The Young Men's Christian Association had been established in Boston eight years previously. When the women proposed the organization of the Women's Christian Association, the clergy of various denominations viewed such an addition to church-supported benevolent associations as a threat, speculating that the work might result in further diminishment of focus by congregational members on their own churches. A letter of protest was sent from the clergy to the leaders of the proposed establishment (Lamson, 1893). Mary and her peers had intended to begin their organizing work the very next week, but after they received the message from the leading clergy in Boston, they were forced to refrain.

Mary Swift Lamson later wrote about these circumstances. In addition to viewing the benevolent associations as a potential diminishment of focus by congregational members on their own churches, clergy saw it as an unpleasant connection with the "fallen."

Twenty-five years ago, few women thought their duties extended beyond their houses and churches and I begged for help for months in vain, always calling on people who were in any way brought to my mind. At last a note from Mrs. Abuer Kingman (Anderson) was received saying she had heard what I was trying to do, had been long praying that some one might be raised up for the work and would be very glad to aid me in any way she could. About the same time other ladies expressed their willingness to co-operate. Mrs. Kingman & myself in consultation decided that for a work so new it would be very desirable to have on our list of managers the names of the wives of some prominent clergy men of the city & we divided the denominations each of us taking two to call upon. We thought it wisest to lay the matter before their husbands also.

I called on Rev. Edwin Johnson and he entirely disapproved of the whole matter, objecting to it on the grounds of it being likely to bring us into unpleasant connection with the fallen etc. and especially that the churches ought to be doing their work. He concluded the conversation by saying that he should not be willing that his wife should give her name. My next call was on Rev. Mr. Stockbridge, Baptist, and was a repetition of the preceding. Mrs. Kingman had no better success with her Episcopalian but a hearty "Good speed" from Rev. Mr. Dadmuer of the Methodist Church. Amazed and puzzled by this aspect of things, as the thought had never occurred to us that we should have anything but a most cordial endorsement from the clergy. I went with confidence to my own pastor Mr. Stow, only to find that he disapproved on similar grounds. The next Monday it was discussed at the Minister's meeting and word was sent me by Mr. Stow that the thing must stop. Darkness shut down upon me and I could not then see for what all the lessons of a year had been given me. Was God or man to be doubted? (M. S. Lamson, personal communication, November 3, 1884)

During the seven years that followed the clergy-based opposition to the first attempt to form such an organization, no progress was made on the Young Women's Christian Association in Boston. The well-being of working girls also seemed to decline in the city. Mary and others subsequently wondered if a change of sentiment might have occurred among the clergy and again broached the topic of starting the Young Women's Christian Association. A change of sentiment had taken place and with the hearty cooperation of the clergy, the Young Women's Christian Association was formed in 1866.

Seven years went by and then I received an invitation to attend a prayer meeting called by a lady working among fallen women not connected with any society who was overwhelmed by the condition of things in the city. Absence from town prevented my attendance. She told her stories and the result was that those present asked divine guidance as to what could be done, the impression being that the remedy must be applied before the fall. One lady present remembered my interest in the subject and suggested that I could probably tell them just what to do and I was invited to attend the next meeting. The old plans for work were presented and accepted and in a month we were ready to form the Board and had secured Mrs. Durant's acceptance of the presidency. March 1866 was the date of the organization. M. S. Lamson. November 3/84. (M. S. Lamson, personal communication, November 3, 1884)

Mary was a leader and founding member of the Boston Young Women Christian Association, along with several other elite and socially conscious women who had ties with Boston Protestant churches. The goal of the association was to do all things possible for the elevation of women—physically, mentally, morally, and spiritually. A boarding home was opened in Boston. Classes were organized that focused on book keeping, typing and stenography. Libraries and reading rooms opened in various locations. Bible classes and prayer meetings were held. On April 11, 1867, the Boston Young Women's Christian Association was officially incorporated and recognized by the House of Representatives in Massachusetts. The first annual meeting of the association was held in the Old South Chapel, in Freeman Place, on March 4, 1867. The Honorable William Claflin, then Lieutenant Governor of Massachusetts, presided over the meeting. Mary Swift was elected to serve as one of the six vice presidents (Board of the Young Women's Christian Association, 1867, pp. 3–4). Another vice president was the wife of Lieutenant Governor Claflin. A Mrs. Henry Durant was elected president. Meetings of the Board of Managers were held on the first Monday of every month (Board of the Young Women's Christian Association, 1867, p. 6). Mary became a life member of the Boston Young Women's Christian Association in 1867 and two years later, her daughters, Helen and Kate, also were recorded as becoming life members (Board of the Young Women's Christian Association, 1869, p. 29). Mary remained involved with the association for the next 40 years. Between 1882 and 1905 she was listed as serving on a special executive committee of the organization (Board of the Young Women's Christian Association, 1882, 1889, 1890, 1896, 1898, 1899, 1902, 1904, 1905). Between 1882 and 1906, a period of 24 years, she also served consecutively as a vice president (Board of the Young Women's Christian Association, 1882, 1889, 1890, 1896, 1898, 1899, 1902, 1904, 1905).

Although the association aimed to support the elevation of all women, there were some restrictions. For example, full YWCA membership required church membership. The constitution of the Young Women's Christian Association stated that "Any Christian woman, who is a member in regular standing of an Evangelical church, may become an active member of this Association, by the payment of one dollar, annually. Active members only shall have the right to vote, and be eligible for office. Any young woman of good moral character, may become an associate member of this Association, by the payment of one dollar, annually" (Board of the

Young Women's Christian Association, 1867, p. 4). Upon applying, women needed to present two letters of reference attesting to their character. An implicit understanding was that applicants must be Protestant women (Cote, 2004). Although membership requirements were explicitly stated, a review of the annual reports suggests that the formalities of membership did not always preclude other women from receiving services from the association.

After the Young Women's Christian Association was officially started in Boston, Mary communicated with women in other cities throughout the United States to encourage expansion of the movement. Soon, similar undertakings were underway in Providence, Hartford, Cleveland, Minneapolis, and St. Louis. By 1870, ten cities had established a Young Women Christian Association. Yearly conferences of the associations began to be held. Connections were established in Europe, and Mary attended meetings of the International Young Women's Christian Association. At the Columbian World Exposition in Chicago in 1893, aimed to celebrate the 400th anniversary of Christopher Columbus' arrival in the New World, Mary was present to read the history of the Young Women's Christian Association (Lamson, 1893).

In an 1874 letter to family friend Charles Finney, Mary's husband, Edwin, wrote, "Mary's time as *usual* is much occupied—much time is devoted to the Y. Womens C. Asso" (E. Lamson, personal communication, August 5, 1874). Edwin continued to serve as a deacon at Park Street Church. He had, however, officially retired from his merchant and ship business in 1868. When he retired, he, Mary and their children traveled to Europe where they spent several years. They also purchased a mansion in Winchester, Massachusetts during that time. The family had acquired wealth as a result of Edwin's business. In a *New York Times* article on November 3, 1851, titled "Sixteen Days Later From California: Arrival of the Cherokee Over Two Millions of Gold," Edwin Lamson and his business partner, Twombly, were listed as receiving shares from proceeds of the California Gold Rush.

In a letter to Charles Finney in 1870, Edwin described his new home, but he also indicated that he did not know if they would remain there long term.

Boston 2 Nov. 1870

My Dear Rev. Finney,

We arrived at our home in Winchester 8 miles from Boston . . . Since then we have been occupied with various duties. It is our legal place of abode, but, what the future will require of us, we have little idea now.

(E. Lamson, personal communication, November 2, 1870)

In this letter Edwin also reflected on their easy life in Europe in comparison with that which they faced in America. He suggested that he went to Park Street Church less frequently and that he felt some displeasure with the minister. He also wrote that Mary largely was occupied with organizational work. In addition to her work with the Young Women's Christian Association, Mary had become a school committee member in Winchester. Edwin described to Finney the threshold that was crossed by that new responsibility.

> And lastly she is one of the school committee of Winchester chosen for 2 years. She did not see how she could find the time for this new appointment but the public will was too strong to be disregarded. That not to accept endangered it was thought the experiment of having this trust shared by the sexes in common. Between you and me, there was unmistakable need of such a change. It cannot issue them otherwise in good to the schools. Two other ladies are associated with her in connection with as many gentlemen. (E. Lamson, personal communication, November 2, 1870)

In this same correspondence, Edwin also mentioned the possibility of sending their son, Gardner, to Oberlin to study, but he wrote to Finney that Gardner had decided on another course of action. Edwin felt somewhat apologetic to Finney, when discussing Gardner's life choice of a vocation. Gardner's choice was still evolving and by 1874 he would finish his first year at Harvard (Harvard College, 1940).

Mary had grown to know that changes take place in both professional and private circles and that life is accompanied by loss. Her father had died in November of 1866. In February of 1876, she received notice that Samuel Gridley Howe had died (Trent, 2012, p.1). He was a man who had a powerful influence on Mary's life. Mary wrote a letter to Laura Dewey Bridgman and in return received a response. Laura wrote:

> There is good comfort [and] in it much sunshine, though it tries my feelings in [the] thought of never meeting & grasping my best & noble friend Dr. Howe on earth. The path seems so desolate & void without sight of him to us all . . . I think much of Dr. H. day & night with sorrow & gratitude & love & sincerity. (as cited in Trent, 2012, p. 3)

Six months later notification arrived that Mary and Edwin's friend, the Reverend Charles Finney, also had died. Mary and her husband had desired to see him before his death, but circumstances prevented it. Edwin, grieved by his death, immediately began to compose a letter that could be read at Finney's funeral. In that letter, Edwin reflected on Finney's great ministerial work, as well as on his strong misgivings about the work of the controversial Reverend Theodore Parker from Boston. Edwin, as well as Charles Finney, was part of the group who considered Parker a heretic. They had tried to stop some of his orations at Music Hall in Boston (Grodzins, 2002). They were in opposition to those, including Mary's close friends from the normal school and Mary's mentor Samuel Gridley Howe, who considered Parker a saint.

Yet, this series of losses had not yet come to their conclusion. On the next day after hearing of Finney's death, after an illness of only half an hour, Mary's husband, Edwin Lamson died of a heart attack. Edwin's obituary appeared in numerous newspapers in Massachusetts and in New York.

> Deacon Edwin Lamson. The many friends of this well-known gentleman will regret to hear of his sudden death on Sunday at his residence in Winchester under circumstances that forcibly illustrate the uncertainty of life. He had been of late in his usual robust health and on Sunday morning attended church. On retiring to his chamber at night he appeared in excellent spirits, conversing pleasantly with his wife and giving no indication of the slightest indisposition. A few minutes afterwards he started up suddenly, complaining of great heat and distress in his chest. A cordial was administered to revive him, but he grew worse and in a half an hour of the attack he expired. A physician was called but death ensued before his arrival. The cause of his death is attributed to the stagnation of blood in some of his principal arteries, the attack being of an apoplectic nature. An autopsy will be held tomorrow. (unknown author, 1876)

Edwin was 65 years old when he died. Mary, at 54 years, was a widow and mother of three children; her son Gardner was due to graduate from Harvard College that year, having first prepared at the Greylock Institute in South Williamstown (Harvard College, 1940). The Finney letter, penned by Edwin, subsequently was sent to Reverend Finney's funeral without signature. Mary was in shock. It took some time before she could write about it to others. Following her husband's death, she received letters from Laura Dewey Bridgman. Mary's former student from the Perkins Institution offered her support during one of her times of greatest grief.

> Hanover Oct. 13th 1876
>
> My Dear Mrs. Lamson,
>
> I am sitting up in my snug room & feeling the gladdening ray of sun which is more beneficial in my frail health than the heat of fire that is built by the hand of man. Your letter came to me with ardent welcome last evening. I longed for a reply from you many times but thinking of not your feeling disposed to write why for a long while after the grievous event of decease of your dear husband. I fear that you did not feel really able to write a long letter though I thank you truly for making the great effort to write so much for my comfort & happiness. I hope that you will be well & strong by the spirit of grace of our heavenly Father.
>
> (L. D. Bridgman, personal communication, October 13, 1876)

Following Edwin's death, there likely were times when Mary looked at the portraits in their home that had been painted of the both of them by Matthew Wilson, an English artist who had immigrated to the United States (Fehrenbacher & Fehrenbacher, 1966, p. 503). Wilson had been commissioned to paint President Abraham Lincoln's portrait in 1865. The portraits Wilson had painted of Mary and Edwin were small in size, but of a beautiful quality.

Figure 11.2   Mrs. Mary Swift Lamson. Courtesy of the Massachusetts Historical Society, Boston, MA.

Figure 11.3   Mr. Edwin Lamson. Courtesy of the Massachusetts Historical Society, Boston, MA.

Following her husband's death, Mary began to write and eventually published a book about Laura Dewey Bridgman entitled *Laura Dewey Bridgman: The Deaf, Dumb and Blind Girl.* She had remained in touch with Laura since she first served as her teacher. Laura continued to reside at the Perkins Institution throughout her adult life, a place that Mary could travel to for visits. Mary also had developed strong academic skills and was equipped to manage the writing project about Laura. In writing the book, Mary acknowledged her debt to Samuel Gridley Howe. She suggested that she had received requests from across the country to write the book so that the work undertaken with Laura would not be lost. In the preface to her book she wrote:

> Most reluctantly have I yielded to these requests, appreciating fully my own inability to fill the place which rightfully belonged to him who first devised a way to pour light into a mind thus darkened. My aim will be simply to state facts, and in making selections from the daily reports of her teachers to omit nothing which can be of service to any department of science. (Lamson, 1881, p. xxxi)

Mary's book was reviewed widely in publications such as *The Academy: A Weekly Review of Literature, Science and Art* a publication out of London, *The Atlantic Monthly, The Dial: A Monthly Review and Index of Current Literature, Trubner & Companies Monthly List,* and *The Critic.* Mary's book was judged to be a critical and popular success. The Critic review stated that, "this profoundly interesting book can hardly fail to find a hearty welcome where-ever the miracle of Laura Bridgman's education has ever been heard of. Mrs. Lamson writes from full knowledge, having been her special instructor for three years, and intimately acquainted with her for thirty-seven years" (The Critic, 1881, pp. 118–119). In future years, *Laura Dewey Bridgman: The Deaf, Dumb and Blind Girl* would be referenced when other books about Bridgman were written. Mary would be referred to in encyclopedias of education and handbooks of psychology.

The book largely was a record of diary entries which Mary had written while she was Laura's teacher, along with entries of journals kept by some of Laura's other teachers. While working with Laura, Mary had grown accustomed to keeping paper and pencil at hand so she could record words and phrases of interest to Laura. In her book, Mary also referenced Howe's published reports of his work with Laura, some of which were nearly out of print (Lamson, 1881).

After the book was published Mary, along with her two daughters, Helen and Kate, traveled back to Europe. There she wrote long, extensive letters to her family, at times reflecting on the general reception of her book about Laura. In one letter, she discussed a review that Professor Stanley

Hall had written in the *New York Nation*. Hall was a pioneering psychologist whose work focused on childhood development. He had received the first doctorate in psychology in the United States, awarded by Harvard College. After leaving Harvard, he studied at the University of Berlin.

> I have also had another letter from Prof. Hall who is in Berlin. He says he has written a review of my book for the N. York Nation & that the editor of Mind—a London paper has requested him to prepare an article on Laura for that paper for Jan. 7. He does not know yet whether he wishes a review or an independent article. If any of you see the Nation send it to me please. I have written him a long letter in answer to his this morning. I have a pile of unanswered letters which makes me groan but I am trying to get off one a day until they are done. (M. S. Lamson, personal communication, unknown date)

It appeared, in his letters, that Hall questioned Mary's book and whether she had left out information that might have changed the narrative. Mary answered Professor Hall's inquiries in a subsequent letter dated October 14, 1878.

> Dear Sir,
>
> Yours of the 6th was duly received, and I thank you for your kind expressions of interest in my book. I should like to read your review in the Nation but suppose that paper is not to be had here.
>
> To yourself & also those who are making a study of Laura, I do not doubt that the whole . . . would have had interest, but I was writing for the general reader. I was therefore obliged to call from my store thing of greatest interest, that the story need not be tediously long. Were all my own & Laura's journals printed, there would have been two volumes instead of one. My aim was, however, to omit nothing which I could see had any bearing on any question in psychology. The temptation was great to express my opinions more freely on various subjects but I decided that it was better to let the story tell itself in as simple a manner as possible.
>
> Perhaps you are not aware that at the time when Laura was my pupil there was much feeling on the question of the methods of teaching deaf . . . Each year when Dr. Howe's reports appeared there was great interest amongst all deaf mute teachers to know what the year's teaching had done for her & sometimes there were very hard things said even to the expression of a doubt whether Dr. Howe were telling the truth about her progress. Although this is a thing of the past, yet many of the same men still live & in my selections writing I had always in view the desirability of so connecting the account of her intellectual training & coursework development, as to carry to the minds of this class of readers the conviction of the entire truth of the details. All this to you may have no interest. I mention it only to share you my reasons for making selections as I did. I hope that your comparison of the book with the journals in the matter of things selected for insertion

or omission does not leave in your mind an impression of unfairness in any particular, for certainly my only aim was to be entirely candid....Your trouble seems to be in discrepancies you find. If I knew on what pages of the book they occur I could probably explain it satisfactorily. I made use of her own journals, sometimes I have omitted sentences & have not always put the . . . between thinking in this case it was not necessary, as I wished to give all that she had written on our subject connectedly . . . I went carefully over the journals that Anagnos knew of & failed to find in these source things which had already been printed in Dr. Howe's reports. This led me to a second revision with the aim to fix the dates when these journals were written.

(M. S. Lamson, personal communication, October 14, 1878)

Mary's children continued to be a strong focus in her life. Her daughter, Helen, studied music at the Conservatorium fur Musik in Stuttgart. She was developing into a very accomplished pianist. Kate in contrast took a strong interest in the efforts of the Young Women's Christian Association. Gardner Lamson eventually became an opera singer (Harvard College, 1940).

Mary and her daughters, traveled extensively in Europe during this period. While in Bologna, Italy they visited a cathedral that Mary thought was beautiful. They traveled to see the Passion Play in Germany. Throughout this time, Mary continued to correspond with Laura, whose health was increasingly frail.

Boston, Jan. 26 79

My Dear Mrs. Lamson,

I wish you a gay New Year & Christmas. It is a great task for me to write this letter because my health is so frail. I cannot accomplish as much as I should like for it tires my nerves more than it used to. I was ill in bed a few days in Dec. The Dr. called on me . . . I suffer more ill spells. . . . Your letter was joyfully received at my home in Aug or before. I sold a few books for 2 dollars & pieces. I had a letter & a check from Mrs. Hubbard awhile ago. . . . Last Thursday Mrs. Morton called on me. Is well. We spoke of you specially . . .

Your loving friend,

Laura

(L. D. Bridgman, personal communication, January 26, 1879)

The trip to Europe was a period of recovery for Mary, a healing from the loss of her husband. The active period of Mary's own life, however, had not concluded. On a subsequent return trip to Europe in 1889, Mary received a letter from Harriet Rogers, sister of Eliza Rogers, regarding a blind and deaf child named Ragnhild Kaata. At the age of 16, Ragnhild Kaata had been admitted to the Institute for the Deaf at Hamar, Norway, and her instructor, Elias H. Hofgaard, was teaching the child to learn to speak through the touch of the lips. While in Europe, Mary arranged to meet with Kaata and her instructor. What she learned from these interactions later shaped Mary's role in encouraging Helen Keller to learn to orally communicate with the outside world (Deland, 1908).

When Mary returned to the United States in 1889, she set out at once to meet Helen Keller to tell her about the Norwegian child whom she had met. Helen had come to the Perkins Institution in 1888, after she had started to work with her teacher Anne Sullivan in 1887. Helen's introduction to the Perkins Institution came about through Alexander Graham Bell whose wife, Mabel Hubbard, attended Harriet Rogers' school. Mary had been influential in starting this school. Helen's teacher, Anne Sullivan, was present at the meeting with Mary in 1889. When Mary shared the news about the Norwegian child, Helen responded with earnestness. She wanted to improve her conversational powers. In *The Story of My Life*, a book that Helen Keller would later write, she revealed that "Mrs. Lamson had scarcely finished telling me about the girls' success before I was on fire with eagerness" (Keller, 2010, p. 59) Although Helen would later write enthusiastically about her interactions with Mary, it is unclear how enthusiastic Helen Keller's teacher, Anne Sullivan, was about the course of events. Helen said that she would not rest satisfied until her teacher took her to meet with Miss Sarah Fuller who was the principal of the Horace Mann School. Miss Fuller thereafter taught Helen Keller to speak, with lessons starting in March of 1890. In a letter that Sullivan subsequently wrote to Mr. Anagnos, son-in-law of Samuel Howe, she described how Helen learned to speak and how she had been exposed to religion.

Tuscombia, July 7, 1890

Dear Mr. Anagnos,

I cannot seal this letter without telling you how very sorry I am that you did not have the pleasure of hearing first from Helen herself that she had learned to talk. You certainly had a right to expect that you would be kept informed of Helen's doings and you should have been was it not for an odd lot of circumstances which combined to prevent. You must not think that is was due to thoughtlessness on Helen's part for it was not. She said many times how delighted Mr. Anagnos will be when he hears my beautiful secret. And if you had received a letter which I sent, more than a month ago you would understand that I did not intentionally keep the good news from you. But I have not the heart to enter into details which are so unpleasant again. I see no reason why my letter failed to reach you. It seems especially strange as you mention in your last letter to Helen having received a paper from Miss Lane which was mailed several days later than my letter.

I enclose a letter which I sent to the trustees before leaving Boston. It explains itself. No one can regret more than I do your absence from home this year. I wish you could have watched Helen's wonderful development—as I have done. . . .

You will see from her letter that she knows about God. It was impossible to keep the knowledge from any longer. She had met with so many references to religious things in books that her curiosity was awakened. What could I do but satisfy her thirst for this new knowledge in as broad and Christian way as I could. I went to Mr. Brooks for advice and I found him very willing to help both Helen and myself. I shall guard Helen very carefully against those notions and opinions which made Laura's religion so repulsive to all but the most narrow of Christians.

Please excuse me for taking so much of your time, and believe me,

Very truly yours,

Anne Sullivan

(A. Sullivan, personal communication, July 7, 1890)

As Mary provided encouragement to Helen Keller to learn to orally speak, her daughter Kate continued to work with the Young Women Christian Association, and attended the Bible readings regularly. There Kate met Anna Wade, daughter of parents who had been slaves. This event too would shape Mary's remaining years.

Born in 1862 in Georgia, Anna described the white family to whom her mother belonged as kind and humane. After emancipation, Anna and her family continued to live with this family who then paid wages and fed them. The family taught Anna to read, write, and spell. She recalled that she read the works of Scott, Shakespeare, and Milton.

The white children from this family eventually went to college and Anna remembered dreaming that she might also go one day. Instead, at age 13 she took an exam for a teaching license in Georgia before assuming her first school of 50 children. At age 13, however, she was still a child herself. With the money earned from teaching school, Anna subsequently was able to attend Atlanta University, founded in 1865 by the American Missionary Association, where she studied for several years. Atlanta University and Clark College later merged in 1988 to form Clark Atlanta University.

Needing respite from a nervous condition, Anna Wade had traveled to Boston for free medical care. While in Boston, she studied at the Girls' High and Latin School and eventually met Kate Lamson, Mary's daughter, who she described as her "loving friend." After two years in Boston, Anna returned to Georgia where she started a school for African American children, which quickly grew in numbers. Funds for the school were needed and subsequently were received from the Young Women's Christian Association and the American Missionary Association. The Lamson family was closely connected to the Young Women's Christian Association, and Kate Lamson had become affiliated with The American Missionary Association. The school that Anna Wade started received financial assistance from Kate, likely with help from Mary. Mary's interest and involvement with this school, subsequently named the Lamson Normal School, was one of the final undertakings of her life. Anna Wade later wrote "A Word to The Friends of Lamson Normal School," and suggested, "I shall pass through this world but once. Any good thing therefore that I can do, or any kindness that I can show to any human being, let me do it now. Let me not defer it or neglect it, for I shall not pass this way again" (Richardson, 1900). Anna Wade's school eventually was renamed the Lamson-Richardson School, to include the name of Anna's future husband. Over the next century, the school would evolve into a public school in Georgia, offering educational experiences for thousands of school-aged children.

12

Networks, Reunions, Visits, and Legacies

Beginning in 1849, the tenth year after completion of their studies, the first class of the Lexington School normalites started to meet formally each year for reunions, and continued to do this for the remainder of their lives. During these reunions they kept records of their proceedings. At each reunion, they recorded those who were present and maintained copies of the addresses that were given. They preserved notes regarding their peers' professional endeavors, as well as some of the personal activities that were reported. If children joined the normalites at reunions this too was recorded. At these gatherings, the normalites accepted that "changes have come to us, the alterations of joy and sorrow, the full fruition or the disappointment of our most cherished hopes. Yet with our hearts still glowing with their youthful freshness of affection we meet each other today with all the ardor or the disappointment of our most cherished hopes" (Lamson, 1903, p. 2). The normalites reflected on the strength that was needed for the strenuous labor of teaching, they laughed about the study hours that they broke while at the normal school, and they spoke about how much the bonds of friendship meant to each another. As the years passed, when death

Normalites, pages 185–194
Copyright © 2014 by Information Age Publishing
All rights of reproduction in any form reserved.

entered some of their homes, in the depth of distress, their normalite sisters' sympathies had power to sooth the bitter sorrow (Lamson, 1903, p. 3).

When Cyrus Peirce joined the women at these reunions, he often reminded them that they should, "Live to the Truth"—a sentiment they had long ago internalized. At a reunion in the 1850s Louisa Harris reflected on her former teacher's physical condition. She thought that old age and feebleness had "somewhat dimmed the intellectual brightness of him." She thought he was "sinking behind the cloud where he will rise radical and glorified" (L. Harris, personal communication, journal entry, January 15, 1858). The normal school movement had succeeded, however. It was shaping the country in profound ways. Mr. Peirce had played a key role.

In addition to meeting at reunions, the normalites on occasion met for tea. Mr. and Mrs. Peirce remained in contact with them, staying as guests in their homes at times. The normalites also stayed connected through letters. Louisa Harris penned in her journal on July 23, 1857 that "I always look with a kind of morbid anxiety for letters from the old, familiar world I have left" (L. Harris, personal communication, journal entry, July 23, 1857). In 1858, when Louisa's brother Elbridge relocated to Syracuse, New York, she traveled to visit with him and his family and stayed for several weeks, wading in nearby creeks, running from pet cows and enjoying the time with family. While with Elbridge and his family, she received letters, valued notes of correspondence from normalites, including Mary Hall and Addie Ireson. Upon receiving Addie's correspondence she reflected that Addie, well-developed, practical and accomplished in the arts that beautify a home, ought many years ago have become the center of such an institution. Louisa, in contrast recorded in her journal that she thought she was, "born to be a purposeless, aimless, individual, a warf floating hither and thither, finding some . . . pleasures—unlawful, because I have purchased no right to them and that I am filling my destiny most lamentably" (L. Harris, personal communication, journal entry, unknown month, circa 1858). It is unclear which pleasures, deemed unlawful, Louisa meant.

At times, the normalites met for holidays. In 1856 Louisa Harris spent Thanksgiving at Lydia Drew's house in Halifax, Maine (L. Harris, personal communication, journal entry, January 9, 1857). The normalites also traveled on trips together. In 1859, for example, Louisa traveled to Syracuse to her brother Elbridge and his family, crossing the Green Mountains by stage and taking the cars from Manchester to Albany. She wrote that she never spent a happier three weeks in her life. She walked the city streets and shopped in stores. She met a Dr. Cove, a philosopher from Sweden, who kept her up late two nights, expounding and teaching for her special benefit. She wondered why he should deem her worthy. Hannah Damon, a normal school peer, and her sister visited Louisa while in Syracuse. During that trip Louisa also traveled further to visit Niagara Falls and recorded that the Falls looked more glorious every hour that she stayed at them. While a normal school scholar, Louisa Harris and her peers had looked at streams running down hills and wondered about the great Niagara Falls. In 1859, when she was at the Falls, she went out early in the morning to see the sun rise. Crossing the bridge athwart the Falls, she trembled over the rapids, yet saw the advancing sun fill the whole scene until "the mighty rush of the waters seemed perfectly glorified." She recorded in her journal that she watched the "varying aspects of the rainbow, until the perfect arch appeared and I could have looked forever." It was a morning she would remember and be grateful for eternally (L. Harris, personal communication, journal entry, unknown month, 1859).

Eleven members were present at the normal school reunion in 1865. Mary Swift joined the festivities with her husband and three children. Other members came with their spouse and children. Lydia Stow came from Fall River, without her family on that occasion. Hannah Damon, Eliza Rogers, Adeline Ireson, members of the first class, also were in attendance. Like Louisa Harris they were single (Lamson, 1903). Marital status had great importance on how women were viewed in the nineteenth century. Louisa Harris felt discomfort with not having entered into matrimony. However, Addie Ireson, another normal school scholar was not apologetic.

Sadly, by then, death had rendered their ties with some of the normalites. Eliza Pennell, niece of Horace Mann died in 1857 at the age of 35. Her sister Rebecca adopted her child. Rebecca Pennell did not attend the reunion due to distance and to reasons of a more personal nature. In 1857 and 1858 disagreements arose between the religious groups at Antioch College, at which Rebecca was a professor, and led to a general sense of unsettledness. There also were tremendous financial problems at the institution, which led to a lack of regular salaries for the faculty. Pennell's husband, the treasurer of Antioch, was accused of falsifying financial records. His commissions were scrutinized and probed. Subsequently the reputation of Pennell was questioned which led to conflict between Pennell and Horace Mann and subsequently between Pennell and Mary Mann (Kolodny, 2010). Mann grew frail and Rebecca became known to speak in his place. Some questioned whether Pennell, and not Mann, served as president of the college. The stress associated with his work was all consuming for Horace Mann (Kolodny, 2010). In 1859, he died, surrounded by his wife, children and Rebecca (M. Mann, personal communication, September 5, 1859). After Mann's death Rebecca Pennell left Antioch College, with her husband and adopted child and relocated to St. Louis where she worked at the Mary

Institute in Washington University. Her brother, Calvin, secured a job there as school principal, where he was enticed by the promise of a larger salary.

The 1865 normal school reunion was held in the Marlboro Hotel in Boston. Although the weather was rainy and dull on that day, Louisa Harris thought the reunion was pleasant. After a dinner in the main dining room, the normalites read letters from those who were absent from the occasion. Louisa was asked to deliver the address and was pleased to say some remarks. At the reunion, Louisa reflected with her class members that she knew many of their journeys to the reunion had been longer than hers. A day's monotonous ride by rail-car would often leave one feeling weary and seasick. Their attendance was valued, however (Lamson, 1903, p. 102).

During a normal school reunion in 1871 the normalites met on Nantucket. Their teacher, Father Peirce, had died and his wife wanted them to visit his grave. Lydia Stow made the journey from Fall River. Mary Swift made the trip with her daughter Kate (Daisy). Others in attendance included Louisa Harris, Addie Ireson, Sarah Wyman, and her family, Eliza Rogers, and invited guests. They parted for Nantucket from New Bedford, docking at Martha's Vineyard for a few hours and then resumed their voyage and landed in Nantucket in the early evening. At the start of the following morning they met at Mrs. Peirce's home and then traveled to the gravesite of Cyrus Peirce, each carrying a small bouquet of flowers. As they stood at the grave, they remembered his warm character and the influence his life had on theirs. They saw the stunted pines which grew out of the sandy soil surrounding the grave, and the broad blue ocean in the distance that gleamed gloriously (Lamson, 1903, p. 115). The epitaph for Peirce's grave read, "Live to the Truth" (Nantucket Historical Association, 2013). At this reunion, the normalites had settled into the middle years of their lives; they were then between 49 and 51 years old.

In 1889, 50 years had passed since the normalites had commenced their studies. They prepared for one of their final reunions. Throughout all those years the normalites had conversed through letters, traveled for reunions, and attended weddings and funerals when they could. The semicentennial celebration of the first class of students of the first state normal school was held on July 2, 1889 on Bare Hill in Framingham, the new and final location of the school. They convened in Normal Hall. May Hall, a four story structure composed of red bricks with graceful arched entrances, was in the process of being constructed. It was to be the place where they would not only hold one of their final reunions, but in a sense some of their final, formal conversations. Eleven members of the first class still lived and eight were able to attend the event. Mary Swift and Louisa Harris were present. Rebecca Pennell, niece of Horace Mann, made the journey from

Minnesota where she then lived with her adopted child, son of her sister Eliza Pennell. Others, such as Adeline Ireson, traveled a shorter distance to take part in the festivities (Lamson, 1903, p. 169).

Figure 12.1   Normal Hall. Courtesy of Framingham State University, Archives and Special Collections, Framingham, MA.

Figure 12.2   May Hall. Courtesy of Framingham State University, Archives and Special Collections, Framingham, MA.

While preparing for the 50th reunion, Lydia Stow corresponded about her class with Mary Peirce, a student who attended the normal school at a later time. In her letter to Mary, Lydia wrote that she did "not wonder that you are much puzzled over the imperfect records of nearly fifty years ago" (L. Stow, personal communication, April 29, unknown year). She shared that her journal from 1840 was still in existence, though she had several times proposed committing it to the flamer. Drawing from her journal records, she wrote that she would be happy to help contribute to filling out the catalogue of records. In her letter Lydia also shared some reflections on her peers. She recorded that, "Miss Swift was very bright—a great favorite of Father Peirce." She reflected on the normal school movement. "How *slowly* the public became interested in this Normal School. The Board of Education had to stand the fight of ignorant prejudice." She concluded her letter with a personal reflection about her own participation saying that, "Certainly I thank those who directed me in coming under such influences to mould my life, a mortal of the immortal first class" (L. Stow, personal communication, April 29, unknown year).

Lydia Stow died on August 26, 1904. She was 82 years old and had been spending time in a summer home in Tiverton, Rhode Island. She was buried in the Oak Grove Cemetery in Fall River, Massachusetts. After she died, Mary Swift carefully penned notes about her in her copy of *Records of the First Class of the First State Normal School in America Established at Lexington, Massachusetts 1839*. Mary had published a copy of the records in 1903. Mary wrote, "In her death many residents of Fall River realize the departure of one of the most excellent and most useful women of her times" (M. S. Lamson, personal communication, journal entry, unknown date). She suggested that Lydia and her husband had sacrificed social prestige, and given money, time and labor in the promotion of the anti-slavery movement, affording shelter to those who were pursued because they were slaves. "The speaker for freedom was always welcomed to their board, whether black or white, orthodox or heterodox" (M. S. Lamson, personal communication, journal entry, unknown date). She further wrote that Lydia, during the Civil War, had been an earnest worker for the Sanitary Commission. She was a specimen of the finest type of New England womanhood. In addition to her work in abolitionism and the Civil War, she was active in the cause of working women. In 1904, the year that Lydia died, three Fall River women provided a lot of land at the corner of Rock and Franklin Streets where a red brick building was erected, a center for the Women's Union activities (Fall River Women's Union, 2006).

Louisa Harris died of a stroke on April 30, 1906, at the age of 82. She had become blind, yet she still wrote poetry which made its way to the hands of her normal school peers and would later be found in their personal collections. On her death certificate her occupation was listed as an authoress, although she spent a lifetime as a teacher. She was buried in the First Parish Cemetery in Needham, Massachusetts beside the graves of her parents. Throughout her teaching career, she had boarded around. Mary Swift, too, had remembrances of Louisa in her record book, specifically a hand written poem that Louisa had composed during her eighty-second year. Louisa had attended every reunion of the normalites, all 23 formal gatherings, the last of which occurred in 1895. Fifty-five years after they first met, she drew from their company. Perhaps the care and concern she acquired through the friendships with the normalites as a 15 year old student were as important to her as the academic and pedagogical education she had received while at the normal school.

Mary Swift died on March 2, 1909 at the age of 86. She was buried in the Mount Auburn Cemetery in Cambridge, Massachusetts in a family grave site. Her final resting place was beneath a sturdy, quercus rubra red oak, located within sight of Horace Mann's grave and a short walk from that of Samuel Gridley Howe. Mary had first visited the Mount Auburn Cemetery when she was a normal school student. She was with her teacher and fellow normal school peer, Lydia Stow. On August 29, 1839, she penned in her journal "Mr. P took a carriage & conveyed us all to Mount Auburn, about a mile & a quarter from Cambridge. We occupied all our time which was very short, in rambling about... The scenery was much more beautiful than I anticipated" (as cited in Norton, 1926, p 99). A pioneer in the normal school movement, Mary also was one who forged new ground in the field of education for the deaf and blind and with social movements for working women.

For The Class of 1839
Presented at the Semi-Centennial Reunion
Louisa E. Harris

We're nearing now the sunset's glow,
Our eastern sky grows pale and dim;
Our morning chimes sound faint and low,
And near and sweet our vesper hymn.
And as we now, in sober gladness,
Salute this younger, gayer throng,
Remembering that tones of sadness
Make discord with their matin song,

We fain would ask for them the boon
We cherish from our Normal days –
Friendships, as true beyond life's noon
As in its earlier morning rays.

We find not here our early shrine,
But in the old heroic town,
Where firmly planted was the vine
Whose purple grapes your borders crown.

We helped the planting of that vine,
Grown vigorous on this golden day,
And drink with you the generous wine
Pressed from its vintage, while we may.
We do not come with golden spurs
To greet this bright, rejoicing throng;
None deems the victor's laurel hers,
Or dares essay the victor's song.

Though not all loyal have we proved
To fair ideals that charmed our youth,
The visions that our hearts then moved
Have helped our "living to the truth."
Those fair ideals, so cherished then,
Though never reached, still lure us on;
'Mid sternest Real they shine again,
Though "Youth's sweet purple light is gon."

We see a host beyond your ken,
And voices, hushed before your time,
Come to our ears from noble men
Whose fames was in its glorious prime.

Great hearts, with anxious, fond desire,
Watched well the germ they planted here,
And stirred us nobly to aspire
And help to bring this golden year.
Names written large upon the roll
Of those who served with holy zeal
The State we love, and whose control
Helped on our country's truest weal,

To us were pleasant household names,
Recalling who whose presence brought
Something besides their stately fames,
Beyond their stern, majestic thought.
The sage of Concord sometimes came,
And made our youthful hearts aspire;
Brave Horace, with his soul aflame,
Enkindled ours with sacred fire.

His wit was keen as his of Rome,
His eye as clear to read his time;
He wrought to make his land a home
For virtue, knowledge, love sublime.

And he, the Bayard of our day,
As poet called him, in whose face
We read romance and courage gay,
And knightly service for his race.

The saintly Follen sweet and strong,
His kindly critic word bestowed,
Alert to right e'en school-girl's wrong,
Pure lead on the upward road.
And that was deemed a joyful day
When came, as guest to grace our board,
The earnest, gentle, genial May,
A many by you and old adored.

Rantoul of Essex, Stetson, Sparks,
Putnam of pulpit fame so rare,
And many, being honored marks
From life's great battlefields were there.
The guide who led our youthful feet
Along the steep and rugged way,
Amid the burden and the heat
Gave strength and purpose to our day.

"Live to the truth"—his motto high –
Was no vain badge to grace our walls;
We deemed him strong to dare and die
For truths he taught within those halls.
Our kindred aims with those rare men
Whose high discourse so charmed our ear,
As from the past they rise again,
He stands beside them as their peer.

And she, whose sweet and steadfast soul
Was linked with his in each high aim,
Who swayed our hearts by Love's control,
Is now a dear and honored name.
With gentle mien and eyes of light,
With accents low, but sweet and clear,
She moved a presence pure and bright,
With words of wisdom and good cheer.

That was a bright, awakening hour
When strains heroic filled the air;
A grant, resistless, cleansing power
Was rousing men to do and dare.
To some old truths men waked anew,
The Nazarine taught us to long ago;
The human then diviner grew,
And love for man found richer flow,

A wave swept o'er the inner life
Of souls of truest fiber wrought,
And stirred, amid the worldly strife,
To finder issues, grander thought.
The voices, since familiar grown,
The prophet voices of our day,
Rang out their fresh and youthful tone,
Prophetic of their grander lay.

Their words half battles later grew,
As giant wrong its crest high reared,
And wrought for Freedom's cause anew,
Averting woes the timid feared.
Those voices reached our calm retreat
Within the old, heroic town,
And mingled with the brave drum-beat,
That later noises could not drown.

We read upon the engraven stone
The story tyrants trembling heard;
The soil, so dear and sacred grown,
Reechoed Freedom's latest word.
With grateful hearts we own the sway
Of influence, strong and deep and pure,
That helped to brighten all our way,
And shaped our friendships to endure.

Each heart that beats a welcome here
Knows deeper draughts of joy and pain,
Knows larger hope, more anxious fear,
Knows heavier loss and sweeter gain,
Than when, in breezy, school-girl hour,
It rose and fell with changing mood,
Now, dewy fresh as new-waked flower,
Now, drooping 'neath dark Fancy's boord.

The march through weary toil and strife,
Life that the Grecian hero knew,
Must bring the rapturous, sparkling life
Of God's full sea to meet our view.
The guiding hand we know divine,
Whether it leads through smiles or tears,
And, having pledged to auld lang syne,
We'll also pledge to coming years.

Hail and farewell are quickly said;
The fairest day has fleetest hours,
As in old poet's line we've read,
How light Time's footfall on the flowers.

Archives, Libraries, Historical Societies, and Associations

American Antiquarian Society, Worcester, MA

Boston Public Library Rare Books Room, Boston, MA

Concord Public Library, Concord, MA

Dedham Historical Society, Dedham, MA

Fall River Historical Society, Fall River, MA

Fall River Public Library, Fall River, MA

Framingham State University, Archives and Special Collections, Framingham, MA

Gilder Lehrman Institute of American History, NY

Haverford Library, Quaker and Special Collections, Haverford College, Haverford, PA

Houghton Library at Harvard University, Cambridge, MA

Independent Association of Framingham State Alumni, Framingham, MA

Lexington Historical Society, Lexington, MA

Massachusetts Historical Society, Boston, MA

Nantucket Historical Association, Nantucket, MA

Normalites, pages 195–196
Copyright © 2014 by Information Age Publishing

National Archives and Records Administration in Washington, DC

New England Genealogical Society, Boston, MA

Oberlin College, Oberlin, OH

Perkins School for the Blind, Watertown, MA

Rhode Island Historical Society, Providence, RI

Schlesinger Library at Harvard University, Cambridge, MA

The Henry W. and Albert A Berg Collection
of the New York Public Library, NY

University of Rochester, River Campus Libraries,
Rare Books, Special Collections and Preservation, Rochester, NY

Washington University in St. Louis, MO

Bibliography

Primary Sources

Adams, E. (1873–1874). *Personal journals*. Framingham State University, Archives and Special Collections, Framingham, MA.

Adams, I. (1845, July 19). [Letter to Robert Adams]. Adams Family Papers, Rhode Island Historical Society, Providence, RI.

Adams, L. (unknown year, April 29). [Letter to Mary F. Peirce], Lydia Stow Adams Papers, Framingham State University, Archives and Special Collections, Framingham, MA.

Adams, L. S. (1845, November 3). [Letter to Maria S. Chapman]. Boston Public Library Rare Books Room, Boston, MA.

Adams, W. (1843, February 27). [Letter to Robert and John Adams]. Adams Family Papers, American Antiquarian Society, Worcester, MA.

Alcott, L. M. (no date). [Book of handwritten poems to Sophia Foord]. Louisa May Alcott Collection, Henry W. and Albert A. Berg Collection of the New York Public Library, NY.

Blake, E. (1812, January 26). [Letter to Esther Foord]. Dedham Historical Society, Dedham, MA.

Boyd, L. (1858). [Letter to Charles Scudder]. Young Women's Christian Association Papers Schlesinger Library at Harvard University, Cambridge, MA.

Bridgman, L. D. (1876, October 13). [Letter to Mary Swift Lamson]. Laura Dewey Bridgman Papers, Perkins School for the Blind, Watertown, MA.

Bridgman, L. D. (1879, January 26). [Letter to My Dear Mrs. Lamson]. Lamson Family Papers, Massachusetts Historical Society, Boston, MA.

Combe, G. (1842, November 30). [Letter to Samuel Gridley Howe]. Samuel Gridley Howe Papers, Perkins School for the Blind, Watertown, MA.

Douglass, F. (1888, March 23). [Letter to Robert Adams]. Boston Public Library Rare Books Room, Boston, MA.

Normalites, pages 197–210
Copyright © 2014 by Information Age Publishing

Douglass, F. (1891, November 12). [Letter to Robert Adams]. University of Rochester, River Campus Libraries, Department of Rare Book and Special Collections, Rochester, NY.

Drew, L. (1839, November 28). [Letter to Mother], Lydia Drew File, Independent Association of Framingham State Alumni, Framingham, MA.

Drew, L. (1840, February 18). [Letter to Samuel Gridley Howe]. Samuel Gridley Howe Papers, Perkins School for the Blind, Watertown, MA.

Drew, L. (1840, March 6). [Letter to Samuel Gridley Howe]. Samuel Gridley Howe Papers, Perkins School for the Blind, Watertown, MA.

Fall River Daily Globe. (1900, April 3). Robert Adam's death. Robert Adams Papers. Fall River Historical Society, Fall River, MA.

Foord, S. (1837). [Signature on Pamphlet titled The American scholar]. American Antiquarian Society, Worcester, MA.

Gardner, M. T. (1839, July 18). [Letter of recommendation for Lydia Stow], Lydia Stow Adams Papers, Framingham State University, Archives and Special Collections, Framingham, MA.

Harris, L. (1840–1905). Personal Journals. Framingham State University, Archives and Special Collections, Framingham, MA.

Jenks, S. (1840, February 9). [Letter to daughter]. Laura Dewey Bridgman Papers, Perkins School for the Blind, Watertown, MA.

Johnson, S. (1840–1842). Personal Journals. Lexington Historical Society, Lexington, MA.

Lamson, E. (1863, February 6). [Letter to my dear friend]. Lamson family Papers, Massachusetts Historical Society, Boston, MA.

Lamson, E. (1870, November 2). [Letter to Charles Finney]. Finney Papers, Oberlin College, Oberlin, OH.

Lamson, E. (1874, August 5). [Letter to Charles Finney]. Finney Papers, Oberlin College, Oberlin, OH.

Lamson, M. S. (no date). [Collections of Sea Moss]. Lamson Family Papers, Massachusetts Historical Society, Boston, MA.

Lamson, M. S. (no date). [Letter to family]. Lamson Family Papers, Massachusetts Historical Society, Boston, MA.

Lamson, M. S. (1861, April 12). [Letter to Edwin Lamson]. Lamson Family Papers, Massachusetts Historical Society, Boston, MA.

Lamson, M. S. (1861, April 20). [Letter to Edwin Lamson]. Lamson Family Papers, Massachusetts Historical Society, Boston, MA.

Lamson, M. S. (1861, April 29). [Letter to Edwin Lamson]. Lamson Family Papers, Massachusetts Historical Society, Boston, MA.

Lamson, M. S. (1861, July 10). [Letter to Samuel Gridley Howe]. Samuel Gridley Howe Papers, Perkins School for the Blind, Watertown, MA.

Lamson, M. S. (1878, October 14). [Letter to Stanley Hall]. Lamson Family Papers, Massachusetts Historical Society, Boston, MA.

Lamson, M. S. (1884, November 3). [Personal account of the origin of the B.Y.W.C.A.]. Young Women's Christian Association Papers, Schlesinger Library at Harvard University, Cambridge, MA.

Mann, M. (1859, September 5). [Letter to Sophia Hawthorne]. Horace Mann Collection, Microfilm Edition, The Massachusetts Historical Society, Boston, MA.

Peabody, E. (1841). [Letter to Samuel Gridley Howe]. Samuel Gridley Howe Papers, Perkins School for the Blind, Watertown, MA.

Peabody, E. (1842, July 26). [Letter to Samuel Gridley Howe]. Samuel Gridley Howe Papers, Perkins School for the Blind, Watertown, MA.

Peirce, C. (1839, August 5). [Letter to My Dear Young Friends]. Nantucket Historical Association, Nantucket MA.

Peirce, C. (1843). [Letter to Electa Lincoln]. Peirce Papers, Nantucket Historical Association, Nantucket, MA.

Pennell, C. (1852, October 17). [Letter to my dear sister]. Horace Mann Collection, Microfilm Edition, Massachusetts Historical Society, Boston, MA.

Pennell, R. (1833, April 3). [Letter to Horace Mann]. Horace Mann Collection, Microfilm Edition, Massachusetts Historical Society, Boston, MA.

Phillips, W. (circa 1850). [Letter to Robert Adams]. Gilder Lehrman Institute of American History, NY.

Photograph of Commonwealth of Massachusetts return of a death certificate. (1885). Dedham Historical Society, Dedham, MA.

Photograph of Pennsylvania State Marriage Certificate of Edwin and Mary Lamson. (1846, June 22). Lamson Family Papers, The Massachusetts Historical Society, Boston, MA.

Robbins, L. M. (1839, August 7). [Letter to Maria Weston Chapman]. Boston Public Library Rare Books Room, Boston, MA.

Stone, H. (1863, April 24). [Letter to my dear little Kate]. Lamson Family Papers, Massachusetts Historical Society, Boston, MA.

Stow, L. A. (1840–1843). Personal Journals. Framingham State University, Archives and Special Collections, Framingham, MA.

Sullivan, A. (1890, July 7). [Letter to Mr. Anagnos]. American Antiquarian Society, Worcester, MA.

Swift, D. G. (unknown date). [Recording of an event]. Lamson Family Papers, Massachusetts Historical Society, Boston, MA.

Swift, P. (1839, March 2). [Letter to William Coffin]. Swift Papers, Nantucket Historical Association, Nantucket MA.

Swift, P. (1840, April 10). [Letter to Samuel Gridley Howe]. Samuel Gridley Howe Papers, Perkins School for the Blind, Watertown, MA.

Swift, P. (1841, November 7). [Letter to Samuel Gridley Howe]. Samuel Gridley Howe Papers, Perkins School for the Blind, Watertown, MA.

Unknown author. (1876, August 24). Obituary Deacon Edwin Lamson. Lamson Family Papers, The Massachusetts Historical Society, Boston, MA.

Village Register, Dedham. (1824, September 30). Copy in possession of author.

Secondary Sources

Abbot, J. (1875). *Moral influences employed in the instruction and government of the young*. New York: Harper & Brothers, Publisher.

Adams House. (no date). *The history of the Fall River home for aged people*. Fall River, MA: Adams House.

Adams, R. J. (1842, October 19). Bookstore and bindery. *The Fall River Monitor*, Volume XVIII, p. 43.

Alcott, L. M. (1885, April 11). In memoriam of Sophia Foord. *The Woman's Journal, XVI*(15).

Austin, W. (1912). *Tale of a Dedham tavern: History of the Norfolk hotel, Dedham, Massachusetts*. Cambridge, MA: Riverside Press.

Barnard, H. (1851). *Normal schools and other institutions, agencies and means: Designed for the professional education of teachers*. Hartford, CT: Cace, Tiffany and Company.

Bartoletti, S. (2001). *Black potatoes: The story of the great Irish famine 1845–1850*. Boston, MA: Houghton Mifflin.

Beecher, C. (1842). *A treatise on domestic economy: For the use of young ladies at home and at school*. New York: Harper & Brothers, Publishers.

Bernard, R. M., & Vinovskis, M. A. (1977). The female school teacher in antibellum Massachusetts. *The Journal of Social History, 10*(3), 332–345.

Beyer, R. (2011). *The Lexington revolutionary experience: First shot*. Lexington, MA: Lexington Historical Society.

Biklen, S. K. (1990) Confiding woman: A 19th-century teacher's diary. *History of Education Review, 19*(2), 24–35.

Blight, D. (2006). *Passages to freedom: The underground railroad in history and memory*. New York: HarperCollins.

Board of the State Industrial School for Girls. (1866). *By-laws and statutes for the government and regulation of the State Industrial School for Girls*. Boston, MA: Press of Geo. C. Rand & Avery.

Board of the Young Women's Christian Association. (1867). *First annual report of the Young Women's Christian Association of Boston presented March 4, 1867*. Boston, MA: Press of T. R. Marvin & Son.

Board of the Young Women's Christian Association. (1869). *Third annual report of the Young Women's Christian Association of Boston presented March 1, 1869*. Boston, MA: J. M. Hewes, Printer.

Board of the Young Women's Christian Association. (1882). *Sixteenth annual report of the Young Women's Christian Association of Boston presented March 6, 1882*. Boston, MA: Frank Wood Printer.

Board of the Young Women's Christian Association. (1889). *Twenty-third annual report of the Young Women's Christian Association of Boston presented March 4, 1889*. Boston, MA: Frank Wood Printer.

Board of the Young Women's Christian Association. (1890). *Twenty-fourth annual report of the Young Women's Christian Association of Boston presented March 3, 1890*. Boston, MA: Frank Wood Printer.

Board of the Young Women's Christian Association. (1896). *Thirtieth annual report of the Young Women's Christian Association of Boston presented March 2, 1896*. Boston, MA: Frank Wood Printer.

Board of the Young Women's Christian Association. (1898). *Thirty-second annual report of the Young Women's Christian Association of Boston presented March 7, 1898*. Boston, MA: Frank Wood Printer.

Board of the Young Women's Christian Association. (1899). *Thirty-third annual report of the Young Women's Christian Association of Boston presented March 6, 1899*. Boston, MA: Frank Wood Printer.

Board of the Young Women's Christian Association. (1902). *Thirty-sixth annual report of the Young Women's Christian Association of Boston presented March 3, 1902*. Boston, MA: William B. Libby Printer.

Board of the Young Women's Christian Association. (1904). *Thirty-eighth annual report of the Young Women's Christian Association of Boston presented March 7, 1904*. Boston, MA: The Garden Press.

Board of the Young Women's Christian Association. (1905). *Thirty-ninth annual report of the Young Women's Christian Association of Boston presented March 6, 1905*. Boston, MA: The Garden Press.

Boston Daily Atlas. (1851, January 4).The new clipper ship John Bertram of Boston. *Boston Daily Atlas.*

Boston Transcript. (1900, April 3). *Robert Adams: Fall River. Boston Transcript.*

Bridgers, L. (2006). *The American religious experience: A concise history.* Lanham, MD: Rowman & Littlefield Publishers, Inc.

Bruce, R. (1973). *Bell: Alexander Graham Bell and the conquest of solitude.* Boston, MA: Little, Brown, Publishers.

Bullough, R. (1998). Musings on life writing: Biography and case studies in teacher education. In C. Kridel (Ed.), *Writing educational biography: Explorations in qualitative research* (pp. 19–32). New York: Garland Publishing.

Butts, R. F., & Cremin, L. (1953). *A history of education in American Culture.* New York: Holt, Rinehart and Winston.

Chapman, M. W. (1839). *Right and wrong in Massachusetts.* Boston: Dow & Jacksons Anti-Slavery Press.

Clark, A. H. (1912). *The Clipper Ship Era.* New York: G.P. Putnam's Sons.

Clarke, C. (1995). *The communitarian movement: The radical challenge of the North Hampton Association.* Amherst, MA: University of Massachusetts Press.

Clarke, G. K. (1912). *History of Needham Massachusetts, 1711–1911.* Cambridge, MA: The University Press.

Clarke, T. (2010). *South of Boston: Tales from the coastal communities of Massachusetts Bay.* Charleston, SC: The History Press.

Clay. (1844, October 12). Letter from Mr. Clay. *The Fall River Monitor.* Volume XVIII (42), p.1.

Combe, G. (1841). *Notes on the United States of North America during a phrenological visit.* Philadelphia, PA: Carrey & Hart.

Conway, J. K. (1996). *Written by herself, volume II: Women's memoirs from Britain, Africa, Asia and the United States.* New York: Vintage Books.

Conway, J. K. (1998). *Exploring the art of autobiography: When memory speaks.* New York: Vintage.

Conway, J. K. (2005). Politics, pedagogy & gender. *Daedalus. 134*(4), 134–144.

Cote, J. (2004). Class and the ideology of womanhood: The early years of the Boston Young Women's Christian Association. *Historical Journal of Massachusetts, 32*(1), 1–20.

Cushman, S. (1859). *Young ladies' seminary and boarding school, Highland Avenue, Somerville, Mass.: To parents and guardians.* Somerville, MA: Sine Nomine.

Dedham Historical Society. *Images of America: Dedham,* Dedham, MA: Dedham Historical Society.

Deland, F. (1908). *Dumb no longer: Romance of the telephone.* Washington City: Volta Bureau.

Dickens, C. (1842). *American notes.* London: Chapan and Hall.

Douglass, F. (1845). *Narrative of the life of Frederick Douglass, an American Slave.* Anti-Slavery Office.

Douglass, F. (2000). *Frederick Douglass: Selected speeches and writing.* Chicago, IL: Chicago Review Press.

Dubois, E. C. (1998). *Woman suffrage: Women's rights.* New York: New York University Press.

Earl, H. (1877). *A centennial history of Fall River, Mass: Comprising a record of its corporate progress from 1566 to 1876.* New York: Atlantic Publishing and Engraving Company.

Eddy, M. B. (1889). *Science and health with key to scriptures.* Boston, MA: Published by the author.

Emerson, R. W., Rusk, R., & Tilton, E. M. (1939). *The letters of Ralph Waldo Emerson.* New York: Columbia University Press.

Enoch, J. (2008). A woman's place is in the school: Rhetorics of gendered space in 19th century America. *College English, (70)*3, 275–295.

Essex Institute. (1906). *Essex Institute historical collections.* Salem, MA: Printed from the Essex Institute, Peabody Essex Museum.

Fall River Daily Globe. (1904, August 26). *Mrs. Adams dead: She was always prominent in good works. Fall River Daily Globe.*

Fall River School Committee. (1842). *Report of the general school committee of the town of Fall River.* Fall River, MA: Tripp and Pratt, Printers.

Fall River Women's Union. (1882). *8th annual report of the Fall River Women's Union, January 1, 1881–January 1, 1882.* Fall River, MA: Press of Almy & Milne, Printers and Publishers.

Fall River Women's Union. (1895). *21st annual report of the Fall River Women's Union, January 1–1894 January 1, 1895.* Fall River, MA: Press of Almy & Milne, Printers and Publishers.

Fall River Women's Union. (1897). *23rd annual report of the Fall River Women's Union, January 1 1896–January 1, 1897.* Fall River, MA: Press of Almy & Milne, Printers and Publishers.

Fall River Women's Union (2006). *Constitution & Bylaws: Adopted January 23, 2006 5th Revision.* Fall River, MA: Sine Nomine.

Fay, F. (1901). *The population and finances of Boston: A study of municipal growth.* Boston, MA: Municipal Printing Office.

Fehrenbacher, D., & Fehrenbacher, V. (1966). *Recollected works of Abraham Lincoln.* Stanford, CA: Stanford University Press.

Fishburn, E. (1947). *The first state normal school in America: Personal growth leaflet number 15.* Washington, DC: The National Education Association.

Foord, J. (1843, July 15). Letter from editor. *The Fall River Monitor,* Volume XVIII, p. 1.

Fox, V. (2000). Lydia Stow: Self-actualization in a period of transition. *The Journal of Psycho History, 28*(1), 62–71.

Framingham State Alumnae Association. (1914*). Historical sketches of the Framingham state normal school.* Framingham, MA: Framingham State Alumnae Association.

Framingham State Alumnae Association. (1959). *First state normal school in America: The state teacher's college at Framingham Massachusetts.* Framingham, MA: The Alumnae Association of the state teachers college at Framingham Massachusetts.

Freeberg, E. (2001). *The education of Laura Bridgman: First deaf and blind person to learn language.* Cambridge, MA: Harvard University Press.

Freeman, R., & Klaus, P. (1984). Blessed or not? The new spinster in England and the United States in the late 19th and early 20th centuries. *The Journal of Family History, 9,* 394–414.

Gamber, W. (2007). *The boardinghouse in nineteenth-century America.* Baltimore, MD: John Hopkins University Press.

Gifford, S. N., & Marden, G. A. (1876). *Commonwealth of Massachusetts: A manual for the use of the General Court: Containing the rules and orders of the two branches.* Boston, MA: Wright and Porter State Printers.

Gitter, E. (2001). *The imprisoned guest: Samuel Howe and Laura Bridgman, the original deaf blind girl.* New York: Farrar, Straus, and Giroux.

Glen, M. (1984). *Campaigns against corporal punishment: Prisoners, sailors, women, and children in Antebellum America.* New York: State University of New York Press.

Gormley, B. (1995). *Maria Mitchell: The soul of an astronomer.* Grand Rapids, MI: Wm. B. Eerdmans Publishing.

Golden, J., Meckel, R. A., & Prescott, H. (2004). *Children and youth in sickness and in health: A historical handbook and guide.* Westport, CT: Greenwood Publishing Group, Inc.

Graham, G., Poe, E. A., & Batchelder, J. D. (1842). *Graham's lady's and gentlemen's magazine,* (XX) 2. Philadelphia, PA: George Graham.

Gormley, B. (1995). *Maria Mitchell: The soul of an astronomer.* Grand Rapids, MI: Wm. B. Eerdmans Publishing.

Grodzins, D. (2002). *American Heretic: Theodore Parker and transcendentalism.* North Carolina: University of North Carolina Press.

Guarino, R. (2011). *Beacon Street: Its buildings & residents.* Charleston, SC: The History Press.

Hambrick-Stowe, C. (1996). *Charles G. Finney and the spirit of American Evangelicalism.* Grand Rapids, MI: WM. B. Eerdmans Publishing, Co.

Hanson, R. (1990). *Churches of Dedham, Massachusetts: Admissions, dissmissions, adult baptisms, and preceedings under the half-way covenant 1638–1844.* Maryland: Heritage Books Incorporated.

Hanson, R. (Ed.). (1997a). *Vital records of Dedham, Massachusetts 1635–1845: Revised and expanded edition.* Camden, ME: Picton Press.

Hanson, R. (Ed.) (1997b). *Vital records of Needham, Massachusetts 1711–1845:* Camden, ME: Picton Press.

Hanson, R. (Ed.) (1998). *The diary of Dr. Nathaniel Ames of Dedham, Massachusetts 1758–1822.* Camden, ME: Picton Press.

Harding, W. (1962). *The days of Henry Thoreau.* New York: Dover Publications.

Harris, L. (1861). *Robert Harris and his descendants with notices of the Morey and Metcalf families.* Boston, MA: Printed by Henry W. Dutton & Son.

Harris, L. (1900, June 14). The art of forgetting. *The Christian Register,* pp. 652–653.

Harris, L. (1903). *Poem for semi-centennial celebration.* In M. Lamson (Ed.), *The first state normal school in America: Records of the first class* (pp. 170–171). Boston, MA: Printed for the class.

Harris, M. (2003). *The a to z of Unitarian universalism.* Landham, MD: The Scarecrow Press.

Harvard College. (1940). *Gardner Lamson.* Cambridge, MA: Harvard College.

Haverford Alumni Association. (1892). *A History of Haverford College for the first 60 years of its existence.* Prepared by the committee of the alumni association. Philadelphia, PA: Porter & Coates.

Herbst, J. (1989). *And sadly teach: Teacher education and professionalization in American culture.* Madison, WI: The University of Wisconsin Press.

Hill, D. G. (1896). *The record of the town meetings an abstract of birth, marriages, and death in the town of Dedham, Massachusetts 1887–1896.* Dedham, MA: Transcript Steam Job Print.

Hilldred, H. (1876). *Norfolk County manual and yearbook for 1876.* Dedham, MA: Sine Nomine.

Howe, J. W. (1876). *Memoir of Dr. Samuel Gridley Howe.* Boston, MA: Albert J Wright.

Howe, J. W. (1900). *Reminiscences, 1819–1899.* Boston, MA: Houghton, Mifflin and Company.

Howe, M., & Hall, F. H. (1903). *Laura Bridgman: Dr. Howe's famous pupil and what he taught her.* Boston, MA: Little, Brown and Company.

Hudson, J. B. (2006). *Encyclopedia of the underground railroad.* Jefferson, NC: McFarland and Company.

Hunter, S. H. (2013, October). Sailing on. *Cape Cod Life,* 40–47.

Hutt, F. W. (1924). *A history of Bristol County, Massachusetts, Volume 1.* New York: Lewis Historical Publishing Company.

Johnson, C. (1904). *Old-time schools and school-books.* New York: The MacMillan Company.

Jordan, R. (2004). Quakers, comeouters, and the meaning of abolitionism in the Antebellum free states. *Journal of the Early Republic, 24*(4) 588–608.

Karttunen, F. R. (2005). *The other islanders: People who pulled Nantucket's oars.* New Bedford, MA: Spinner Publications.

Katz, M. (1976). *A history of compulsory education laws.* Bloomington, IN: Phi Delta Kappa.

Keller, H. (2010). *The story of my life: Helen Keller.* New York: Signet Classics.

Kelly, G. (2008). *Lydia Sigourney: Selected poetry and prose.* Ontario, Canada: Broadview Press.

Kelsey, R. W. (1919). *Centennial history of Moses Brown School 1819–1919.* Providence, RI: Moses Brown School.

Kridel, C. (1998). Qualitative research and educational biography. In C. Kridel (Ed.), *Writing educational biography: Explorations in qualitative research* (pp. 13–18). New York: Garland Publishing.

Kollen, R. (2004). *Lexington: From liberty's birth place to progressive suburb.* Charleston, SC: Arcadia Publishing.

Kolodny, K. (2010). The social networks of Rebecca Pennell: An early woman college professor to have equal pay with her male colleagues. *Vitae Scholasticae, 27*(2), 105–122.

Lamson, M. S. (1881). *Life in education of Laura Dewey Bridgeman, the deaf, dumb, and blind girl.* Boston, MA: Houghton, Mifflin and Company.

Lamson, M. S. (1893). *The history of the Women's Christian Associations and Young Women's Christian Associations:* Paper read before the congress auxiliary to the World's Columbian Exposition, Chicago, 1893. Philadelphia, PA: Sine Nomine.

Lamson, M. S. (1903). *Records of the first class of the first state normal school in America established at Lexington, Massachusetts 1839.* Boston, MA: Printed for the class.

Laurie, B. (2005). *Beyond Garrison: Anti-slavery and social reform.* New York: Cambridge University Press.

Lawrence, R. M. (1922). *Old Park Street and its vicinity.* Boston, MA: Houghton Mifflin Company.

Leach, R. J., & Gow, P. (1997). *Quaker Nantucket: The religious community behind the whaling empire.* Nantucket, MA: Mill Hill Press.

Leach, W. (1980). *True love and perfect union: The feminist reform of sex and society.* New York: Basic Books.

Linebaugh, B. (1978). *The African school and the integration of Nantucket public schools 1825–1847.* Boston, MA: Boston University: Afro-American Studies Center.

MacMullen, E. (1991). *In the cause of true education: Henry Barnard & nineteenth century school reform.* New Haven,CT: Yale University Press.

Mann, H. (1840). *Lecture on education.* Boston, MA: Marsh, Capen, Lyon, and Webb.

Mann, H. (1852). *The institution of Slavery: Speech of hon. Horace Mann, of Massachusetts, on the institution of slavery, delivered in the U.S. House of Representatives, August 17, 1852.* Retrieved from the Cornell University Library Digital Collections.

Marshall, M. (2005). *The Peabody sisters: Three women who ignited American romanticism.* Boston, MA: Houghton Mifflin Company.

Marshall, M. (2007). Why biography? *Common Place.* Retrieved from http://www.common place.org/vol-08/no–01/:INTERNET.

Marshall, M. (2013). *Margaret Fuller: A new American life.* Boston, MA: Houghton Mifflin Harcourt.

Martin, J. R. (1994). *Changing the educational landscape: Philosophy, women, and curriculum.* New York: Routledge.

Martin, J. R. (2011). *Education reconfigured: Culture, encounter, and change.* New York: Routledge.

Martins, M., & Binette, D. (2010). *Parallel lives: A social history of Lizzie A. Borden and her Fall River.* Fall River, MA: Fall River Historical Society.

Massachusetts Board of Education. (1840). *Third annual report of the board of education together with the third annual report of the secretary of the board.* Boston, MA: Dutton and Wentworth, State Printers.

Massachusetts Board of Education. (1841). *Fourth annual report of the Board of Education with the fourth annual report of the secretary of the board.* Boston, MA: Dutton and Wentworth State Printers.

Massachusetts Board of Education. (1844). *Seventh annual report of the Board of Education, together with the seventh annual report of the secretary of the board.* Boston, MA: Dutton and Wentworth State Printers.

Massachusetts Board of Education. (1845). *Eighth annual report of the Board of Education, together with the eighth annual report of the secretary of the board.* Boston, MA: Dutton and Wentworth State Printers.

Massachusetts General Government. (1829). *The Massachusetts register of the United States calendar for the year of our lord.* Boston, MA: Richardson & Lord and James Loring.

Massachusetts Teachers Association. (1873). *The Massachusetts teacher: A journal of school and home education.* Boston, MA: Published by Alfred Mudge and Son.

May, S. (1856). *Liberty or slavery, the only question: Oration: Delivered on the fourth of July, 1856, at Jamestown, Chautauque [sic] co., New York.* Retrieved from the Cornell University Library Digital Collections.

May, S. J. (1857). *Memoir of Cyrus Peirce, first principal of the first state normal school in the United States.* Hartford, CT: F.C. Brownell.

May, S. (1861). *The fugitive slave law and its victims.* New York: Published by the American Anti-Slavery Society.

McClure, A. W. (1847). *The Christian Observatory: A religious and literary magazine.* Boston, MA: J. V. Beane & Co.

Messerli, J. (1972). *Horace Mann: A biography.* New York: Alfred A. Knopf.

Methodist Episcopal Church. (1837). Mrs. Sigourney's letters. *The Methodist Review,* VIII, 51–66.

Myerson, J., Shealy, D., & Stern, M. (1995). *The selected letters of Louisa May Alcott.* Athens, Georgia: The University of Georgia Press.

Nagel, P. C. (1997). *John Quincy Adams: A public life, a private life.* New York: Knopf.

Nantucket Historical Association. (1905). *Proceedings of the Nantucket Historical Association, eleventh annual meeting.* Waltham, MA: Waltham Publishing Co., Printers.

Nantucket Historical Association. (2013). Online Barney Geneological Record. Nantucket, MA. Retrieved from http://nha.org/library/genealogy.html.

Nash, M. (1997). Rethinking republican motherhood: Benjamin Rush and the Young Ladies' Academy of Philadelphia. *Journal of the Early Republic, 17*(2), 171–191.

Nash, M. (2005). *Women's education in the United States: 1780–1840.* New York: Palgrave Macmillan.

National American Woman Suffrage Association Collection. (1851). *The proceedings of the Woman's Rights Convention, held at Worcester, October 15th and 16th, 1851.* Boston, MA: Prentiss & Sawyer.

National Center for Educational Statistics. (2012). Digest of Education Statistics: 2011. Retrieved from http://www.nces.ed.gov.

Noddings, N. (1995). Teaching themes of care. *Education Digest, 61*(3), 24.

Norton, A. (1926). *The first state normal school in America: The journals of Cyrus Peirce and Mary Swift.* Cambridge, MA: Harvard University Press.

Ogren, C. (2005). *The American state normal school: An instrument of great good.* New York: Palgrave Macmillan.

Peabody, E. P. (1835). *Record of a school: Exemplifying the general principles of spiritual culture.* Boston, MA: James Munroe and Company.

Pellico, S. (1931). *My prisons: Memoirs of Silvio Pellico.* Cambridge, MA: University Press.

Philbrick, N. (1994) *Away off shore: Nantucket Island and its people, 1602–1890.* New York: Penguin Books.

Philbrick, N. (2001). *In the heart of the sea: The tragedy of the whale ship Essex.* New York: Penguin Books.

Phillips, A. S. (1945). *The Phillips history of Fall River: Ecclesiastical and educational history, welfare, agencies and charities, financial structure, industries and public utilities.* New York: Dover Press.

Phillips, D. (1997). *The founding fathers on leadership: Classic teamwork in changing times.* New York: Warren Books.

Preston, J. (1993). Domestic ideology, school reformers, and female teachers: Schoolteaching becomes women's work in 19th century New England. *The New England Quarterly, 66*(4), 531–552.

Provenzo, E. (2008). Time exposure. *Educational Studies, 43*(3), 278–279

Reynolds, D. (2006). *John Brown abolitionist: The man who killed slavery, sparked the civil war and ceded civil rights.* New York: Vintage Books.

Richardson, A. (1900). *A word to the friends of Lamson Normal School, Mashallville, GA.* Mashallville, GA: Sine Nomine.

Richardson, R. D. (1995). *Emerson: The mind on fire: A biography.* Berkeley, CA: University of California Press.

Rodriguez, J. (2007). *Slavery in the United States: A social, political and historical encyclopedia.* California: ABC-Clio.

Rosell, G. (2009). *Boston's historic Park Street Church: The story of an Evengelical landmark.* Grand Rapids, MI: Kragel:

Rothermel, B. A. (2002). A sphere of noble action: Gender, rhetoric, and influence at a 19th century Massachusetts state normal school. *Rhetoric Society Corderlly, 33*(1), 35–64.

Roxbury School Committee. (1848). *The annual report of the school committee on the public schools of the city of Roxbury 1848.* Roxbury, MA: Joseph G Torrey, City Printer.

Roxbury School Committee. (1850). *Report of the examination of the public schools in the city of Roxbury, for the year 1850.* Retrieved from https://archive.org/stream/citydocuments508roxb/citydocuments508roxb_djvu.txt.

Rutledge, L. V. (Ed.). (1912, August 1). Extracts from the journals of three ladies from Billerica, Mass., in time of our Civil War, 1864. *Billerica, 1*(3), 5–7.

Salitan, L., & Perera, E. (1994). *Virtuous lives: Four Quaker sisters remember family life, abolitionism, and women's suffrage.* New York: The Continuum Publishing Company.

Saxton, M. (1977). Louisa May Alcott: *A modern biography.* Boston, MA: Houghton Mifflin Company.

School Committee of the City of Boston. (1870). *School committee of the city of Boston.* Boston, MA: Published by Alfred Mudge & Son.

School Committee of the City of Fall River. (1872). *Annual report of the school committee of the city of Fall River together with the 6th annual report of the superintendent of public schools, 1871–1872.* Fall River, MA: Fiske & Munroe, Book and Job Printers.

School Committee of the City of Fall River. (1875). *Annual report of the school committee of the city of Fall River together with the 9th annual report of the superintendent of public schools, 1874–1875.* Fall River, MA: Almy, Milne & Co., Steam Printers.

Senate Historical Office. (No date). *The senate's civil war.* Washington D.C.: Senate Historical Office.

Sigourney, L. (1837). *Letters to young ladies.* NY: Harper & Brothers.

Sklar, K. (1995). *Florence Kelley & The nation's work: The rise of women's political culture, 1830–1900.* New Haven, CT: Yale University Press.

Sklar, K. (2000). *Women's rights emerges within the antislavery movement 1830–1870.* Boston, MA: Bedford\St. Martin's.

Slafter, C. (1905). *A record of education: The schools and teachers of Dedham, Massachusetts 1644–1904.* Dedham, Massachusetts: Dedham Transcript Press.

Small, S. (1979). The Yankee schoolmarm in Freedmen's schools: An analysis of attitudes. *The Journal of Southern History, 45*(3), 381–402.

Spring, J. (2006). *American education* (12th ed.). Boston, MA: McGrawHill.

Spurzheim, J. G. (1846). *Phrenology or the doctrine of mental phenomena* (5th ed.). New York: Harper & Brothers, Publishers.

State Board of Charity of Massachusetts. (1874). *Tenth annual report of the State Board of Charity of Massachusetts.* Boston, MA: State House.

State Normal School Framingham. (1900). *State normal school Framingham, Mass.: Catalog of teachers and alumni 1839–1990.* Boston: Wright & Potter Printing Co., State Printers.

Stern, M. (1994/1962). *We the women: Career firsts of nineteenth century America.* Lincoln, NE: University of Nebraska Press.

The American Stationer. (1922, January 7). Adams Bookstore Celebrates Eightieth Anniversary. *The American Stationer, XC*(1) 40.

The Critic. (1881). Books. Life and education of Laura Bridgman: The deaf; dumb, and blind girl by Mary Swift Lamson. *1*(8), 118–119.

The New York Times. (1851, November 3). Sixteen days later from California: Arrival of the Cherokee over two millions of gold. *The New York Times.*

The New York Tribune. (date unknown). Senator Sumner in Baltimore. Copy in possession of the Lamson Family Papers, Massachusetts Historical Society, Boston, MA.

Thompson, O. (1832, July 31). Dr. Thompson's celebrated eye-water. *Hopkinsian Magazine,* IV (10) 448.

Titus, F. (1881). *Narrative of sojourner Truth: A bonds woman of olden time.* Battle Creek, MI: Published for the author.

Trent, J. (2012). *The manliest man: Samuel G. Howe and the contours of 19th century American Reform.* Amherst, MA: University of Massachusetts Press.

Trustees of the Perkins Institution. (1841). *Ninth annual report of the trustees of the Perkins Institution and Massachusetts Asylum for the Blind.* Boston, MA: John H. Eastburn, Printer.

Trustees of the Perkins Institution. (1844). *Twelfth annual report of the trustees of the Perkins Institution in Massachusetts Asylum for the Blind, to the corporation.* Boston, MA: Dutton and Wentworth's Print.

Trustees of the Perkins Institution. (1845). *Thirteenth annual report of the trustees of the Perkins Institution and Massachusetts Asylum for the Blind.* Boston, MA: John H. Eastburn, Printer.

Trustees of the Perkins Institution. (1847). *Fifteenth annual report of the trustees of the Perkins Institution and Massachusetts Asylum for the Blind.* Boston, MA: John H. Eastburn, Printer.

Truth, S. (1997). *Narrative of Sojourner Truth* (Dover Thrift Editions). New York: Dover Publications.

Tuttle, J. H. (Ed.). (1897). *Dedham Historical Registrar, Volume VIII.* Dedham, MA: Printed by the society.

Tuttle, J. H. (Ed.). (1901). *Dedham Historical Registrar, Volume XII (2).* Dedham, MA: Printed by the society.

United States Federak Census. (1850). *Census and voter lists.* Retrieved from Ancestry.Com. Website http://www.ancestry.com/.

Urban, W., & Wagoner, J. (1996). *American education: A history.* New York: McGrawHill.

Wallace, J. (1996). The feminization of teaching in Massachusetts: A reconsideration. In S. Porter (Ed.), *Women of the Commonwealth: Work, family, and social change in 19th century Massachusetts* (pp. 43–62). Amherst, MA: University of Massachusetts Press.

Warren, D. (1974). *To enforce education: A history of the founding years of the United States Office of Education.* Detroit, MI: Wayne State University Press.

Wayne, T. (2007). *Women's roles in nineteenth century America.* Westport, CT: Greenwood Press.

Weigley, R. F. (1982). *Philadelphia: A 300 year history.* New York: W.W. Norton & Company.

White, G. S. (1836). *Memoir of Samuel Slater: The father of American manufaturers.* Philadelphia, PA: Printed at No. 48 Carpenter Street.

Williamson, J. (1896). *A bibliography of the state of Maine from the earliest period to 1891.* Portland, Maine: The Thurston Print.

Wilson, S. (2003). *Boston sites and insights: An essential guide to historic landmarks in and around Boston.* Boston, MA: Beacon Press.

Winsor, J. (1881). *The memorial history of Boston including Suffolk County, Massachusetts: 1630–1880* (vol. III). Boston, MA: James R. Osgood and Company.

Wolff, K. (2009). *Culture club: The curious history of the Boston Athenaeum.* Amherst, MA: The University of Massachusetts Press.

Woodbridge, W. C. (1831). Art. VI—Seminaries for Teachers in Prussia. *American Annals of Education and Instruction and Journal of Literary Institutions, I*(II), 253–257.

Yellow Springs Bicentennial Committee. (2005). 200 years of Yellow springs: A collection of articles first published in the Yellow Springs news for the 2003 bicentennial of Yellow Springs, Ohio. Yellow Springs, OH: Yellow Spring News.

Zsuzsa, B. (2000). 'The best or none!' Spinnsterhood in 19th century New England. *The Journal of Social History,* Summer, 935–957.

CPSIA information can be obtained at www.ICGtesting.com
Printed in the USA
BVOW04s0038020514

352326BV00005B/30/P